Between Celan
and Heidegger

SUNY SERIES
LITERATURE...IN THEORY

SERIES EDITORS

David E. Johnson, *Comparative Literature, University at Buffalo*
Scott Michaelsen, *English, Michigan State University*

SERIES ADVISORY BOARD

Nahum Dimitri Chandler, *African American Studies, University of California, Irvine*
Rebecca Comay, *Philosophy and Comparative Literature, University of Toronto*
Marc Crépon, *Philosophy, École Normale Supérieure, Paris*
Jonathan Culler, *Comparative Literature, Cornell University*
Johanna Drucker, *Design Media Arts and Information Studies, University of California, Los Angeles*
Christopher Fynsk, *Modern Thought, Aberdeen University*
Rodolphe Gasché, *Comparative Literature, University at Buffalo*
Martin Hägglund, *Comparative Literature, Yale University*
Carol Jacobs, *German and Comparative Literature, Yale University*
Peggy Kamuf, *French and Comparative Literature, University of Southern California*
David Marriott, *History of Consciousness, University of California, Santa Cruz*
Steven Miller, *English, University at Buffalo*
Alberto Moreiras, *Hispanic Studies, Texas A&M University*
Patrick O'Donnell, *English, Michigan State University*
Pablo Oyarzun, *Teoría del Arte, Universidad de Chile*
Scott Cutler Shershow, *English, University of California, Davis*
Henry Sussman, *German and Comparative Literature, Yale University*
Samuel Weber, *Comparative Literature, Northwestern University*
Ewa Ziarek, *Comparative Literature, University at Buffalo*

Between Celan and Heidegger

Pablo Oyarzun

Translated by
D. J. S. Cross

Foreword by
Rodolphe Gasché

Cover image: *Für Paul Celan*, 2005. Oil, emulsion, acrylic, charcoal, chalk, wood, metal, and plaster on canvas, 190 × 280 cm. Copyright Anselm Kiefer. Photo: Atelier Anselm Kiefer. Collection Albertina, Vienna.

The English translation of this book is possible due to the permission of Editorial Metales Pesados © 2013.

Published by State University of New York Press, Albany

© 2022 State University of New York

All rights reserved

Printed in the United States of America

No part of this book may be used or reproduced in any manner whatsoever without written permission. No part of this book may be stored in a retrieval system or transmitted in any form or by any means including electronic, electrostatic, magnetic tape, mechanical, photocopying, recording, or otherwise without the prior permission in writing of the publisher.

For information, contact State University of New York Press, Albany, NY
www.sunypress.edu

Library of Congress Cataloging-in-Publication Data

Names: Oyarzun R., Pablo, 1950– author. | Cross, Donald J. S., translator. | Gasché, Rodolphe, foreword.
Title: Between Celan and Heidegger / Pablo Oyarzun ; translated by D. J. S. Cross ; foreword Rodolphe Gasché.
Other titles: Entre Celan y Heidegger. English
Description: Albany : State University of New York Press, [2022]. | Series: SUNY series, literature . . . in theory | Includes bibliographical references and index.
Identifiers: LCCN 2021041525 | ISBN 9781438488370 (hardcover : alk. paper) | ISBN 9781438488387 (ebook) | 9781438488363 (pbk. : alk. paper)
Subjects: LCSH: Celan, Paul—Criticism and interpretation. | Heidegger, Martin, 1889–1976—Criticism and interpretation. | Aesthetics. | Literature—Philosophy. | Poetry.
Classification: LCC PT2065.E4 Z725913 2022 | DDC 831/.914—dc23/eng/20211216
LC record available at https://lccn.loc.gov/2021041525

10 9 8 7 6 5 4 3 2 1

*For Roxana,
by all paths*

Contents

The Idiom *of* the Poem: A Foreword   ix
   Rodolphe Gasché

Translator's Note   xxxiii

Prologue   xxxvii

1. "Dialogue"   1

2. "Place"   17

3. "Art"   33

4. "Language"   45

5. Pain   61

6. Doit   77

7. "Dialogue"   93

Notes   109

Bibliography   151

Index   159

The Idiom *of* the Poem

A Foreword

Rodolphe Gasché

Compared to most of modern poetry, which has been qualified by its tendency toward muteness, Paul Celan's poems pose a particular challenge to the reader. Indeed, according to *The Meridian*, Celan's sole text on poetry, "the poem does speak" (Celan, *Meridian*, 31a). And yet, his poems, especially the later ones, are held to be impenetrable, obscure, or hermetic. However, on the other hand, obscurity and hermeticism are considered to be essential characteristics of modern poetry.[1] Therefore, the question to be asked in the case of Celan concerns the kind of obscurity of his poems, especially since the poems speak in a language that has gone "through terrifying muteness, through the thousand darknesses of murderous speech" (Celan, *Collected Prose*, 34; translation modified). What kind of intelligibility characterizes an obscurity associated with poems that go through a language that experienced its own loss as a result of "what happened [*das, was geschah*]" and that are dialogically "headed toward," that is, "toward something open, inhabitable, an approachable you, perhaps, an approachable reality" (35)? What kind of impenetrability might characterize a poem for which this experience is one that can no longer be attributed to some epochal distinction such as "modern" but also, even though it is closer to Hölderlinean poetry than to Goethean, no longer fits the Mallarméan striving for the absolute and universal poem? When, in the Bremen speech, Celan famously speaks of the poem as a letter in a bottle thrown out to sea, he emphasizes not only that it speaks in hopes of an addressee but also, and especially, that the poem is always a singular address rather than an instance of an epochal genre, modern or not; in other words, the poem is not "wearing a uniform" (Dostoevsky, *Writer's Diary*, 52), to quote in this context an unlikely source. If what is new about the poem today is that it "stays mindful of its dates," this does not mean that it is "modern" but, rather, that it in a way belongs to a genre all by itself (Celan, *Meridian*, 31a). Perhaps this would even be something other than a genre to begin with! If, moreover, such a letter headed toward an Other is obscure, how does this destination shape its intelligibility? If, in all its obscurity, the poem is intelligible, it is because its singularity consists not in an individual personality and his or her purely personal or even idiosyncratic nature but, rather, in a resistance to all forms of understanding that, already in advance, have decided its meaning. Needless to say, since such singularity resists all appropriation, it inevitably remains obscure, but it is also, for this very reason, (minimally) intelligible as the universal trait of a singularity in all its irreducible uniqueness. This is thus an obscurity that must be respected, one that solely manifests itself in readings that themselves can and must remain singular. The reader of this foreword will by now already have understood that, hereafter, I will be interested in the readability and intelligibility of a poet who is also, as we will see, a thinker.

Pablo Oyarzun's *Between Celan and Heidegger* is a philosopher's book on Paul Celan. There is nothing particular in this respect, since a number of prior thinkers have been drawn to the study of poetry. Within the present context, Martin Heidegger's interpretation of Friedrich Hölderlin—but also of Rainer Maria Rilke, Georg Trakl, and Stefan George—is a case in point. Furthermore, though Heidegger's interest in Celan's poetry did not materialize in a written philosophical commentary on his work, Celan's own complex and subtle debate, both in *The Meridian* and in his poetry, with Heidegger's thought and understanding of language is testimony to what has been called a dialogue between the poet and the thinker. Celan's poetry has certainly attracted considerable attention from literary critics, philologists, and poetologists, but remarkable in his case is the consistent attention his work has drawn from philosophers and philosophically sophisticated literary critics. With this, the question arises: what is it in Celan's writings that challenges philosophical thought? Among its many accomplishments, Oyarzun's study not only engages the philosophers' accounts of the poetry in question, along with the poet's relation to the thinker, but also inquires into what motivates this philosophical interest in the first place. In short, it is an inquiry into the stakes of the philosophical encounter with poetry.

The Idiom *of* the Poem: A Foreword

The Meridian, a speech given by Celan on the occasion of receiving the Büchner prize in 1960, is not only devoted to Georg Büchner's reflections on art and poetry, as the circumstances demanded, but also a debate with the poetological speeches of several previous recipients of the prize, among whom figures—to name only one—Gottfried Benn. Taking his point of departure from Büchner's reflections on the complex relation between art and poetry, indeed, the singular occasion of the award presents Celan with the unique opportunity of elaborating on the nature of the poem and, more precisely, "the poem *today*" (Celan, *Meridian* 32a; emphasis mine). Because of his concern with the poem's datedness, Celan's speech already, unlike speeches made by previous recipients of the prize, ceases to be poetological: it is not a theoretical speech on poetry in general or on poetry from an epochal perspective like, for example, "modern" poetry. Its prose, it has been observed, is also that of the poet as a poet.[2] But what does this mean in the specific case of Celan? First and foremost, Celan's is a "speech," that is, a performance that, as Kristina Mendicino remarks, must be approached on its own terms and through the position it assumes "within a tradition of public speaking, while resisting and participating in the tradition of rhetoric" (Mendicino, "Other Rhetoric," 633). This intrinsic resistance of the speech to its own public form manifests itself in several ways. First, the talk anaphorically repeats the rhetorical figure of the apostrophe ("Ladies and gentlemen"), especially toward the end, where, "from a transparent means of opening the speech," this figure turns into "an insistent poetic figure" (633–34). Furthermore, "the pervasiveness of citation throughout the address," whose aim as a rhetorical device is to "[bring] a witness to the fore" in view of persuasion, "overwhelms the speaker's voice" to such a degree, indeed, as to "render it impossible to locate from whom this speech comes in any univocal way" (634–35). In short, through the "intensification of a rhetorical technique" required by public speech, *The Meridian* turns this technique "into something else, threatening to obscure the rhetor rather than submit to his purpose" (635). In both cases, Celan's rhetoric or, rather, what Mendicino calls "an 'Other' rhetoric," an altering rhetoric, one that "speak[s] *in the cause of an Other*—who knows, perhaps in the cause of a *wholly Other*," "bends his speech toward poetry" (635, 643–50).

Yet, in *The Meridian*, Celan also enlarges on a subject matter. What, then, about this text's discursive dimension? How does Celan meet the challenge of discoursing in his sole text on what he terms "the poem today"? Even supposing that one could make the distinction between the rhetorical and the discursive dimensions of a public speech, the latter would still have a rhetoricity of its own. And yet, no one particular figure dominates it—say, for example, the figure of inversion. Indeed, if it is true that, as Celan advances in his text, the poem's images are "what is perceived and is to be perceived once and always again once, and only here and now," it follows that "the poem would be the place where all tropes and metaphors want to be carried ad absurdum" (Celan, *Meridian*, 39b). Furthermore, what is true of the poem in all its uniqueness is no less true of a prose text such as *The Meridian*. Not through any one particular rhetorical figure but, rather, through what I call, for better or worse, the "deconstruction" of rhetoric as a whole does a text like this accomplish its aim, namely, opening up on the level of discursiveness a space not for dialogical consent or for the fusion of self and other but, rather, for an encounter that preserves that which divides it in order for it to take place. However, as we learn from *Between Celan and Heidegger*, such a "deconstruction" of rhetoric is in no way a nostalgic return to an immediacy of encounter. Nor does it amount to an annihilation of one extreme by its opposite. On the contrary, it consists in tracing a line through opposite poles, a line that keeps them vacillating in their "between."

As is obvious from *The Meridian*, while meeting the challenge that the occasion represents by taking as his starting point writings on poetry by Büchner, according to whom art (distinct in a complex way from poetry) is the business of market criers, barkers, or monkeys and marionette players, Celan also engages the tradition of the more academic and technical poetological approaches to poetry and their established conventions. This characterization of art and theorizing about it is, unmistakably, indebted to Büchner. The same obtains when Celan observes that art, along with discourses about it such as that of Büchner's Lenz in the story of the same name, "creates I-distance [*Ich-Ferne*]" (Celan, *Meridian*, 20d). Yet, when we read:

> Ladies and gentlemen, please, take note: "One wishes one were a Medusa's head" in order to . . . grasp the natural as the natural with the help of art! / *One* wishes to does of course not mean here: *I* wish to,

it is shown that, though citing Lenz and apart from discussing art according to Büchner, Celan is also in the same breath arguing that art, at its most fundamental, belongs to the realm of the Heideggerian *Man*, a realm of inauthenticity that *The Meridian* characterizes in terms of uncanniness (*Unheimlichkeit*), a realm in which the *I* is not at home (16a–b).

With Gottfried Benn in mind, Celan qualifies as "artistic" not only the latter's art but also, implicitly, his technical elaborations on "modern lyric." The predicate "artistic" refers to academic discourse's nature as a public theatrical spectacle and intellectual entertainment. Celan evokes this artistic, artificial, and mechanical dimension of modern poetry in what seems, at first, to be a rejection. Moreover, it also has all the appearances of the entirely conventional gesture by which natural immediacy and the merely private or personal are construed as the opposites of art. But the specificity of the accomplishments of *The Meridian* begin to come into view when one pays attention to the fact that, rather than one of these opposites, Celan seeks to secure the space between them and in which he locates the place of poetry and of "the poem today." In spite of the rejection of art, poetry needs art. It must "tread the route of art" in order to set itself free from it and, thus, make "the step" to address itself (*spricht sich zu*) to not only the human other but also any "opposite [*Gegenüber*]" (Celan, *Meridian*, 21, 35a). In distinction from the "distance of the I" that characterizes art and the discourse about it, however, does poetry need the private or the personal? No doubt, but only on the condition that, in the Celanian perspective, one understands poetry as dated, singular, and yet as having a universality of its own, one that resists not only universality as we know it but also its opposite in the immediacy of the particular. Rather than a rejection, the Celanian approach to the poem is of the order of a resistance against embracing art, subjectivity, or both.

Poetry, according to *The Meridian,* is not artlike, and—unlike art—one cannot endlessly chat about it. It originates in a certain lack of understanding of what is said about art, suddenly, in the same way as Lucile's counterword, "Long live the King," irrupts in Büchner's *Danton's Death*. Rather than "a declaration of loyalty to the 'ancien régime,'" the exclamation is, by contrast, "an act of freedom," a "step" that "intervenes" in the struggle between the right and the leftist defenders of the revolution, a "step" that has something personal about it, not in the sense of the private but, rather, in that it consists in the singularity of the individual (Celan, *Meridian*, 6c–8a, 31f). This something personal has "direction and destiny," while its "absurdity" is the index of its specific intelligibility compared to that of the words piled upon words in artful fashion by all the defenders of the revolution (5b). As Celan remarks, Lucile's counterword is testimony of "the presence of the human" in the face not only of the Regime of Terror but also of the rhetoric of those who are its victims—"homage . . . to the majesty of the absurd" (8c). Lucile's exclamation, her counterword (*Gegenwort*), is "absurd" because of the insistence of presence (*Gegenwart*), of the now in all its singularity, and because of its being dated. Celan writes: "That, ladies and gentlemen, has no name fixed once and for all, but I believe that this is . . . poetry" (9).

This is, then, what Celan understands by *Dichtung*, along with what about the latter is *precise*: its concern with the singular and the datedness of its "step."[3] Not unlike Lucile, "one who is blind to art" (Celan, *Meridian*, 6c) and whose sudden interjection interrupts the artful words and theatrical speeches of her former companions who are being driven to the place of the revolution to be executed, Pablo Oyarzun *resists* the highly, often astoundingly brilliant and intimidating scholarship on Celan in *Between Celan and Heidegger*. In doing so, in an equally brilliant fashion, Oyarzun's text makes us hear and see in Celan's poetry not only what cannot be reduced to a Heideggerian interpretation but also what withstands Celan scholarship, however learned it proves to be. Again like Lucile, Oyarzun has heard and acknowledged the language of scholarship, but, having heard it spoken, he also distances himself from it and refuses to understand it if, however critically, understanding means to subscribe to the interpretations that it offers. The uniqueness of Celanian poetry, he holds, is that it literally winds itself out of the Western mode of thinking about poetry, a mode of thinking presupposed by any reading that seeks to understand it in the frame of a purported dialogue with Heidegger, and into an other space. This does not mean that there has not been something like a dialogue between Heidegger and Celan. But such a dialogue has only taken place, indeed, if it can be shown that Celan resisted Heidegger's Western bent and, in a way similar to what Lucile achieved with her counterword, that this dialogue is interrupted by something that "intervenes"—the "between" of something non-Western.

Rather than hasten to conclusions, however, I wish to turn to the importance that *The Meridian* plays in Oyarzun's text. In this respect, a reflection on the title of Celan's speech may first be warranted, not simply because *Between Celan and Heidegger* is a thorough exposition of this speech, but also because the way this title punctuates Oyarzun's elaborations may already point to what is at stake in his reading of this text. Even before asking what the one (*einen*)—that is, also the singular—meridian is that, at the end of his talk, Celan claims to have found and touched again, we must ask what "a" meridian is in the first place, although "one should not see in *The Meridian*," as Oyarzun remarks, "the essence of a sovereign word" (*Between Celan and Heidegger*, 17).

Known as an avid reader of dictionaries, in all likelihood, Celan may also have consulted them in the context of preparing his speech. I do so, too, and learn that the origin of this foreign word "meridian" makes it, indeed, a very complex one. From the dictionary, I take it that the term derives from the Latin *meridianus*, itself the adjective of *meridies*, meaning midday or noon. *Meridianus* signifies "*of* or *belonging* to mid-day," noon, that is, "the meridian hour" (*meridies*), but it also signifies in its figural sense "the *middle* of a given time" (Lewis and Short, *Latin Dictionary*, 1137), that is, the time midway between the times of sunrise and sunset, *medius* signifying "middle" (or "south"). The word "meridian" thus refers to the midday line, the line that connects all places on the earth that simultaneously share midday and where, during that time, the position reached by the sun is at its highest. In short, then, geographically or terrestrially speaking, the meridian corresponds to the line or degree of longitude that cuts the equator at a right angle.[4]

Yet, I learn also from the dictionary that the word has a double sense, astronomical and geographical. In geography, the meridian, or midday circle, signifies "a great circle [of the earth] which passes through the equator in two opposed points, and which passes as well through both poles, dividing the globe of the earth in each place where it is drawn into an *eastern* and a *western* part. Each place has its meridian. In other words, from each place I can draw a circle, which cuts through the equator and the poles" (*Brockhaus Conversations-Lexikon*, 3:126). In astronomy, the meridian designates "the great circle of the celestial sphere that passes through its poles and the observer's zenith" (*Webster's*, 1203). However, before further exploring the word's celestial sense, let me take note of the fact that, when the dictionaries also—on the basis of Latin literary references—identify the meridian as a *circulus meridianus* with the equator, the meridian as the greatest among the latitudinal lines is not only seen to be the line that divides the earth into a northern and southern hemisphere; it also has connotations of what, geographically, is situated in the south or belongs to the south. Furthermore, as the equator, the *circulus meridianus* is thus also understood in view of the equator's equalizing properties, in the sense that it not only partitions the earth's surface in two equal halves, south and north, but also divides all its hours through their middle. Finally, this circle may also occur midway between the earth and the sky.

Indeed, distinct from its geographical or terrestrial meaning, the meridian also has an astronomic or celestial meaning. As the midday circle, it is the great circle that, in the celestial sphere, passes through the north and south poles (of the celestial sphere), as well as through the zenith and nadir in whose plane the terrestrial observer is situated, dividing the plane into the latter's upper and lower meridian. In the same way that, stretching from one pole to the other, the terrestrial longitudinal semicircle stands vertically on the equator, the celestial semicircle "stands [also] vertically on the observer's horizon and cuts the latter at its north- or midnight point, as well as at its south or midday point," and it is thus perpendicular to the celestial equator. "Both points are connected with one another through the *midday-line*. By passing through the meridian, the stars are for their observer at their highest position (meridian-, midday-height), or, twelve hours later, at their lowest height (midnight-low)" (*Brockhaus Enzyklopädie*, 425). Finally, since an astronomical meridian is in the same plane as the terrestrial meridian projected onto the celestial sphere, its number of meridians is also infinite.

It should be clear by now that the word "meridian" is not just any word. If "each place has its meridian," then it is a word that has to be thought on the basis of all its meanings, which imply connections that divide and divisions that connect all places and all times, such as south/north, east/west, upper/lower, day/night, sunrise/sunset, and in particular the divide between the terrestrial and the celestial, the earth and the sky. It is a word that also names the middle, the "between"—midday, midnight—and is itself situated between the poles that it interlinks while at the same time keeping them at a distance, resisting their proximity. Is this word, which Celan has found and touched, not perhaps a counterword—a *Gegenwort*—to the term "das Geviert," a counterword against the unifying and harmonizing movement of the Heideggerian "fourfold"? Like Lucile's "absurd" exclamation with which Celan opens his speech, then, he closes it with reference to a word just as provocative.

Undoubtedly, Celan's speech is a debate with the academic discourses on poetry, but it is also, as several scholars—including Oyarzun—have noted, a debate with the Heideggerian conception of language and poetry. At the end of his speech, Celan "undertake[s] some topos research" into the four regions or topoi from whence Karl Emil Franzos and Reinhold Lenz came, two figures to whom he refers in the speech and whom he "met on the way here and in Georg Büchner," but this is also a study of "the place of [his] origin" (Celan, *Meridian*, 49a–b). These four topoi are places of origin, regions from whence all four named—Franzos, Lenz, Büchner, and Celan himself—come. Notwithstanding the fact that none of these regions can be found, since none of them exist, Celan claims to find something: "I find something—like language—immaterial, yet terrestrial, something circular that returns to itself across both poles while—cheerfully—even crossing the tropics: I find . . . a *meridian*" (50c). Rather than a region whose poles or extremes are gathered in one unifying ring (*Reigen*), as in Heidegger's fourfold or topology of Being, Celan finds a meridian in pursuing the study of topoi. What exactly is meant here by a meridian is not easy to understand. But let me emphasize that Celan finds *a* meridian, a singular meridian, and not *the* meridian! Needless to say, if this meridian traverses both poles and returns to itself, crossing and even crossing out (*Durchkreuzendes*) with the tropics also all *topoi*, that is, all accommodating (*Commode*) commonplaces, it is barely distinct from the gathering ringing of the Heideggerian fourfold.[5] Therefore, it is crucial to understand the almost nothing—or to use Celan's word, to which Oyarzun devotes a whole chapter of his study, the "doit [*Deut*]"—that separates this meridian from the gathering fourfold. Seemingly made in passing, Celan's remark that, by crossing the tropics, the meridian also "merrily [*heiterweise*]" crosses out all topoi shows this meridian to be of the order of language—more precisely, for Celan, the order of what language is and does. Indeed, what he claims to find after "having . . . taken this impossible route, this route of the impossible," the path of the study of topoi on which he embarked in the presence of his audience, "is something . . . like language" (Celan, *Meridian*, 50a–c). That is, what he claims to find is not language as it is commonly understood but rather something that, by crossing out language as constituted by topoi, is language in another sense—"language actualized [*aktualisierte Sprache*]" rather than "language as such [*Sprache schlechthin*]" (33a–b). "I find what connects and leads, like the poem, to an encounter" (50b).[6] What distinguishes the singular meridian—that which Celan holds to have touched "just now again"—ever so slightly from something like the fourfold is, first, that it is found only in the singularity of its occurrence and, second, that it is the object of something as singular as a touch. Furthermore, the traversing and the crossing out of which it consists are what binds, and it binds by separating and dividing. A meridian is a singular happening, just like the poem, and like the poem it enables an encounter. It is the happening of an encounter, and it is also, as a movement that returns to itself like a circle, the "between" or nondialectical middle of all the places and commonplaces that it crosses and crosses out. It is the u-topic place not of a community to come but, rather, of a community that comes into being in the fragile moment of the encounter.

All of this does not make *The Meridian* a poem—the difference is preserved—but *a* meridian has made this speech the event of an encounter like that effectuated by the poem. At this juncture, I wish to evoke a remark made by Emmanuel Levinas about Celan's speech. Having described it as a text "in which Celan gives us what he is able to perceive of his poetic act," Levinas adds that it is "an elliptic, allusive text, constantly interrupting itself in order to let through, in the interruptions, his other voice, as if two or more discourses were on top of one another, with a strange coherence, not that of a dialogue, but woven in [*ourdie selon*] a counterpoint that constitutes their immediate melodic unity—the texture [*tissu*] of his poems" (Levinas, *Proper Names*, 41). If, indeed, Celan's speech—a prose text, as well as a discursive engagement with poetry and its relation to art—is interwoven by way of a counterpoint, if not even several counterpoints like the fabric of his poems, then his poems become instrumental to the interpretation of the speech's vibrant formulations. In *Between Celan and Heidegger*, Oyarzun engages in precisely such a reading of *The Meridian* that allows it to be interrupted in all its moments by its counterpoints. Yet, rather than poetizing the speech by weaving Celan's poems into the discursive text, his reading breaks down the classical divide between discursive speech and poetry. It is from the complex tissue that the text of *The Meridian* reveals when read in this manner, rather than being interpreted, that Oyarzun engages several among the most sophisticated interpretations, mostly philosophical, of Celan's work.

As I have already noted, Celan is generally considered to be cryptic, impenetrable, in short, a "hermetic poet" (Gadamer, *Gadamer on Celan*, 164). His poetry is exposed to "the 'idiomatic' threat: the threat of hermeticism and obscurity," and his poems, consequently, are "completely untranslatable, including within their own language" (Lacoue-Labarthe, *Poetry as Experience*, 56, 13). All "the approaches traditionally employed in literary interpretation" (Szondi, *Celan Studies*, 27) fail in the face of poems that challenge intelligibility vis-à-vis these traditional tools. Right from the beginning of his reading, Oyarzun takes issue with these claims, noting that "obscurity" is, first of all, the inevitable correlate of a hermeneutic approach to the poems, one that understands itself as concerned with an intended meaning of literary texts that, through interpretation, is to be brought to light in univocal clarity. It is not by accident, therefore, that *Between Celan and Heidegger* opens and closes with chapters devoted to explicitly hermeneutic approaches to Celan's writings: first that of Hans-Georg Gadamer, and then, in the concluding chapter, that of Peter Szondi. It is this assumption that the poem intends a unitary and transparent meaning different from its linguistic formation that drives "the zeal of hermeneutics" and explains, in Oyarzun's words, "Gadamer's grandiose deafness to what the poem says" (Oyarzun, *Between Celan and Heidegger*, 3, 4–5).[7] Distinct from Gadamer's emphasis on the univocity of the poem is Szondi's hermeneutic approach, which conceives of itself as a hermeneutic reading rather than a hermeneutic interpretation. As Szondi holds, reading is the only appropriate response to a poem that has ceased to be mimetic—no longer a representation of something real but likewise, I add, not merely formal, as so much of modern poetry—and that is to be understood as a text "projecting itself, constituting itself as reality" (Szondi, *Celan Studies*, 31). "The language of reading," Szondi states, is the only appropriate approach to a poem when the latter is "neither verbal nor discursive" (38). As his reading of Celan's "Engführung" demonstrates in an admirable fashion, reading requires untiring attention to the nonsemantic complexity of the poem, such as the structure of the words themselves, their own tissue. This is true especially in the case of Celan's considerably expanded vocabulary through compounded words (*paranomasia*), as well as the textual tissue deriving from their undecidable syntactic relations to one another, the caesuras that punctuate the poem, the hiatuses and ellipses that interrupt it, the movements of its rhetorical figures, the movements of inversion, *correctio*, or *obscuritas* that affect these figures themselves, and so forth. With a poem, one is from the start in a territory other than that with which one is familiar, a territory of "ambiguity [which is] neither a defect nor purely a stylistic trait, [but] determines the structure of the poetic text itself" (29). Since an "essential ambiguity" characterizes the territory of the poem, to ask what its words mean is to disregard the laws of their composition—or as Szondi holds, in the case of "Engführung," their musical composition (66–67). In reading a poem such as "Engführung," it is not "a matter of selecting one of several meanings, but of understanding that they *coincide*, rather than differ. Ambiguity, which has become a means of knowledge, shows us the unity of what only appeared to be difference" (82). Compared to Gadamer's hermeneutics of univocity, then, Szondi's hermeneutic reading is one of polysemy whose unity, furthermore, is of Hegelian inspiration. It is, Szondi holds, the result of "the mediation and thus the negation of [. . .] opposed elements, the negation of negation" (80).

Oyarzun's reading of Celan is suspended *between* these two poles of hermeneutics. In the opening chapter, he distances himself from an interpretation that claims that each Celanian poem has a distinct unity of meaning, and in the concluding chapter he distances himself from a reading that, despite its admirable complexity, also reunifies the plurality and ambiguity of meanings despite having been called "essential." In what follows, I wish to engage the space of reading *The Meridian* and Celanian poetry—the "between"—opened up by Oyarzun's text, which returns at its end to its beginning, in order to search for what Oyarzun, in turn, finds along this trajectory.

Let us, then, also take note of the titles of the beginning and concluding chapters. They are identical: "Dialogue." The central chapter, chapter four, is titled "Language." Suspending these titles between, to quote *The Meridian*, "'Hasenöhrchen' [hare's ears], that is, something not completely fearless, that listens beyond itself and the words" (Celan, *Meridian*, 48c), the quotation marks are also an indication that both are translations from the German: *Gespräch* and *Sprache*, respectively. From the opening chapter to the concluding chapter, while passing through the tropics of language or, more precisely, through Celan's resistance to a topical understanding of language—what he calls "metaphor-flurry" in a poem from *Breathturn*—a more profound understanding of "dialogue" will have emerged (Oyarzun, *Between Celan and Heidegger*, 135 note 22). For the time being, however, it is certainly appropriate to note that *Between Celan and Heidegger* is also about a particular "dialogue" that began in 1967 with Celan's first visit to Heidegger in Todtnauberg, a dialogue that, while it "delighted the thinker" (Petzet, *Auf einen Stern zugehen*, 209), left the poet bitterly disappointed, as demonstrated by the poem of the same name ("Todtnauberg"), as well as testimony from some of those involved.[8] Hailed as a summit talk of *the* thinker and *the* poet and described by one of its witnesses—Gerhard Neumann—as an epochal event, the meeting has been the subject of numerous scholarly discussions. Let us note that such an interpretation of the event is, from the start, already an interpretation from a Heideggerian perspective. Oyarzun's intervention in this discussion resists not only the pathos with which a number of scholars have spoken of it but also the idea that the encounter that took place was, indeed, a dialogue. If an encounter took place between both, between thought and poetry, it was an "encounter without encounter," and not a dialogue but rather, at best, "something like a dialogue" occurred at the occasion (Oyarzun, *Between Celan and Heidegger*, 6 and 9, 10). Since there is no question that Celan's poetry and his thought of the poem—and *The Meridian* is a case in point—were always defined by not only a certain proximity to Heidegger's thought but also, at the same time, an extreme distance from the latter, Oyarzun assiduously focuses on the "between" opened up by the impossible encounter and dialogue. In question is an examination not of the abstract intermediate space presupposed by all encounter and dialogue but, rather, of the "between" of this complex exchange in all its radical singularity, owing to what Oyarzun calls Celan's "incarnated resistance, a resistance that comes imposed and surpasses all sentiment or certainty even of proximity" and that is "prior to every purpose, intention, or will" (8). If the author can speak of "the experience of the 'between'" (10), it is because this "between," which opens the space of all being-with and togetherness, is rooted in the resistance that singularity, not to be confused with privacy, represents as such. This peculiar "between" is also the language of the poem, which in Oyarzun's words is "the place to which an other and all others are called" (10). The place of the "between," the place "of *inter-esse*, which makes possible *Mitsein* and *Miteinandersein*" (10), is something like a dialogue. In the same way as, according to *The Meridian*, the poem resists and frees itself from art in order to be a poem, for something worthy of the name "dialogue" to occur, it must resist what is commonly understood by the term. In other words, the dialogue that took place between Celan and Heidegger, the former's poetry and thought having always been in an intimate relation with the latter's thought, has thus been a dialogue in resistance to a dialogue about language, about language in general, in the name of individuated speech, in the name of what Oyarzun, with Celan, also refers to as a wound and, in particular, as the "raw [*Krudes*]" (8), which resist all translation.

At this point, I wish to bring into greater relief what I believe to be a fundamental gesture and remarkable tonality of not only Oyarzun's reading of the hermeneutical attempt to reduce the so-called obscurity of Celan's poetry and his prose by establishing the unity of its univocal or polysemic meaning but also his reading of a variety of outstanding philosophical discussions of Celan's work—in particular by Philippe Lacoue-Labarthe, Emmanuel Levinas, Werner Hamacher, and Jacques Derrida—intent on dispelling some of its obscurity. First, however, I should emphasize that, although Oyarzun acknowledges his own indebtedness to these brilliant readings, it is precisely their brilliancy that, for him, is at issue. Indeed, the accounts of Celan's poetry that Oyarzun takes on stand out not only for their impeccable scholarship and the impressive discipline of their readings but also for their striking lucidity. If Oyarzun guards against these readings, whose impressive rigor he nonetheless adopts, it is certainly not because they would promote a facile lucidity, however laborious, but rather because their very lucidity risks the paradox of covering over what shines forth through the obscurity of the poems themselves. Take, for example, Oyarzun's response to Levinas's emphasis that Celan's poetry is to be understood in terms of the relation to the Other that precedes all dialogic forms. Undoubtedly, Levinas has "hit upon" something crucial, Oyarzun acknowledges (*Between Celan and Heidegger*, 14). Yet, as Oyarzun also remarks, "in this enhancement,

I perceive an excessive force," a force brilliant to the point of breaking the balance of the constant fragile oscillations between self and Other, and "the more and less than being" (14). From the beginning of *Between Celan and Heidegger*, Levinas's interpretation serves as a reference point for Oyarzun's acknowledgement that, in the following chapters, his readings will "take more or less distance" from the major commentaries on Celan and his poems (15). At first, such a caveat would seem to be a function of the attitude one expects from a scholar or critic, and yet something else is at stake here. At times blunt, at times subtle, Oyarzun's resistance or reticence to adopting the conclusions of other readings, however philosophically astute, serves to prevent the "between," with which he associates Celanian singularity, from fading from view. As Celan's several encounters with Heidegger demonstrate, as well as the poem "Todtnauburg" and the speech *The Meridian*, something like a "dialogue" took place between the two, but it was in fact already taking place from the beginning of Celan's work. Oyarzun inscribes a warning, the warning to preserve "the quotation marks around 'dialogue,'" a warning that "does not affirm or negate the dialogue but, rather, holds it in suspense" (15). To approach the *Gespräch* between Celan and Heidegger as a dialogue is to fall into the temptation to take Celan's poems and his elaborations on the poem in his speech in Darmstadt as philosophical statements. Oyarzun's goal is to remain aware of the "extreme, intolerable friction between what Celan says [about language, in particular] . . . and what Martin Heidegger thinks" (45). As already pointed out, it is not a dialogue between *the* thinker and *the* poet; if, however, it is indeed a dialogue, then it is a dialogue between one who thinks and one who writes poems, that is, between singular individuals.[9]

A certain proximity between Heidegger and Celan is evident. Indeed, Celan was deeply familiar with Heidegger's works and had been in contact with him by letter. They also exchanged their publications. Yet, as Oyarzun observes, unless the quotation marks around "dialogue" are kept in place, to assume that there was a dialogue between them "can become completely deceiving" (39). Unlike the hermeneutically motivated readings of Celanian poetry, the aim here is not simply to keep the poem free from what is foreign to it, such as personal interpretations or anecdotal information; instead, by resisting all "emphasis foreign to Celan's poetry," Oyarzun's aim is to bring out persistently and seek to keep open the "between" that, within their "*vacillating opposition*" (13), the poems are unfolding and thus to avoid deciding in favor of one pole over the other, in which case the "between" would become invisible.

Oyarzun's study takes issue with the claim that Celan's poetry is obscure. In no way, however, does he therefore hold that it would not be difficult to understand. But what is it, precisely, that one expects from poetry and in view of which Celan's poems are judged to lack transparency? Thinkers in the hermeneutic tradition have linked this obscurity to the poet's break with the mimetic tradition, that is, to the fact that his poetry is no longer involved in representation. Celanian obscurity would thus be a function of an interpretive approach to the poetry in question, which demands, rather than interpretation, the practice of a certain reading. Undoubtedly, formidable skills are required to read Celan's poetry, since what one may call the semantic core of the poems cannot, to put it in simple terms, be separated from what they accomplish linguistically and syntactically, which keeps all semantic content in indefinite suspense. But, then, a seemingly naïve question also arises: is this not what one should expect from any poem worthy of its name? Is not the meaning that a poem offers, either in its immediacy or after some excruciating deciphering, deceitful from the start because it has been found at the expense of the poem as linguistic artifact and linguistic event? Celanian poetry is, perhaps, more demanding, but the technics of reading for which it calls might prove only somewhat more demanding and more radically demanded than those required by any poem. The unmistakable difficulty that these poems present is that they are neither "modern" nor instances of a genre, such as the lyric (a word, furthermore, that Celan does not mention even once in *The Meridian*). Their difficulty resides in their datedness, in short, in what Celan refers to as their "one, unique, punctual present" that results from "a radical individuation [of language]" (Celan, *Meridian* 36b, 33b; translation modified). Werner Hamacher has characterized this datedness of the poems as "the movement of [their] infinite singularization" (Hamacher, "Second of Inversion," 252). Indeed, in *The Meridian* Celan writes: "Poetry, ladies and gentlemen: this infinity-speaking full of mortality and to no purpose" (*Meridian*, 44). There is something "raw" about these poems, something that resists translation and even thinking. Consequently, attending solely to the syntax of these poems does not yet suffice to do justice to them. Their very idiomaticity, which threatens them with obscurity, requires meticulous attention to the rules by way of which they achieve their singularity. Only on this condition does the obscurity that they exhibit become transparent. If the poem "wants to head for the Other" and, in order to do so, must pay careful "attention . . . to everything it encounters," and if it has a "sharper sense of detail, outline, structure, color," then the way by which the poem secures its datedness begins with such "attention," which Celan, citing Walter Benjamin citing Nicolas Malebranche, qualifies as "the natural prayer of the soul" (*Meridian*, 35a–d). Everything Celan does to language semantically and syntactically—his undoing of its tropological and rhetorical common nature, its spatial and temporal disarticulation—is at the service of accomplishing a poem that has the status of a singular address to an Other. The obscurity that results from such undoing of the structures of language in general is the price to pay for the poem to be an address and for an encounter to become possible. Its unintelligibility is intended to bring about a response. Thus, rather than bemoaning opaqueness, Celan clearly "demands the risk," as Lacoue-Labarthe suggests (*Poetry as Experience*, 56), that comes with it.

If, as I hold, this radical singularization of language in a poem that seeks to reach the Other in his, her, or its radical singularity and that, therefore, inevitably comes with obscurity explains the fascination that Celan's poetry has exerted on philosophers and philosophically astute literary scholars, the particular kind of obscurity involved certainly warrants greater attention. As we have already seen, rather than a deficiency, this obscurity is a positive aspect of the poem. It is not simply an effect of the poem's reaching toward the Other; rather, it is meticulously produced by the transcendence in question. It is not produced hazardously but rather according to rules, which much of Celan scholarship has sought to elucidate. It is thus a very particular obscurity. As Szondi notes, *obscuritas* is also a rhetorical figure, one of which, without a doubt, Celan's poetry makes occasional use. From the dictionary, we learn that *obscuritas* does not signify complete darkness but, rather, "the wanly twilight in which the contours of things and beings, after a while, can be made out" (Walde et al., "Obscuritas," 358). Let us remind ourselves that, as a rhetorical figure, *obscuritas* intentionally aims at concealment and lack of clarity in speech, not merely to draw the attention of the addressee to the subject matter effectively but also, paradoxically, "to render a specific subject-matter all the clearer" (363).[10] Even though there is thus a rather fluid limit between *obscuritas* and *perspicuitas*, the task of reading, as Szondi holds, cannot consist in seeking to explain the intentional obscurity in question completely. Instead, reading has "to note and attempt to characterize this obscurity without losing track of what, both despite and because of this obscurity, is becoming apparent [*in Erscheinung tritt*]" (Szondi, *Celan Studies*, 65). Indeed, the Celanian obscurity with which I am concerned is of another order than that of a figure of rhetoric, even that of *obscuritas*. Let me put it this way: in the so-called obscurity of Celan's poetry, the meticulous disarticulation of language and its tropological and rhetorical structure so as to be able to pay attention to minute detail and to possess what is expected of a poem that seeks to reach the Other, namely, precision—a disarticulation that, as all the good readings of the poems demonstrate, can be reconstructed in equal detail—is what the specific obscurity of his poems offers to understanding. Since all the procedures of such a disarticulation can be identified, the specificity of the obscurity in question consists, paradoxically speaking, in its very intelligibility.

To secure this paradoxical intelligibility of Celanian obscurity, a debunking of all attempts to lift it precipitously, pretending that the poems are about this or that, becomes necessary. This, in my view, is the great accomplishment of Oyarzun's work. From the first lines of this foreword, I have pointed out that, even though in his speech in Bremen Celan refers to a certain experience only in an extremely discrete and reserved formulation as "what happened," this experience is, for Oyarzun, undoubtedly a major concern of Celan's poetic writing. But this indelible experience, in view of which one would thus be able to situate or determine his poetry as a variation within the genre of poetry, is not what Celan's art seeks to verbalize. Rather, it is an experience concerning poetry itself; since, moreover, there is no longer anything as such after the unnamable event that has happened, it is an experience of the poem and, more precisely, an experience of the idiom *of* the poem.[11] Not of a poetry after the unnamable, that is, but rather of a reshaping—after and in light of "what happened"—of poetry in its totality, singularizing the poem and shaping it as an address, thus recasting the idiom of the poem today. For this reason, Celan's poetry is not simply confessional or testimonial. It cannot simply be explained by "what happened." As Szondi notes, the secret credo or guiding word of his poetry has "an essentially nonconfessional, impersonal character" (Szondi, *Celan Studies*, 74).

If the preposition "of" is italicized in the expression "the idiom *of* the poem," which I borrow from Szondi, it is not to highlight the double genitive indicating a belonging.[12] Rather than thus highlighting the ambiguity of the genitive and the ensuing equality of the subjective and objective, not to speak of an eventual dialectical relation between the two, I wish to bend the expression entirely in the direction of the poem. For Szondi the poem is idiomatic insofar as what it accomplishes "is neither verbal nor discursive" (Szondi, *Celan Studies*, 38). By contrast, by highlighting the "of" in "the idiom *of* the poem," I wish to emphasize that, as far as its total structure is concerned, *the* poem—"the poem today"—is not simply predictable in terms of general rules constitutive of what to expect from poetry as a genre.

The poem, in a Celanian sense, is marked by objective idiomaticity; it is in its very existence and its very essence idiomatic, each time unique, and it stands apart from all other poems. As we know from *The Meridian*, "the poem is lonely" (Celan, *Meridian*, 34a). It is *idios*, uniquely itself, and "speaks always only on its own, its very own behalf" (31a), and it is by implication separate and alone. However, this aloneness peculiar to the poem without a genre or an epochal variation of a general form that would make it generally meaningful, this (if I may dare say) "material" idiomaticity that is at the same time the poem's manner of speaking "exactly *on another's behalf*" (31b)—this is, precisely, what needs to be thought.

Compelled by a profound respect for the singularity of Celan's poetry and for the equally singular understanding that it represents of the poem in all its constitutive datedness and precision, Oyarzun observes a methodological reservation, a profound awe before the very singularity of the Celanian poem and what the poet himself says about it, an awe that is, as I have suggested, manifest in the systematic resistance to all interpretations that presumptuously seek to fix its cause and what it says. This respect for what it is that Celan has "found"—"poetry as experience," to cite the title of Lacoue-Labarthe's commentary—even prevents Oyarzun from reducing it to an experience of the Holocaust. Even Oyarzun's own observations, when they venture forth to make interpretive statements, are almost always modulated by a "perhaps," consistently seeking to keep open the "between" and its space of "vacillating opposition."

Since the dialogue that supposedly took place between Heidegger and Celan has to a large extent shaped the way in which the latter's thought and poetry have been received, let me now return to the question of dialogue and, more specifically, to this particular dialogue. For reasons to which I have already alluded, there has been, undoubtedly, an exchange between Heidegger and Celan; yet, since it did not occur in a dialogic and discursive fashion, it is also one that is unmistakably still going on between their works. Oyarzun's study is a case in point. It is an exchange that, as demonstrated by the ongoing Celan scholarship, has not come to a rest and whose form is not dialogical in the ordinary and philosophical sense. In the same way that the poem intervenes in any conversation about art, "something does interfere [*kommt dazwischen*]" in this dialogue; something interrupts it (Celan, *Meridian*, 1c)—namely, the resistance of Celan's poetry, as well as *The Meridian*, to concerns that might at first glance be misunderstood as indicative of a certain proximity to Heidegger's philosophy. *The Meridian* is certainly, in some of its parts, an engagement with Heidegger's thought.

But Heidegger's thought is countered here, and it is countered not in an argumentative but, rather, first and foremost in a singular fashion, namely, countered with "the poem today" in all its singularity. In other words, what Celan opposes to the thinker's thought is not an argument but, rather, the singular poem or individuated speech, that is, a speaking that does not allow itself to be gathered into one—into one unified sense concerning Being—and that therefore, as a counterword, amounts to barely nothing, to a doit, as it were, incapable in its "absurdity" of being sublated and resistant to any meaningful standstill.

So far, it should be clear that Oyarzun, too, resists any attempt to arrest the exchange between Heidegger and Celan and, in particular, such an attempt in the form of a Heideggerian reading of Celan. Yet, by insisting on the fact that Celan "only" counters Heidegger's thought by way of the poem, this also excludes "counteracting Heidegger with supposed Celanian theses" (Oyarzun, *Between Celan and Heidegger*, 94).[13] The poem opposes the Heideggerian notion of *Sprache* with a *Sprechen* that is not that of "language" but, rather, that of the singular poem. At stake in this controversy is thus language itself—language and *its* saying. Although in his talk in Bremen Celan utters confidently that, notwithstanding what happened and in spite of the absence of words for it, language "had to go through terrifying muteness, through the thousand darknesses of murderous speech," but was still the only thing that "remained reachable, close and secure amid all losses" (Celan, *Collected Prose*, 34; translation modified), nothing—after all—is less certain. Rather than the language that, while preceding all singular speech acts, opens within itself the horizon of a world destined for a people, what remained was only the language allowing the poem to speak. With language at stake, however, is Celan not also resisting the very matrix that the gathering essence of language imparts to dialogue—to a dialogue between thought and poetry—even though it may, as Heidegger's analyses of Trakl have shown, preserve the singularity of what is gathered into a meaningful whole?

Heidegger's statement "die Sprache spricht" lies, Oyarzun writes in the book's central chapter titled "Language," "in the gravitational center of my reflections . . . ; its powerful force of attraction, it seems to me, should be emphasized if one seeks to discover the relation between Celan and Heidegger" (Oyarzun, *Between Celan and Heidegger*, 129n3). If the statement in question occupies the "gravitational center" of the book's reflections, it is because here the "between" of a dialogue between Celan and Heidegger is decided. This is the case, first, because a dialogue, strictly speaking, requires that one speak about the same: that *Sprache* be a self-identical sameness, that the protagonists of the *Gespräch* speak in the same language, and that they are determined to address this one sameness. Yet, the abrupt and disruptive exclamation in *The Meridian*—"But the poem does speak [*Aber das Gedicht spricht ja*]!" (Celan, *Meridian*, 31a)—opens a space of confrontation, a "between" that is not dialogical. With the claim that it is the poem that speaks, "the possibility not only of *Sprache* but also of its sameness . . . is definitively suspended in Celan and Heidegger's *Gespräch*," Oyarzun avers (*Between Celan and Heidegger*, 11). With the "but" (*aber*) of the interjection, a partitioning line—a meridian, perhaps—is drawn, thus opening the space from whence the singular poem speaks, countering and resisting Heidegger's understanding of language as what speaks—that is, countering and resisting one of Heidegger's central thoughts.

Thematically speaking, more than merely one theme is, of course, at stake in the dialogue between Heidegger and Celan. On the basis of *The Meridian*, it can be shown that topics such as—among others—the relation of art and poetry, the centrality of Hölderlin's poetry and thought for Heidegger's understanding of poetry, and the status of "place" with respect to the poem occupy an important place. However, all of these topics converge in that they make gathering—the unification of everything in itself and of everything into a meaningful whole—the center of Heidegger's thoughts not only on poetry but on language, as well. The word, or language, *is* a gathering, one that lets Being appear in beings. Yet, Oyarzun asks, "is the essential experience of [Celan's] poetry not the word's literally unheard-of break, an unsayable break in any of the modes in which saying is—still—possible? A break that does not permit the thread that ties thing, word, and world in the word *is* (*es ist*)" (*Between Celan and Heidegger*, 75)? That which resists gathering by the word, or through language, is for Celan something indelibly anterior to the anteriority of gathering, something to be thought as the unthinkable, "the thought of the raw, knowledge of the raw" (70), something that cleaves the dialogue, exacerbates the "between," and prevents its poles from losing their distinctness.

This between-space is a space other than that of the medium of language—of language understood as a medium—in which some dialogue between Celan and Heidegger could have taken place and could have found its place; it is the space for another way of being-with (*Mitsein*), where language is the singular way of reaching out to the Other, an encounter that is always only actualized in a punctual and punctuating way, that is, always only in the form of an interrupting interjection resistant to the conventional dimension of language and as "absurd" as Lucile's sudden exclamation,

"Long live the King!" Let us remind ourselves that the meridian is "a partitioning line" (Oyarzun, *Between Celan and Heidegger*, 34). If, to conclude his speech in Darmstadt, Celan exclaims that he finds something, that he finds a meridian, that the meridian is "what connects and leads, like the poem, to an encounter" (Celan, *Meridian*, 50b), then the meridian names language—not, however, language as something to which one belongs but, rather, language as it speaks in the dated poem and opens up a reaching toward the Other in an always singular way, always anew, and always for the first time. Let us also remind ourselves that, as midday (*meridies*), a meridian is the moment when the sun stands at its highest, the climax between sunrise and sunset. This between-space opened by a meridian—by a certain language—is, therefore, "the time of inescapable clarity" (Oyarzun, *Between Celan and Heidegger*, 17). It is an *actual* and individuated space, a space defined by the time at which (or as which) it occurs and whose extreme clarity—or meridianity—is as improbable, impossible, absurd, and u-topic as the between-space and between-time in question. In other words, in its very obscurity, the language of the poem radiates extreme clarity.

As I have suggested, *Between Celan and Heidegger* is an assiduous effort to resist all interpretations and readings of Celan tempted to locate and fix his work and thought in a stable place. From what we have seen so far, the Celanian conception of place—the topos of his study of topoi—is that of a "between." It comes as no surprise, therefore, if Oyarzun also confesses that he does "not feel inclined" to validate Derrida's "Jewish theory of the poem" (*Between Celan and Heidegger*, 102). Oyarzun resists opposing to a German theory of the poem and its place, such as Heidegger's, and by extension also to a Greek paradigm an other determined paradigm—more precisely, a paradigm of the Other construed along the predictable and conventional lines of the divide between Greek and Jewish thought. Needless to say, rather than situating Celan's work in one direction or the other, however plausible, Oyarzun wishes in this case as well to endure the "between" of both alternatives. However, more is at stake, and in conclusion I wish to highlight another outstanding concern of the book that, I believe, makes Oyarzun's contribution a singular one.

It is certainly not by accident that the concern in question is broached in the central chapter devoted to "Language." Throughout this chapter, Oyarzun argues that the Celanian poem seeks to extricate itself from "the occidental mimetic tradition," to uproot itself from "the metaphorical regime of occidental language" (*Between Celan and Heidegger*, 54), and to leave the Heideggerian—that is, the Western—conception of the absolute anteriority of language behind. What has been said so far regarding the nonrepresentational nature of the language of Celan's poems must suffice here. By contrast, the dense and intense pages of chapter 4, in which this departure from the tradition's mimetic conception of poetry is shown to be intertwined with a reconsideration of the function of image and metaphor, would require careful attention. In brief, Oyarzun submits here that "the form and dominant format of poetry in the occidental tradition" (54) are decided in Celanian poetry by the latter's treatment of the image or metaphor. As a movement of transportation and thus of reaching beyond, he argues, meta-phor "is the condition under which, in the circle of occidental languages, the possibility of the relation to the other has been established, predefining that relation as communication" (54–55). However, when Celan claims that, in the poem, the images are "what is perceived and is to be perceived once and always again once, and only here and now," the poem becomes "the place where all tropes and metaphors want to be carried ad absurdum" (Celan, *Meridian*, 39b). Thus practiced, though they remain repeatable, the images and metaphors of language are also "only here and now" (39b) in the poem—that is, in the singular in all its uniqueness—and are therefore subtracted from their universal availability in the arsenal or "garden of rhetoric" (Oyarzun, *Between Celan and Heidegger*, 54). In short, uprooted and destroyed, the metaphor's general citability and its power of taking one beyond oneself toward the Other, which is the very condition of the occidental understanding of language as communication and of the peculiar clarity that it possesses, are renounced to the benefit of thinking and practicing what Celan calls "*the mystery of the encounter*" (Celan, *Meridian*, 34b), an encounter that, qua *ainigma*, seems to be shrouded in extreme obscurity. In other words, intent on securing a relation to the Other in all his, her, or its singularity, Celan's poetry undoes the occidental mode of relating to the Other that, as a meta-phoric transportation, has a universality under which all differences are subsumed in the brightest of lights, which as such is a light that, by forcing the Other into its brightness without shelter, paradoxically stifles all encounter.[14]

The "dialogue" between Heidegger and Celan, if it is a "dialogue," is marked by a resistance on Celan's part to Heidegger's "absolute postulation of the 'anteriority'" of language (Oyarzun, *Between Celan and Heidegger*, 129n3) and its speaking through both thinking and poetizing. As we have seen, it is to this anteriority, on the basis of which and through which we *are*, that Celan responds by interjecting: "But the poem does speak!"—not poetry as such but, rather, the individual poem as an inauguration of an address to the Other in advance of language's anteriority. Now, Oyarzun's point is that, with this statement, Celan breaks with "the Greco-Germanic matrix of dialogue" that Heidegger developed through his interpretations of Hölderlin and, by extension, with the Western matrix of dialogue, and this break occurs in view of "a different possibility of dialogue" (96–97). However, this possibility is not hastily to be associated with any determinate non-Western position, including—as we have seen—the Jewish paradigm. In the book's final chapter, titled "Dialogue" in the same way as the opening chapter, Oyarzun stresses not only that "*the political* is a principal key for all Celanian poetry" but also that "political" here is to be taken "in the highest and most radical sense" (95). The stakes of his reading of Celan thus become explicit: its aim is to rethink the nature of dialogue, which Heidegger's interpretation of Hölderlin has shaped into the constructive principle of community, as one that instead differs from its Greco-Germanic matrix and, in view of a non-Western conception of the dia-logical, has place for a plurality of logoi.

Again, the point is not that Celanian poetry has effectively broken with the occidental philosophical and rhetorical tradition regarding language, dialogue, and community and already speaks from another space, the space of the Other, as if this space could be definitively located. On the contrary, it is a u-topic, improbable, impossible, if not "absurd" space that is not to be confounded with any other so-called space and that can only be reached, without being reached once and for all, through or by way of a traversal of the Western paradigm that it suspends but does not therefore destroy. Celan's poetry goes the way of the Western tradition to free itself from it and thus perhaps to be able to take a step in the direction of what is other, an operation that occurs exclusively in, or as, the suspended "between."

By resisting the brilliance of so many astute readings and interpretations of Celanian poetry and thought, Oyarzun resists not only what he terms "the regime of eloquence," that is, "the occidental law of language," but also the light that prevails in it, "a light, a certain light, a law of light that forces clarity: *Lichtzwang*" (*Between Celan and Heidegger*, 57). In this foreword, I have been concerned with the alleged obscurity of Celanian poetry and the question concerning what sort of obscurity it is. From what we have seen, this poetry is a challenge to *lightduress*, to compulsive clarity, which also means that it is a challenge not to universality as such but, rather, to a certain form of the universal. Inevitably, such a challenge would necessarily seem to give in to obscurity. Yet, when Oyarzun avers that, in the face of forced clarity, "one must also affirm another mode of light [. . . ,] the light of u-topia, of the *absurd* place" (59), it is not a light intent on illuminating the particular at the expense of the universal. For the philosopher whose eyes are inescapably oriented toward the universal, Celanian poetry represents an extraordinary challenge. In order to be capable of thinking how, in the dated and thus individualized poem, that which is "perceived once" is "always again once" what it is "only here and now" (Celan, *Meridian*, 39b), one must think a repeatability of the singular constitutive of its equally singular otherness and its reaching toward and addressing the Other—a repeatability that, at the same time, provides the obscurity of the singular outreach with another kind of clarity and, by extension, another kind of universality for which there is no model. Although no determinate model for such universality can be found in any of the existent forms of the nonoccidental, thought and the poem must traverse the occidental in order to be able to take a step, perhaps, in the direction of this u-topic place.

Translator's Note

If any work worthy of the name is untranslatable, *Entre Celan y Heidegger* inhabits the limit of translation at least twice. For Pablo Oyarzun taps uniquely Spanish resources *not only* in his commentaries on *but also* in his own translations of Paul Celan. In addition to translating into Spanish the German poems and prose analyzed throughout this book's prologue and seven chapters, Oyarzun appends a comprehensive Spanish translation of Celan's *The Meridian* to the original volume of *Entre Celan y Heidegger*. Necessary, perhaps, but neither feasible nor desirable to retranslate Celan into English in light of Oyarzun's Spanish translations, I merely modify—and flag as modified—the extant English translations that lose the subtle tenor of Oyarzun's reading. For Celan's poetry, I include both the original German and the English translation but, since all cited translations are bilingual, I remove Oyarzun's original references to Celan's *Gesammelte Werke*, except where significant discrepancies call for justification. Since some English translator's place Celan's titles in CAPITALS and others in SMALL CAPITALS, following Celan's *Gesammelte Werke* I have systematized all titles as capitals for the sake of consistency.

Most [bracketed] glosses within Oyarzun's quotations are his own. Within citations, I gloss words or formulations only on the rare occasions when I have to modify standard English translations of Celan or his commentators more or less drastically. All bracketed interventions in the main text, however, are mine. More specifically, I add glosses of Oyarzun's original Spanish wherever the semantic or grammatical play isn't readily audible in English; when even a gloss fails to clarify, I add a translator's note. I sign all my endnotes with <—Translator.> and, whenever necessary to add a comment to one of Oyarzun's endnotes, I place my comment in brackets before signing it in the same way.

Oyarzun's commentaries about Spanish translations—his own or those of others—pose particular difficulties. At times, though always in conversation with Oyarzun, I have simply omitted these observations for the sake of this anglophone edition. At other times, however, the commentaries motivate the argument itself and therefore cannot be omitted. In these cases, when I don't manage to graft Oyarzun's comments concerning the Spanish translation onto the English translation, I add an explanatory note. Wherever no English edition is cited, I myself translate the quotation from Spanish, French, or German. With respect to lexical difficulties more generally, I mention here only that I systematically translate *sentido* as "meaning," but I exchange "meaning" for "sense" whenever a certain sensibility is also at stake (e.g., in the discussion of pain in chapter 5) or whenever English idioms demand (e.g., "to make sense"), and I gloss the words wherever this alternation risks confusion. Notwithstanding certain modifications, consolidations, and additions drawn from the new preface, entries in the index at the end of this volume come from *Entre Celan y Heidegger*.

In principle, I stay rather close to Oyarzun's Spanish. The well-known disadvantages of a literal approach to translation are exacerbated in the present case because Oyarzun's syntax is consistently difficult even within a language in itself more syntactically versatile than English. Similarly, he often uses an unexpected, at times even archaic lexicon. Consequently, sentences are often long and dense. Shortening sentences or refashioning their language, however, would run a number of uninsurable risks. To make a dependent clause an independent clause, for instance, gives it an emphasis that the original refuses it. To use an inconspicuous word for one that strikes the reader in Spanish, inversely, neutralizes its emphasis. In short, I have tried to translate not only words and sentences but also the experience of reading them. Suffice one example among many possible:

> Variedad, diversidad de lugares: aquel espacio inquietante (*unheimlich* es la palabra de Celan, y conviene que la inscribamos ya, intraducida, intraducible) en que el arte—que, por otra parte, es también ubicuo—"parece estar en casa," y el lugar "abierto, vacío y libre," "lejano y ocupable," de un "fuera" que es la región de procedencia del Otro, hacia la que se endereza el poema y en cuya cercanía está, quizá; dos lugares "ajenos" que, tan difíciles de discernir, son "acaso, por último, no más que una ajenidad."
> (*Entre Celan y Heidegger*, 39)

My translation runs:

> Variety, diversity of places: that disquieting space (*unheimlich* is Celan's word [*Meridian,* 17a], and it is necessary to inscribe it here already, untranslated, untranslatable) in which art—which, furthermore, is also ubiquitous—"seem[s] to be at home" (17a), and the place "open, empty and free" (36c), "inhabitable distance" (43), of a "beyond" (17a) as the region from which the Other comes, toward which the poem stretches out, and in the proximity of which it perhaps is. (18–19)

This passage comes from chapter 2, "Place," and this sentence is crucial insofar as it maps the topology at stake. The sentence opens by announcing a "variety" or "diversity" of places and then, after a colon, lists the places comprising it: "that disquieting space . . . in which art . . . 'seem[s] to be at home' (17a), and the place . . . from which the Other comes." While I've rearranged clauses and punctuation to meet the demands of English syntax, I haven't shortened, simplified, or "corrected" the sentence by, say, adding a verb. Readers might struggle with the intervening clauses, to be sure, but this struggle is, in a way, precisely the point. At stake is a topology that Celan describes as *unheimlich,* and Oyarzun's description reproduces this disorientation by proliferating clauses, parentheses, dashes, commas, and quotations.

Two final issues merit mention since, at least in ways not comprehended in the traditional concept of translation, they make *Between Celan and Heidegger* a different book from *Entre Celan y Heidegger.* First, upon responding to my queries and reviewing various drafts, Oyarzun took the opportunity to add an occasional reference, detail, or elongation to the translation. As these additions began to accumulate throughout the manuscript, I opted to make a general note of them here at the outset rather than intrusively flag each instance with a translator's note. Second, Oyarzun often quotes Celan's works at length in the original Spanish but, due to issues of "fair use," it was not possible to preserve these quotations. As a translator, I wouldn't presume to make decisions concerning which lines to cut or paraphrase (assuming this is even possible in poetry), and Oyarzun has graciously made the necessary edits for this English edition. As Oyarzun himself noted in the case "Singbarer Rest" in particular, it is especially unfortunate to lose so many parts of a poetry that sings precisely of "remainders."

I warmly thank Rodolphe Gasché for writing the foreword to this English edition. This project would not have been possible without David E. Johnson's support and encouragement from beginning to end. Paula Cucurella Lavín helped track down numerous works in the bibliography and often lent her Chilean ear to my questions. There is perhaps no greater advantage for a translator than the possibility of discussing difficulties with the author him- or herself, and I am very grateful to Pablo Oyarzun for reading through my drafts carefully and patiently responding to all my questions. Any remaining errors or oversights, of course, are my own.

Prologue

I am going to recall things that are all too well known. When Paul Celan read some of his poems in Freiburg im Breisgau on 24 July 1967, Martin Heidegger was in the audience. The next day, they met in the cabin at Todtnauberg, that unadorned refuge annexed to the smooth slope of a hill in the Black Forest to which the philosopher would withdraw in order to immerse himself in his pensive craft—"knit at the secretstocking"[1]—sustained in the rhythm of modest daily labors and walks.

What was said? What happened between the two? Almost from the very moment it occurred, this meeting has incited innumerable commentaries and attempts at interpretation. The more they have intensified, the more famous the entirely decisive significance of Celan's work has become for poetry's situation and for the relations between poetry and philosophy in the epoch of late modernity, and the more complex consideration of Heidegger's thought has become for the situation of philosophy and for its relations to poetry and art within that same horizon. Without having to cave to the temptation of seeing in the meeting "a quasi-mythical episode of our epoch," as Alain Badiou calls it (*Manifesto*, 86), due to the vexing resonance that the allusion to the "mythical" might have precisely in this context (among which numbers, above all, the formulation "myth of the twentieth century" that Alfred Rosenberg uses to characterize Nazism),[2] it cannot be omitted that this meeting is pregnant with signs.

What happened between the two? I asked. Many hypotheses have been ventured with respect to this meeting, the relation between Heidegger and Celan, and the poem—the remarkable poem "Todtnauberg"—that would seem to cipher their relation like a dense abbreviation, along with equally many wagers on the "word / to come" (Celan, *Collected Later Poetry*, 257) onto which the poet's cordial hope opens. It seems entirely vain to me—

vain for me at least—to venture a conjecture with even a minimal aim of verisimilitude concerning this meeting and the other issues intertwined with it. To mention only one issue, I would have no other recourse than drawing up a story in which to make room for my conjecture and, perhaps, supporting this story with the several hints that patience might track in Celan's so densely sedimented writing. Unable to do so, I have limited myself to something else: I have sought to insist upon the "between," to interrogate it assiduously, to weigh it and plumb its depths. This book is not an exercise in fiction but, rather, an attempt to construct that "between" on the basis of its impossibility. For that very reason, I should confess beforehand that I have lost hope of doing justice to the "between"; the book has had to remain necessarily open at its extremities.[3]

Upon entering into the cabin, Celan signed the visitor log that the thinker kept: "Into the cabin logbook, with a view toward the Brunnenstern, with hope of a coming word in the heart."[4] On Maundy Thursday in 1970, Celan and Heidegger met again on the occasion of a reading before a small group. The philosopher proposed taking a walk with the poet in the summer of the same year. On 20 April, once again in Paris, Celan walked toward Pont Mirabeau, which neighbored his room, and threw himself into the Seine with no witnesses; a fisherman found his body seven miles away on the first of May.

1

"Dialogue"

Every attempt to write about the "dialogue" between Paul Celan and Martin Heidegger must be immediately warned of the difficulties, the great and perhaps insurmountable difficulties, that it must treat in order to win even its most basic right. The most basic, indeed, because these difficulties concern not only that to which both Heidegger and Celan attest concerning their absolutely radical experience of and reflection on poetry and thinking, which would already be quite a lot, perhaps too much; they also concern, much earlier, the terrain of dialogue itself and the question of whether there is, in effect, a "dialogue" here or, in other words, how we should conceive that which we call "dialogue" if, by this word, we mean what opens and tenses between Celan and Heidegger.

Without delay or detour, then, let the warning be inscribed here on the portico, a warning taken from one of Celan's poems that—in the margin of polished control and security and only by virtue of the merest inkling—registers, fixes, and circumscribes in a way that is equally definitive and suspended the visit that the poet paid to the thinker at his cabin in Todtnauberg in the summer of 1967.[1] "Todtnauberg" is the title of the poem included in the posthumous book *Lightduress* (*Lichtzwang*). It has been cited, discussed, interpreted thousands of times. The poem's opening verses continue to ring in one's ears—the well, the star-die, the cabin (*die Hütte*), the inscription in the guest book that Heidegger kept there, "the line about / a hope, today" (*die . . . Zeile von / einer Hoffnung, heute*), an intimate hope for just one word that would or could come from a thinker (Celan, *Collected Later Poetry*, 254–57).

A diaphanous and at the same time unapproachable, impenetrable poem. Impenetrable, perhaps, because purely diaphanous. Everything is there in the light, in the *forced light* that prevails in these final poems; everything: including the formfitting reticence in which the poems are gathered. With everything clear, *deutlich*, how could one say that Celan's poetry is hermetic? No, not hermeticism: clarity. So, I do not claim to offer a commentary or to venture a clarifying interpretation—to contribute a sterile light where everything is light—but rather confine myself, as I said, to the warning. The fourth, seventh, and eighth stanzas:

Waldwasen, uneingeebnet,
Orchis und Orchis, einzeln,

[. . .]

die halb-
beschrittenen Knüppel-
pfade im Hochmoor,

Feuchtes,
viel.
(Celan, *Collected Later Poetry*, 256)

forest sward, unleveled,
orchis and orchis, singly,

[. . .]

the half-
trod log-
trails on the highmoor,

humidity,
much.
(Celan, *Collected Later Poetry*, 257)

The inkling, then: Celan and Heidegger, "orchis and orchis," close, separated, singly (*einzeln*), isolated in their pure singularity. And the terrain, that is, the terrain of the "dialogue": forest sward, yes, but harsh; log-trails, but "half- / trod"; miry, muddy ground that, "humidity, / much," makes all walking hard, trammels it—imminent erasure of the roads.

I asked how one could say that Celan's poetry is obscure, impenetrable. How could his own body, his own body of writing, be a sort of *corpus hermeticum*, according to the arcane rules of which unsuspected transmutations of sense would take place? If there is something to the nature of these transmutations, it claims us evidentially as sober and truthful witnesses and not as painstaking decipherers: it claims our thought and not our suspicion or, otherwise, it claims our perception and not our fervor for the occult. Our perhaps blind ear.

I am not speaking of hermeticism, then, but I'm not speaking of univocal clarity either. The zeal of hermeneutics should be situated between the two extremes, as a spiritual discipline that assigns itself the task of mediating between the secret of singularity, the privacy of the idiom, the irremissible dating of what is done [*lo gestado*] on the one hand and, on the other, the universality of knowledge, the publicity of language, the historicity of the deed [*la gesta*]. Such mediation has an obligation to be critical because it must know how to separate not only marks, already closed in their punctual occurrence, from their meanings but also crystalized meanings that a preestablished universality would want merely to re-cognize here from those meanings that have become—even if only latently—an institutional object by virtue of the occurrence.

I leave suspended the question of whether such a mediation could suit Celan's poetry, although doubt has already begun to grow visibly. I want only to evoke a certain disconcerting example of that hermeneutic zeal from Hans-Georg Gadamer's hand. I do so because, it seems to me, this example can better profile what I have named the "inkling" by sharpening the sense of the difficulty. In question is the brief commentary that Gadamer dedicates to the poem cited above over the course of his argument in the essay "Under the Shadow of Nihilism."[2] I said that the example is disconcerting, and I perhaps could have aggravated this epithet by recalling the note in which an angry Philippe Lacoue-Labarthe refers to the text, labeling it "the birth of a hagiography" (*Poetry as Experience*, 94), which will be the hagiography of Saint Heidegger—Saint Martin of the Forest, of course.[3] I am not going to linger on what this staunch critic mentions: the idyllic haze in which the poem and, along with it, the relation between Celan and Heidegger appear bathed, the curative virtue attributed to the cabin's view amid the rural countryside—"little-light balm [*baume luminette*]"—and to the "fountain topped by the / starred wooden die [*la fontaine surmontée du / dé de bois, étoilé*]," as Marc B. de Launay translates and thereby, as Lacoue-Labarthe points out (*Poetry as Experience*, 93), carries out a strange explication of the poetic speech under the influence of the Gadamerian reading.

In terms of my present concern, what I wish to underscore—and, certainly, it has to do with this effect of "explication"—is the surprisingly acritical character that this hermeneutic master's reading assumes, concentrating on what he takes to have been the intention guiding Celan in his visit. He was searching for "a word, a coming word, of hope for today. Carrying this secret hope in his heart, the poet wrote his line" (Gadamer, "Under the Shadow," 122). Hope for a word of hope, a coming word, from Heidegger, from one who thinks, from "a thinker": is this what the poem says? Does a discrete and peculiar displacement not take place here? A displacement that carries from Celan's cordial hope—the hope of his written line or, rather, the hope to which that line belongs, a line written *from* that "hope, today"—to the coming or the perhaps coming word from Heidegger, which would have to be invested, today, with that hopeful virtue? A displacement, then, and even almost a reduction of the hope for a word from the future time of what comes (but is it a question of a simple future in the form of a privation of the present in the negativity of a not-yet?)[4] to the punctually present, current time of today. And one would perhaps have to wonder if this displacement—this slippage that makes the word a hope (or rather that only sketches the word as a hope) that harbors in its present, however fragile and provisional it might be thought, the visitation of what comes, of meaning—is due only to a reading carried away by its intentions or if it does not belong entirely, essentially, to the perspective of hermeneutics. Can hermeneutics think the *to come* (that pure imminence, that *nothing of meaning*) in which—perhaps—the "word / to come [*kommendes*]"[5] consists? Can it, and nothing else, persist in the heart of hope?

In any case, the conclusion of Gadamer's note ends up consummating the displacement in question: "It is a reference to Heidegger's not claiming and not being able to have a coming word, a hope for today—he tried to take a few steps along a risky path" (Gadamer, "Under the Shadow," 123). And this is, precisely, what Celan would have understood *après coup* in the car on the way back: "Only now while they are conversing does the 'raw' become clear to him. What Heidegger said and what Celan at first did not understand: Heidegger's words suddenly take on meaning for him and the other—not for the 'person who drives us'" (123; translation modified).

I will not pause now on the question of the third party, the *witness*, the one who listens but does not understand, although the key to Gadamer's grandiose deafness to what the poem says is perhaps deposited here.[6] Only later will I try to intervene on this point. In the meantime, I limit myself to observing that the third, the witness that lives on in isolation—like another flower—in the sixth stanza, not only administers the poor listening *test*,[7] the counterpoint and the necessary counterproof for a proper understanding, for the truth's intelligence: perhaps precisely *this* listening is required for the "raw" to be made clear.

In the meantime, one can also see that, on the basis of hermeneutics, Gadamer has read the poem as the poem of a hermeneutic experience: Celan's awakening to the well-defined and clear understanding (but what does *deutlich* mean here?[8]) of Heidegger's thinking enterprise. At the risk of somewhat breaking protocols of politeness, I think one would have the right to question whether the trip and the visit were necessary to reach this understanding, whether it was really a pilgrimage (like so many others) to a thinker's solitary keep in search of a word of advice, a guiding oracle, and whether with this exegesis—despite the laudatory flourish that Gadamer subsequently adds in recognition of the poet—the poem's intensity is not trivialized, already converted into an evocation and commentary and, ultimately, homage to the sage in the cabin.[9] One could perhaps say that Gadamer reads the poem from Heidegger and for him; he measures the poem and its saying—and the one to whom it speaks in the comprehensive experience that would have taken place here—on the basis of the fixed, the extremely fixed, center of the Heideggerian enterprise.

But is this what the poem says? Is this the experience in and with it? I do not speak, then, of what the poem *means to say* [quiere decir]: a poem does not *mean* to say anything, probably because a poem is only written when all intent [*querer*] has been nullified, stunned. For the same reason, to claim that one can make a certain pronouncement concerning the intentions that motivated Celan in his visit is, from every point of view, not only illusory but also sterile if one thereby claims to unravel the poem's *signified*. Otherwise, the poem speaks of what is hoped with all possible and desirable precision of "a hope, today," namely a *word*, a word *to come*:

kommendes
Wort.

Not a word of hope, as Gadamer interprets it, but a word that does *correspond* to hope. How? As a coming [*viniendo*] word, the essence of *this* word thus concentrates absolutely in its coming [*advenimiento*]. Not, therefore, a word that says something, not a word that refers, relates, announces, signals, indicates, or manifests something, but rather a word that is only the event of its own coming, of its going to the encounter.

Among all possible and profferable words, conjectures concerning *which word* this word might have been, which it could or should have been, also perhaps belong to the kingdom of intentions and would be, for the same reason, perfectly adventurous and even abusive. Not that knowledge of the circumstances of a poem's gestation in general (to which the intentions, along with many other things, could also belong) are entirely indifferent with respect to what the poem says—and above and before all a poem by Celan; no, this knowledge is not indifferent, and I will soon have occasion to consider this question, but it is not possible to determine these circumstances in the final analysis. Otherwise, it is perhaps not a question of knowing which word, among words, would have corresponded to the hope kept "in the heart"; perhaps the hope concerned a distant relation to the word in which it would be fulfilled—assuming that there would be neither paradigm nor criterion to measure such an occurrence—as the definitively incommensurable event of its coming. And, finally, since it is hope and cannot conjure up what is hoped for, since it cannot bring on that onto which it opens, does the radical unanticipation of the word not belong to this hope's very essence? And is it not precisely by virtue of the fact that this word is, in its essence, absolutely impossible to anticipate and only by virtue of such unanticipation that it—what is called *to come*—might come?[10]

Although I speak on and on, why do I abstain from interpreting? Why do I feel I cannot pronounce anything definitive about what happens in this poem? It is, perhaps, because I want to hold on to the impression—my earliest impression—that there is something *unthinkable* here, and this unthinkable would be the unthinkable (*das Undenkbare*) of an encounter without encounter, without dialogue, on a today that slips over itself (*heute, Feuchtes*), dislodges itself from itself, de-spairs [*des-espera*],[11] drowning, falling on itself (*viel: fiel*). The unthinkable, *das Undenkbare*, imposes the terrible desolation of a forced and essential ingratitude (*Undankbarkeit*),[12] a word's immurement upon itself. The word and the word: Heidegger's and Celan's. Between both words, between both men, between Celan and Heidegger, the "raw" prevails.

And what is the "raw"? Is it what Gadamer supposes: Heidegger's expressions that Celan did not understand at first and penetrated only "later"? But what would the "raw" be in that case? What Heidegger says or its very saying—his tone, for example? Do either one of these or both remain "raw"—thus metaphorically said—while they do not allow themselves to take root in meaning? In which case, clarity would stem from uprooting the "raw" from its rawness, running it through the spirit's fire, incorporating it into the kingdom of meaning, which we tend to identify with the dimension of the human, that space in which we can properly say "us."

Some signs suggest that the latter is the direction of Gadamer's reading, signs that become evident when he speaks of the anecdote and the juncture that occasioned the poem. Of Celan's poetic, which differs from Stéphane Mallarmé's in its adherence to the "particular situation," to the "'existential' reference," Gadamer says: "This reference to a situation, which lends the poem something occasional and appears to demand elaboration through knowledge of the particular situation, is, in truth, elevated to the realm of the meaningful and true, and thereby allows it to become an authentic poem. It speaks for us all" (Gadamer, "Under the Shadow," 123).[13] Earlier, he says: "It [the visit] became a poem because the experience expresses him and us all" (123). The authentic poem is the universal poem, which speak for us all. For and through us.

If so, however, if this is its direction, Gadamer's universalizing hermeneutical reading would forget, it seems to me, its own mediating function, its mission of *hermeneia* if, as I indicated above, this mission contains as one of its necessary moments the (re)cognition that an event—an incision in language inferred, for instance, through an "I" or a "you"—can alter the entire dimension of meaning. Here, in this reading, the universal governs as what is prescribed and as the prescription to conserve it; it is nourished by the essential figure of the *a priori*, which is the *a priori* of "meaningfulness" and importance (*Bedeutsamkeit*). The universal of hermeneutics—which it inherits from the purest metaphysics—rests upon the postulate that every event is such only through the possibility of being inscribed in that dimension. And this postulate will have to be conceded to hermeneutics, I believe, because it is entirely valid if one takes into account that it is not clear how an event could even be indicated in the margins of this constitutive possibility. But one will also have to exercise resistance here, precisely here and without a moment's rest, because the postulate does not do justice to the happening of the event [*al acontecer del acontecimiento*]. It is unjust, because it forgets that the inscription itself is an interruption, an *irruption of nothing* in that dimension,[14] an irruption that exceeds [*desmide*] it—even if only minimally, microscopically—and cannot be measured [*medir*] by it in the incisive moment of its occurrence. Yet, of course, one will argue that I am arbitrarily playing with the fiction of an inscription without history, as if the coming of a word from outside language were possible. And if this were precisely at issue?

I asked, what is the "raw"? But has it not already become clear, well-defined, *deutlich*? Has it not already been shown that, if it primarily withdraws from the dimension of significance [*significancia*] (if one allows me the term), the raw should also escape, without further ado, the domain of every question (questions are the guardians—the customs agents—of this domain)? Might one even say that the raw is unthinkable? Can it be said that the raw *is*? The raw: the unthinkable, *das Undenkbare, das Undankbare*. The raw: live and bleeding flesh that continues testifying to life even in death because it bleeds; the raw: the wound itself.[15] Itself? But wouldn't this therefore make the wound thinkable? Is to say "itself," to think the wound "in itself" and "as such," not already to begin staunching it? Does the poem not speak—or, I might say more timidly, seem to speak—of an inevitable persistence of the raw, of the wound, despite every balsamic virtue? How to think the wound, how to think the wound without healing it into a scar, how to think *that* wound which is impossible to thank?

Here, then, is the difficulty: prior to every purpose, intention, or will, Celan's incarnated resistance, a resistance that comes imposed and surpasses all sentiment or certainty even of proximity [*vecindad*]. For there is a proximity—an extremely tight proximity—between Celan and Heidegger, but a proximity the "between" of which is absolutely uncrossable: a place without passage. The problem, as I was saying, concerns how to conceive the "dialogue" (and this word *Gespräch*, let us recall, divides between them); the problem, as my phrasing implied, concerns how to conceive "dialogue" *in general*. The warning guards us against supposing Heidegger and Celan to be some collaborators or colaborers in discourse, some collaborators or colaborers of the word, eloquent interlocuters of the Same, and it also warns us against believing that this would be a dialogue the *general* possibility of which could be established or, at least, managed. Celan's reticence, his resistance, is *the defense of something irreducible*.

It would seem that I speak of the *Shoah*, the *Holocaust*, that abyss of history. I will say, perhaps, yes and no. The irreducible is and is not the Holocaust: if it could in some way be designated as such, it is that which continues to bleed, raw, in the middle of the general flame. The general is precisely what does not fit here, what can never be offered as the frame within which one might manage to announce, however evanescent and delicate, the irreducible.[16] Hence, neither the extermination of the Jewish population that mutes the poet's word nor the Nazi affiliation that remains indelible in the thinker's silence are "references" that permit one to clarify what "raw" means here (if it means something) or, thereby, the relation between Celan and Heidegger. Every attempt at denominating and recounting the history of this abyss obliterates the raw, giving us the confidence that it would be possible to bring it to the sphere—in the final analysis the consoling sphere—of meaning, of the human, of an "us." Therefore, I believe, nothing would be more misguided than granting this encounter without encounter a symbolic intensity and density toward which, I will not deny it, the scene and the circumstance and also interpretive zeal seduce us. Celan does not speak as the spokesperson for the sacrificed population; nor does Heidegger remain silent as a symptom of the murderous population. Celan is not "the poet"; it is barely an "I" that alludes to his name without uttering it and that, absorbed in the inscription in the visitor's log, no longer knows or did not manage to know which name ended up deposited before his own. Nor is Heidegger "the thinker"; he is only "a thinker" (*eines Denkenden*). Neither represents anything in this scene. They are only two singly (*einzeln*) individuals, placed in the trance of responding each for his own and, thus, of corresponding to each other in the muddy terrain of a single language in which the "we" suddenly became impossible.

In his "Speech" at Bremen, almost ten years before writing "Todtnauberg," Celan says the following about language, that is, about the same language divided between him and Heidegger:

> Only one thing remained reachable, close and secure amid all losses: language. Yes, language. In spite of everything, it remained secure against loss. But it had to go through its own lack of answers, through terrifying silence, through the thousand darknesses of murderous speech. It went through. It gave me no words for what was happening, but went through it. Went through and could resurface, "enriched" by it all.
>
> In this language I tried, during those years and the years after, to write poems: in order to speak, to orient myself, to find out where I was, where I was going, to chart my reality.
>
> It meant movement, you see, something happening, being *en route*, an attempt to find a direction. Whenever I ask about the sense of it, I remind myself that this implies the question as to which sense is clockwise.
>
> For the poem does not stand outside time. True, it claims the infinite and tries to reach across time—but across, not above.

> A poem, being an instance of language, hence essentially dialogue, may be a letter in a bottle thrown out to sea with the—surely not always strong—hope that it may somehow wash up somewhere, perhaps on a shoreline of the heart. In this way, too, poems are *en route*: they are headed toward.
>
> Toward what? Toward something open, inhabitable, an approachable you, perhaps, an approachable reality. (Celan, *Collected Prose*, 34–35)

I would like the echo of this large citation to extend throughout what I have previously said and to continue resonating until another, later citation resumes its tone, its rhythm. I imagine that Lacoue-Labarthe's observation, according to which "Todtnauberg" would be "the poem of a disappointment; as such it is, and it says, the disappointment of poetry" (*Poetry as Experience*, 36), could be related to the disenchantment of the already weakened hope of which this text speaks, the hope for receiving the poem—the shipwreck message—in the heartland (*Herzland*): the hope for dialogue. Sent blindly from a blink in absolutely punctual time, unrepeatable, and delivered to its uncertain destination [*destino*] but also to its tenacious direction in search of something open and occupiable that is, at the same time, the tenacity of its own opening and vacancy for the coming of another word, of the other's word (and of the other as word?), the word-poem is not found with the other's word, not reached with it, because it remains absent, reserved, stubborn. There is no dialogue, then; there was none; it did not occur. The "between" closes, shuts off, and the poem's word stagnates, begins to sink into the swamp. And yet, there would have to be something like a dialogue between Celan and Heidegger, for in something like a dialogue, like *that* dialogue, the fate [*destino*] of the poem *and* of thinking would perhaps play out.

This last affirmation seems to contradict flagrantly what I said about the radical singularity of the scene in "Todtnauberg." Here, however, singularity does not equal privacy; it is not restricted to the narrow circle of what interests only two parties to the exclusion of all others. Here, singularity is the nature of the "between," the place to which an other and all others are called, the primary form of interest, of *inter-esse*, which makes possible *Mitsein* and *Miteinandersein*. And thinking and poetry are perhaps the earliest gestures—and also the last gestures, posthumous gestures—that configure the interest. To persist in thinking and poetry is to expose oneself, even despite oneself, to the experience of the "between." Will it be necessary to recall that Celan's poetry and his thought of the poem were always defined in an intimate "dialogue" with Heidegger's thought? Will it be necessary to recall that what occurs in that "dialogue" not only concerns Celan's work but also, at every moment and with all desirable clarity, constitutes an interrogation, a solicitation, even a provocation of what the hermit in the Black Forest thinks? And for that very reason an interrogation of the "between" that measures both extreme proximity and extreme distance? Without in any way abolishing that interrogation or that "dialogue" (I have returned to quotation marks), on the contrary sharpening it, what Lacoue-Labarthe calls disappointment would weigh in here.

Would this disappointment be the experience of language divided? And would language divided—by the "raw"—be the "dialogue" or the condition of the "dialogue" between Celan and Heidegger? I could not say, not immediately. But I believe, clearly, that this dialogue will not be a "dialogue of language," *ein Gespräch von der Sprache*,[17] the genitive of which does not express solely or primarily an "about," a "concerning which," as if at stake were two wills to discourse—and nothing else—measuring themselves against each other, courting the truth, or undertaking the solidary search for something and converging toward it: language, speech. Rather, this genitive marks the pertinence and gestation of an agreed saying on the basis of the sameness and the reunifying unfolding of *a* language, *Sprache itself*; speech that, in its unfolding, needs interlocutors (*braucht sie*)—those that agree and intonate—appropriating them (for itself) to be said. No, I say, because the possibility of *Sprache* itself—not only whatever it is but also itself, the possibility not only of *Sprache* but also of its sameness—is definitively suspended in Celan and Heidegger's *Gespräch*. It is suspended from its impossibility. In this dialogue a fundamental *but* prevails, a *but* that in Celan's thought concerning the poem, already open as the space of this dialogue, brings the vertigo of the scission between poem and language and, at the same time, the vertigo of the mutual destining [*destinación*] of the splinters: "But the poem does speak [*Aber das Gedicht spricht ja*]!" (Celan, *Meridian*, 31a). This abrupt and disruptive exclamation in *The Meridian* will magnetize much of what I will later attempt to think here. Possibility and impossibility, joined and conjoined at the same time and, at the same time, one after the other, one betraying the other, affirming the other (this is the rhythm of Celan's verse), possibility and impossibility of poem and language. Extreme tension of dialogue, from here on out I would like to remain within this *but* in which I believe I perceive the trace of the raw.

Here, then, not in the suppression of the dialogue before it is even outlined, toward which so much seduces us. Emmanuel Levinas, it seems to me, proceeds in this way in an essay for which admiration is nonnegotiable: "Paul Celan: From Being to the Other," which insists upon all possible points of confrontation between Celan and Heidegger, points organized around Celan's refusal to concede the, let's say, archeological priority of language itself, *die Sprache selbst*, abundant in its prepersonal neutrality. I introduce this new direction to what I have previously outlined in order to round off the warning.

The essay's epigraph from "Cello-entry [*Cello-Einsatz*]" draws attention to a fundamental imbalance that, in its vehement movement, displaces the being of the scale:

> alles ist weniger, als
> es ist,
> alles ist mehr.
> (Celan, *Collected Later Poetry*, 68)

> all is less, than
> it is,
> all is more.
> (Celan, *Collected Later Poetry*, 69)

But the phrase that Levinas begins by citing—from a letter that Celan sends to Hans Bender, which numbers among Celan's few prose writings—marks the itinerary of the entire essay "From Being to the Other": "I cannot see any basic difference between a handshake and a poem [*Ich sehe keinen prinzipiellen Unterschied zwischen Händedruck und Gedicht*]" (Celan, *Collected Prose*, 26).[18] This idea of the poem, of "poetry itself as an unheard-of modality of *otherwise than being*," "more and less than being" (Levinas, *Proper Names*, 46), sustains Levinas's perspective.

> There is the poem, the height of language, reduced to the level of an interjection, a form of expression as undifferentiated as a wink, a sign to one's neighbor! A sign of what? Of life, of goodwill? Of complicity? Or a sign of nothing, or of complicity for no reason: a saying without a said [*dire sans dit*]. Or is it a sign that is its own signified: the subject signals that sign-giving to the point of becoming a sign through and through. An elementary communication without revelation, stammering infancy of discourse, a most clumsy intrusion in the famous "*language*

that speaks," the famous "*die Sprache spricht*": entrance of the beggar into "the house of being." [. . .]

The fact is, then, that for Celan the poem is situated precisely at that pre-syntactic and . . . pre-logical level, but a level also pre-disclosing: at the moment of pure touching, pure contact, grasping, squeezing—which is, perhaps, a way of giving, right up to and including the hand that gives. A language of proximity for proximity's sake, older than that of "the truth of being"—which it probably carries and sustains—the first of the languages, response preceding the question, responsibility for the neighbor, by its *for the other*, the whole marvel of giving. (Levinas, *Proper Names*, 40–41)

In a certain way, everything is already said in these initial passages. In brief and precise outlines, a system of premises has already been installed that possesses the strength and scope to draft a complete exegesis of Celan's poetic project. And this system has, as fundamental points of support, the theses with which Levinas himself opposes Heidegger. One could almost say that Celan becomes an instance of Levinas's persistent, unconceding debate with the master and that the allegation against "so much brilliant exegesis majestically descending from the mysterious *Schwarzwald* upon Hölderlin, Trakl and Rilke, portraying poetry as opening the world, the place between earth and sky" (Levinas, *Proper Names*, 42), might to a certain extent be undermined by a gesture that makes Celan the poetic confirmation of Levinas's radical ethics. I think it would be unfair to put it in these terms, however, and the "almost" restraining the indicated impression is perhaps already unfair: there exists in Levinas's reading a care for the poetic word—and for that word in which the poet reflects upon his own search—that is very far from simply using Celan for purposes of illustration.

Nevertheless, in all of Levinas's sentencings—for they do sound, energetically, like sentencings—an emphasis foreign to Celan's poetry resounds. The incarnation of Celan's poetry is infinitely more fragile. In this incarnation resides the unheard-of figure of what I would venture to call a *vacillating opposition*, which grows not weaker but stronger in the hesitation and stuttering. Levinas has indeed auscultated "Paul Celan's breathless [*haletante*] meditation" (Levinas, *Proper Names* 42; translation modified), that is, the nature of *The Meridian* as an "elliptic, allusive text, constantly interrupting itself in order to let through, in the interruptions, his other voice, as if two or more discourses were on top of one other [*sic*], with a strange coherence, not that of a dialogue, but woven in a counterpoint that constitutes—despite their immediate melodic unity—the texture of his poems" (41). But one already sees that every notion of dialogue ends up discarded here. And not only because the powerful Heideggerian mold ends the dialogue each time one glimpses it there where poem and thinking come into contest but also because, from the Levinasian perspective, the relation to the other—which would be the very entrails of Celan's poetry—precedes all dialogic forms that it could assume: its proper [*lo suyo*] would be touching, trembling proximity, giving without reserve.

Who would assert that this perspective doesn't agree with Celan's poetry? Despite everything, I insist on doubts about the emphasis. I do not claim to suggest, then, that Levinas's interpretation is erroneous. On the contrary: each of the phrases with which the text marks its milestones—"the poem goes toward the other"; "the personal is the poetry of the poem"; "the personal: from myself to the other" (Levinas, *Proper Names*, 41–42)—each of the phrases that conserve all their lapidary exactitude even there where they advance by interrogating, conjecturing, correcting themselves, each of these sharp phrases hits upon Celan's saying, if by "hit upon" we understand not the mere enunciation of correct things but, rather, the enhancement and rendering audible of what in this saying goes beyond everything previously said. But precisely here, in this enhancement, I perceive an excessive force, an accent that no longer suspends, an accent that breaks the balance of the "more and less than being" made of pure fragility and constant oscillation, an accent that breaks that balance in order to recognize transcendence, the "for the other" (*pour l'autre*), in this abyssal fissure.

In what way do the excess and the extra accent occur? Perhaps in a will to origin, which is the will to think the fissure of the origin, the moment of the preoriginary that staves in and fixes the untrespassable limit for all archeology (and Heidegger's thought would obey, precisely, the archeo-logical itch): the will to think the *pre* as an instance of pure proximity, of the immediacy of touching. But there where Levinas writes and affirms a *pre*, right there, I fear, Celan opens the hiatus of a *between*. Not a *before* (which is, at the same time, a beyond) but rather an *interval*, a lapsus of being in being or rather, perhaps, a lapsus of nothing in being (a breath), *nothing-of-being*, neither nothing-of-a-being nor perhaps *autrement qu'être*, nothing-of-being (but is this thinkable?) that would have to be, maybe, "the time of the other."[19]

I have put forth these preliminary considerations so far as a portico. They do not claim to settle the pertinence, opportunity, or scope of the readings from which they nevertheless wish to take more or less distance.[20] In such brief and moreover allusive terms, given that these preliminary considerations have not been directed resolutely toward the assumptions from which those readings arise, no sharp decision could be adopted concerning them, but perhaps the domain in which a decision would be possible has been indicated. This remains to be seen in what follows. In the meantime, as I said at the outset, it is a matter of inscribing a warning. And the warning has been inscribed, I think, with sufficient legibility. In short, the warning is limited to preserving the quotation marks around "dialogue": it does not affirm or negate the dialogue but, rather, holds it in suspense.[21] One would say: as if hung from prophylactic clothespins in expectation of itself, of its possible occurrence, or of its own impossibility. (And how could one know beforehand what the difference is, if there is a difference, and how there is any difference between the two?)

Did I say clothespins? No, not clothespins. Celan speaks of quotation marks at the end of *The Meridian*, and I choose to follow his advice. He speaks of Georg Büchner's invisible quotation marks at the end of *Leonce and Lena*, which frame *commode*, a word borrowed from French (a loan that had already been in use in the German language for many years at that point) in order to describe the word "religion." Quotation marks of a "comfortable" religion, then, that the character Valerio names in an exasperated and utopic effusion that promises to decree the end of all labor and all poverty and the enjoyment of a comfortable life, a "commode" that Karl Emil Franzos believed was best read as a "kommende," a *kommende Religion*, a "coming" religion, just as if the last word of the pathetic speech recuperated its vigor and its opening to hope for the utopia instead of attenuating it irrecoverably into parody and ridicule.[22] Celan prefers "commode"; he prefers quotation marks that, he says, "want to be understood perhaps not as 'Gänsefüßchen' [goose-feet], but rather as 'Hasenörchen' [hare's ears], that is, something not completely fearless, that listens beyond itself and the words" (Celan, *Meridian*, 48c).[23] Scared but also mocking little ears that, "invisibly and smilingly added to the words" (48c), teach one to hear them otherwise—not the "said" but rather the "saying," as Levinas would add, and not even the "saying" but rather its "direction," as Celan would perhaps suggest—to listen to them with the hearing of a third that, there in *The Meridian*, is named Lucile. Little ears, indeed, and perhaps also little and anxiously twitching whiskers of an animal exploring and sniffing around on the ground in unfamiliar terrain.

2

"Place"

First of all, the title: *The Meridian*. Light once again, a forced light, a sort of *Lichtzwang*. It mentions the empire of midday: *meridies*, the time of inescapable clarity.

Such is the name Paul Celan gave to the speech he delivered upon receiving the Georg Büchner Prize, which was established by the German Academy for Language and Literature to honor the most creative literary writers in German during their lifetime. The speech is dated 22 October 1960, the day of the ceremony.[1] The title attests to a discovery Celan made upon writing his address (this is, in any case, how I imagine the circumstances), and the speech itself is in a way the chronicle of an adventure, a meditative exploration, the axis of which lies in this discovery. Already, for this reason alone, one should not see in *The Meridian* the essence of a sovereign word issued on the basis of certainty, perfect knowledge, a lifetime achievement, or an achievement in action, creation, or thought. *The Meridian* is an exposed word, carried to the edge of itself, converted into pure experience and vertigo. Its dimension is extremity, which is also unequivocally signaled by what one calls a "meridian": maximum distance and route, a total trajectory that, as the greatest of all, "returns to itself across both poles" (Celan, *Meridian*, 50c).

A circle, indeed, but not a hermeneutical circle. At the same time, an "immaterial" and "terrestrial" circle (Celan, *Meridian*, 50c).

Hence, the title suggests something else, as well. The speech is not a speech, if one thereby understands stringing "together word upon word" (Celan, *Meridian*, 4b), like those uttered by prisoners sentenced to die while standing on the scaffold during the Reign of Terror.[2] The speech is not a speech: it is a map. From which certain conditions follow for reading it. A map is an instrument of orientation. Whoever consults a map wants to know how to locate themselves in a strange district. The one who designed the map has consigned to it the memory of his or her explorations, movements, and discoveries. A map is a model of experience, but it is also at the same time a discourse by way of its consignation, conventions, and inevitable rhetoric, and it becomes one above all in passing from one hand to the next: a stylization that thins the thickness of experience, that which in experience excites and commits to memory, instituting and at the same time overflowing it. And only because a map is an evocation and a likeness of experience, however remotely, can it also offer itself as a substitute for experience, the same way Kant "traveled" via cartography and travel diaries. A map is a blind knot of experience and representation. Helpless groping underlies it. However hidden it might be, this is the principle of a map's production and decipherment. And, in truth, this principle is never entirely hidden; on the contrary, everyone carries it in the palm of his or her hand:

> Wer mit der Lampe allein ist,
> hat nur die Hand, draus zu lesen.
> (Celan, *Language Behind Bars*, 2)

> Whoever's alone with a lamp
> has only a hand to read from.
> (Celan, *Language Behind Bars*, 3)

. . . to surmise his or her own path. To read Celan's map is to unlearn the regular exercise driven by codes of common knowledge and to learn to read like the blind, feeling the rough surface of experience with fallible finger, reading from one's own hand.

Like others, *this* map is made of routes: routes of art, routes of poetry, routes that from time to time intersect, converge, diverge; I will have to return to all of this later. This map is made of directions and distances; it is made of places. Variety, diversity of places: that disquieting space (*unheimlich* is Celan's word [*Meridian*, 17a], and it is necessary to inscribe it here already, untranslated, untranslatable) in which art—which, furthermore, is also ubiquitous—"seem[s] to be at home" (17a), and the place "open, empty and free" (36c), "inhabitable distance" (43), of a "beyond" (17a) as the region from which the Other comes, toward which the poem stretches out, and in the proximity of which it perhaps is. Two "strange" places that, so difficult to discern, constitute "in the final analysis . . . only *one* strangeness" (42g). And also the place that there is not, that has no place: u-topia. And the narrowest place: the I and its existence. And the abyss, the place of the most tremendous overturning: "He who walks on his head, has the sky beneath himself as an abyss" (26b–c). Will the abyss also—and perhaps above all—be time, as "the most essential aspect of the other" (36b)? Place-time, time-place, and therefore the date?[3]

The Meridian, as I said, is a map. But a map of what? To put it provisionally—very provisionally—for the moment: a map of *Sprache*, a cartography of language. Language, then, as a region or district in which strangeness reigns and toward which the poet moves with his or her existence (*Dasein*), as the Bremen speech says, "wounded by reality [*wirklichkeitswund*]" (Celan, *Collected Prose*, 35; translation modified).[4] This difference between *Dasein* and *Sprache*, which was already implied in the preceding analyses, will have to be a concern later.

In the meantime, *to read* this map is to probe—with a blind and uncertain hand—its places.

Stimmen vom Nesselweg her:

Komm auf den Händen zu uns.
Wer mit der Lampe allein ist,
hat nur die Hand, draus zu lesen.
(Celan, *Language Behind Bars*, 2)

Voices from the nettle-path:

Come to us on your hands.
Whoever's alone with a lamp
has only a hand to read from.
(Celan, *Language Behind Bars*, 3)[5]

And to probe is to write, and to write is to search for direction: let us speak not of topology (we are far from *logos* and its concentrating force here) or of toponymy (places do not have names or, rather, they do and do not have names at the same time) but rather of an anxious topography. Celan never abandons his essential conviction—have I not said so already?—that the poem is a gesture of orientation.

Martin Heidegger also conceives the poem's persistence in *Sprache* in terms of place. The preamble to "Language in the Poem [*Die Sprache im Gedicht*]" (the final essay dedicated to Georg Trakl in *On the Way to Language*) says so as it explains the meaning of *Erörterung*, the "localizing discussion" he undertakes there in order to disclose the most intimate determination of Trakl's poetry.[6] Let us linger on this explication to review the threshold of the "dialogue."

> Every great poet creates his poetry out of one single poetic statement only. The measure of his greatness is the extent to which he becomes so committed to that singleness that he is able to keep his poetic Saying wholly within it.
>
> The poet's statement remains unspoken [*ungesprochen*]. None of his individual poems, nor their totality, says it all. Nonetheless, every poem speaks from the whole of the one single statement, and in each instance says that statement. From the site [*Ort*] of the statement there rises the wave that in each instance moves his Saying as poetic saying. (Heidegger, *On the Way*, 160)

As the only poem from which the poet creates his or her poetry and that, in this condition, remains tacit, *the* poem belongs to a place. Between *the* poem and *the* place, then, there is an essential relation, such that only in their reciprocity can one experience the essence of the poem, the essence of the place. The *Erörterung* should signal toward the place, tend to it, and finally inquire into the locality of place, that is, think place *as such*.

The place of the poem is, as a place, the gathering (*das Versammelnde*) that unites everything in itself and sustains everything in its unfolding.[7] It gathers together, therefore, all the poet's poetizing in the place of the discreet poem from which all the particular poems emerge and to which they remain faithful if the creation achieves its maximum purity and concentration. As a poem, however, it also gathers all places into its own place. Not only because one learns what the poem's place is from the meditation on the placeness of place; the poem itself, in its discreet relation to its place, must orient that meditation from the beginning. And not poetry in its generic being [*entidad*] but rather *this* poem, "Georg Trakl's poem." This calls for explanation.

I have already broached what should be clearly established first of all: Heidegger's thought on poetry has its center in the theme of gathering. It would be a mistake, however, to suppose that this theme is interchangeable with what the occidental metaphysical tradition has characterized and conceived as the universal, which brings together in itself the commonality of a multiplicity of incidents. The gathering is the incidence itself, the most pristine incidence: it is the extreme singularity of the happening, of *a* happening full of possibilities, together with the silent perseverance of this singularity, which makes history itself possible in the first place. Hence, no matter how exemplary, Trakl's poetry is not a "case" to which to apply the *Erörterung* strategy and the notion of "place" as methodical principles and general thematics. The same Traklian poetry first permits one to make for "place"; it convokes thinking to concentrate meditatively on "place," attend to it, and inquire into its locality. To the extent that Trakl intonates his poem in the historical place called the *Abend-Land* (the "Occident"), to the extent that he poetizes "the yet concealed evening land" (Heidegger, *On the Way*, 197), he opens the path toward the absolutely unique happening of this place and makes it manifest as a *destiny*. I want to mark this word in order to take up again later what it encloses here; for the moment, I will not say more on the issue.

I return to the "dialogue." That the question of place should be crucial in this dialogue, it seems to me, is immediately clear. And something has sprouted from the differend that lies between the two modes of referring to place. It will not be idle to insist on this briefly.

In Heidegger's lexicon, the word "place" signals the questionability of being itself. I extract the following passage from the *Seminar in Le Thor* (1969):

> According to the tradition, the "question of being" means the question concerning the being of beings, in other words: the question concerning the beinghood of beings, in which a being is determined in regard to its being-a-being [*Seiendsein*]. This question is *the* question of metaphysics.
>
> With *Being and Time*, however, the "question of being" receives an entirely other meaning. Here it concerns the question of being as being. It becomes thematic in *Being and Time* under the name of the "question of the meaning [*Sinn*] of being."
>
> Later this formulation was given up in favor of that of the "question concerning the truth of being," and finally in favor of that of the "question concerning the place or location of being," from which the name "topology of being" arose.
>
> Three terms which succeed one another and at the same time indicate three steps along the way of thinking:

MEANING—TRUTH—PLACE (τόπος)

> If the question of being is supposed to become clarified [*verdeutlicht*], what binds together the three successive formulations must necessarily be disclosed, along with what distinguishes them. (Heidegger, *Four Seminars*, 46–47)

What binds and distinguishes these three names, steps, or milestones along the "way of thinking"? In what immediately follows, Heidegger very precisely outlines the relation between meaning and truth; with respect to place, it is only necessary—in this context—to extract a few indirect consequences.

According to the doctrine of *Being and Time*, "meaning" is that which Dasein opens projectively in existing, that is, in the "ek-static instancy [*Inständigkeit*] in the openness of being" (Heidegger, *Four Seminars*, 47). The project is executed, carried out by Dasein. The word "meaning," then, preserves a trace of the initiative and spontaneity that characterized the subject of modern metaphysics. Exchanging the name "meaning" for the name "truth," Heidegger says, "emphasizes the openness of being itself, rather than the openness of Dasein in regard to this openness of being. / This signifies 'the turn,' in which thinking always more decisively turns to being as being" (47).

Certainly, however, in *Being and Time* meaning was no longer thought as the giving of meaning, as an attributive act of signification and significancy [*significatividad*]:

> Nevertheless, *Being and Time* does not undertake to present a new signification of being, but rather to open a hearing for the word of being—to let itself be claimed by being. In order to *be* the there [*Da*], it is a matter of becoming claimed by being.
>
> But a question here announces itself: does being *speak*? And do we not already run the danger of degrading being into a being that speaks? But who decided that only a being can speak? Who has so gauged the essence of the word? Obviously these considerations lead directly a new meditation on the word [*zu einer neuen Besinnung auf das Wort*]: *On the Way to Language*. (Heidegger, *Four Seminars*, 47)

To put it very narrowly: in *Being and Time*, "meaning" is still defined on the basis of the projective focus of Dasein, although the latter is determined no longer as consciousness or a bundle of faculties but, rather, in its *performance* of being.[8] "Truth" emphasizes that this projection is only possible on the basis of the previous opening of being as being—from which being is given. "Place" determines the unfolding of the same "giving"; it characterizes the opening as such in its eventive nature. The guiding thread in this succession is language: from the absolutely peculiar relation that, due to its originary installation in the dimension of meaning, existence maintains with language, to understanding truth as the archeological eminence of the *etymon* (which accredits the possibility of understanding truth, no longer in the paradigm of the rectitude of what is uttered, but rather as unveiling and clearing), and from there, finally, to understanding that the opening has the character of the word: *that the word itself is the place*. The "turn" that occurs in this succession is measured by the radical change in sovereignty: the human is no longer conceived as the master of language; rather, language is conceived as the master of the human: *die Sprache spricht*, speaks being [*habla el ser*]. Poetry is the ample credit of this relation; the poem, testament to the interpellation of being; and the dialogue between poetry and thought, the dimension in which hearing this interpellation is maintained and exercised in preparation—incipient, patient, and long in coming—of mortals' inhabitance (having a place) in *Sprache*.

Should all this not lead us to conjecture that precisely here, in the question of place and about it, a fundamental dialogue between Celan and Heidegger is triggered, which would adhere to the pattern that Heidegger foresees and prescribes? Is place not also for Celan the trance of existence to which the poem attests as a gesture of orientation? And is place not, in both Heidegger and Celan, literally sharpened to the extreme, to the decisive point of exposing existence in the dimension opened by interpellation? Is it not, then, the persistence of place as destiny?

But I retrace my steps: is place, in Celan, the trance of existence without further ado? Without further ado: is there a profound inherence, an originary reciprocity, between existence and place? I am afraid not. I am afraid that it would be necessary to take into account a *relation of estrangement*—not an absence of relation, then, but rather a mutual strangeness—between place and existence. It does not happen that, without further ado, existence takes place [*ha lugar*]. *In its radical singularity and its most extreme and unrepeatable punctuality, existence is precisely that which, in a certain sense* (and the restriction just noted, in truth, holds for *all* meaning, that is, for meaning as totality), *is out of place* [no ha lugar]. Whence the *absurdity*. For if place in Heidegger has the nature of gathering and conservation, although without strong presumptions of projectivity, the style of meaning in Celan is determined by a sort of negativity without opposite: it is the absurd, indeed, as "witness for the presence of the human" (Celan, *Meridian*, 8c). The absurd—and we must repeat this word to ourselves, we must listen patiently and assiduously to the multitude of all its deafening resonances, in order to continue tracking the "raw"—the absurd is what is strange to the locality of meaning and, therefore, what is out of place [*no ha lugar*]: the Greeks called it *átopon* or, here in Celan with a different modulation, u-topia. But not u-topia as the wishful representation of the absent because unreachable place but, rather, as the *actuality*—that is to say, as the *meridianity*—of the impossible place, of the place that *does not take* [*el lugar que no ha*]:

> Topos research?
> Certainly! But in light of what is to be searched for: in light
>   of u-topia.
> And the human being? And the creature?
> In this light. (Celan, *Meridian*, 40a–d)

(Which is perhaps not forced but rather free light, the light that knows of shadow, that knows of meaning, but meaning as what is irrecuperable, razed, and also, for the same reason, possible on the desolating condition of the No.[9])

Not discordant in this or that respect but, rather, the essentially discordant, that which absolutely does not suit the essence of the word, the absurd (*ab-surdus*) also marks a fundamental aphasia, a suppression of the word at the root of its possibility and only in the very midst of the trance itself, a larceny of names, and a dislocation of language as such: the instance of "a terrifying falling silent" (Celan, *Meridian*, 29a) that Celan attributes to Lenz's discomfort and diagnoses as the poem's tenacious proclivity today (32a–b). This falling silent "expresses" the mutual strangeness of place and existence (of existence as "nothing of being," pure "between"), a strangeness that cannot be abolished or dissimulated.

Yet, one might perhaps think that there is a way to reconcile this strangeness, to placate it, to smooth its edges a little. By way of the date. The date would be the expedient that would permit existence—no, not existence, but rather the existent in its singularity—to make place *its* place without erasing, obliterating, or covering over the very singularity that is inevitably at stake, "the sign of a radical individuation," "the angle of inclination of [the poet's] Being, the angle of inclination of his creatureliness"

(Celan, *Meridian*, 33b–c). To date is to give testimony: "I was there," "here I am, now," et cetera. Nevertheless,

> Niemand
> zeugt für den
> Zeugen.
> (Celan, *Collected Later Poetry*, 64)

> No one
> bears witness for the
> witness.
> (Celan, *Collected Later Poetry*, 65)[10]

With his or her testimony, the witness (the third party) remains orphaned and uncertain, a foundling exposed [*expósito, expuesto*] at the edge and as the edge of the law *before which*, nevertheless, he or she is constituted.[11] The ex-position of the witness with his or her testimony—his or her liminal and constitutive fragility—makes impossible the targeted appropriation of place through the date's act of consignation.

Will I wander too blindly if I suppose that one of the decisive argumentative axes organizing Jacques Derrida's text "Shibboleth" consists precisely in showing that the strangeness of place and existence is indelible and that the poem, if it essentially gives testimony of something, originates in this tenacity?

The truth, however, is that I do not intend to circumscribe—or circumcise—this difficult and extremely contained text; rather, I intend only to mark a few of its lines. These lines are circular rings that in part intertwine—this becomes increasingly evident to me as my writing advances—with what it is a question of verifying here.

In any case, with respect to tenacity, Derrida elaborates the date as something *undecidable*: "How can one date what does not repeat if dating also calls for some form of return, if it recalls in the readability of a repetition? But how can one date anything other than that which never repeats itself?" (Derrida, "Shibboleth," 2).

I understand that the problem on which Derrida insists is the inherently commemorative structure of the date: upon stamping the singularity of an event, one inseparably disposes it for resuscitation in memory. It follows perforce that the event owes its singularity to the possibility of being repeated as unrepeatable.[12] But Derrida is not interested in uncovering a supposedly transcendental structure of the event (the rigorous concept of which demands thinking it as the fissure of that order) but, rather, in allowing the operation of this reiterative unrepeatability to take shape in the date itself. The repetitive function that would determine the date itself (and here it would be necessary to take its numerical character into account, given that the number is, by virtue of its seriality, the principle of repetition) supposes a loosening of the date from what it dates. A loosening that must not be confounded with the difference that subsists between the sign and what it signifies. A date does not signify an event or the time in which it has taken place: it is limited to *marking it*; it is not given as an intermediary, then, meant to incorporate the event in the sphere of meaning. Released from all links to a "content," in its very intrepidity the date preserves the nonsense and the vertigo of the event's irruption. This loosening, which determines the date as such a date, is the *datum* of the date: that which gives onto dating itself. Nor will one confuse this gift with the act of *instituting* (the highest mode of stamping because it is originary), which always in the final analysis refers to a will that configures that which is by appropriating it.[13] The date's commemorative structure is not the same as the institutional efficacy in the service of which it might be put. Of course, perhaps there are no dates in the margin of a community or even of its mere possibility, but a community is probably constituted and instituted on the basis of the possibility of commemorating the date of its beginning as the date of its not-yet precisely insofar as the date itself—which "*succeeds only in effacing itself* [*n'arrive qu'à s'effacer*]; its mark effaces it *a priori*" (Derrida, "Shibboleth," 49)—supplies the structure of this dilation and delay [*dila(ta) ción*]. The date is as much prepolitical as prereligious ("a religion begins there," Derrida writes, "before religion, in the blessing of dates, of names, of ashes" [37]). Without at all being alien to it, the date does not belong to the regime of the institution; it is, rather, the institution of the institution: the condition of possibility of all *religatio*, whether spiritual (*geistlich*) or secular, sacred or profane—to whatever extent these distinctions are tenable.[14] The date, then, would not only be the memory and auspice of a community but also, in a way, the community itself, the community itself *as a* community. In Derrida, the Jewish community: "Formally, at least, the affirmation of Judaism has the same structure as that of the date" (Derrida, "Shibboleth," 49). But I leave this aside for the moment.

What, then, is the date in Celan? To attempt a first response: it is the inscription of the existent's irreducible singularity, the singularity that is *its* time. This is how *The Meridian* seems to put it with respect to the "true" Lenz—Büchner's Lenz: "Thus had he lived *on*," that is, on toward *his* death.[15]

> He: the true, the Büchnerian Lenz, Büchner's figure, the person we were able to perceive on the first page of the story, the Lenz who "on the 20th January walked through the mountains," he— not the artist, not the one preoccupied with questions about art, he as an I. (Celan, *Meridian*, 24e–f)

And the same inscription defines the condition of the poem, above all the poem that continues to be possible—and imperative—to write today:

> Perhaps one can say that each poem has its own "20th of January" inscribed [*eingeschrieben*] in it? Perhaps what's new in the poems written today is exactly this: theirs is the clearest attempt to remain mindful of such dates [*solcher Daten eingedenk zu bleiben*]?
> But don't we all write ourselves from such dates? And toward what dates do we write ourselves? (Celan, *Meridian*, 30a–b)

"Its own 20th of January" . . . is anything else necessary to begin calibrating how Celan thinks dates operate? The 20th of January: the date of Lenz's excursion, which is (but not only) the chronological heading for one day among many others and at the same time the signature of an experience (but not a sign [*signo*]: a fate [*sino*]), is at the same time—and this second "at the same time" entails the unfathomable—the ominous date of the literally decisive day, namely, the day of the Wannsee Conference in 1942 when Reinhard Heydrich, Adolf Eichmann, and others agreed upon the "Final Solution" that sealed the fate of millions of Jews. And yet, the very atrocity of this coincidence might prove deceptive; it might seem to us that the date's operation depends solely upon this coincidence for Celan. The date, let us recall, is and is not the event that it dates; constitutively separable from the event, the date maintains a sort of strange indifference to the event by virtue of which, however, it is able to mark the difference that the event makes precisely by signaling its irruption in time and as time. This is already insinuated by the double question that ends the series of questions in the passage I just cited; memorial and memorable, the date or the date's writing also encloses—today—the unfathomable future: the destiny of every individual and the common destiny, the latter certainly not as a generic determination but, rather, always as a destiny that is given and completed one by one and one at a time. The date has a structure or a regime that comes not from the character, quality, or "content" of the dated event but, rather, from its temporality: this structure must be made more precise.[16]

After reproducing the "small four-line stanza" he had written "a few years ago," which I cited at the beginning of this chapter, Celan continues:

> And a year ago, in memory of a missed encounter in the Engadine, I wrote down a little story, in which I let a man walk "like Lenz" through the mountains.[17]
>
> On both occasions, I had written myself from one "20th January," from my "20th January," toward myself.
>
> I had . . . encountered myself. (Celan, *Meridian*, 45d–f)

"On both occasions," *das eine wie das andere Mal*, "one time like the other": it would be necessary to meditate patiently upon this formulation as, perhaps, the formulation of the date, the formulation that defines the regime and structure of the date as the regime and structure of return. Dates return; they return annually (*annus*); like Lucile who "comes to you year after year" (Celan, *Meridian*, 5c), they return as many years return, describing the figure of a ring (*anulus*) that connects and separates "at the same time," that connects and separates the "at the same time" at the same time (*das eine wie das andere Mal*), that redoubles the "time" as the secret rhythm—or rapt—of temporality.[18]

Certainly, however, I might provoke misunderstandings if I leave the relation between date and existence on which I have been insisting undetermined. And it is not a matter only of calling on existence and saying that here, in the context of Celan's poetry, only a discourse about *individuated* existence is suitable, not even if it is *radically* individuated existence, because the question falls upon what in principle authorizes one to speak of individuation and *a fortiori* its radicality, which could never be equivalent to the status of subjectivity and ego-ness [*egoidad*] (which is distinct from the "I," by the way, distinct from "him or her as an I") and never equivalent to sovereignty or autodetermination. Due to an inherent tendency, these structures and conditions all keep vigil over or bury the sending and destiny without which those other structures are definitely not thinkable. They all speak of an assured presence and not of the punctuality of an exposed present whose exposition points toward something counter to which and in the encounter with which it occurs, something of which those structures do not want to know: *Gegenwart* and not *parousia*.[19] In the memory and the expectation of the existent, the date is the time of mishap or countertime [*contratiempo*]. It is thus, perhaps, that the date and its inscription, its *incision*, show their decisive impact. For the date dates an encounter; it marks the irruption of alterity.

The incision that *is* the date marks the abyssal fissure of time and thus signs and seals temporality itself, the *enigma* of temporality. By virtue of its indifference, it indicates chronic difference and deferral, as well as the repetition that the same deferral makes possible, but does so precisely by repeating the deferral. So, the incision indicates this difference and deferral as the temporality of time. I suggested that *das eine wie das andere Mal* would perhaps formulate the date in a complex equation sustained and directed by the *wie*, that is, the "as" or "like" (and how is one to think this "wie" that absolutely escapes the law of analogy and rends rather than sutures?); this "like" or "as," this "wie," redoubles the *Mal* ("once" or "time"). Because it is a matter—at the same time—of one time and another, *das eine Mal* and *das andere Mal*: *Mal*, one time, as the mark that marks, once again; *Mal*, the temporal point, the narrowness of existence.[20] Without any knowledge whatsoever that could decide which of the two is the first time. The original separation of the "at the same time" marks the rhythm of temporality: distending it, deferring it in itself, it measures in its dimensions the time of existence, sealing destiny.

If, however, we must inquire into what comes first, if there is in general something first—neither in a temporal sense because time itself unfolds in the repetitive and fickle relation of times [*veces*], nor in a logical sense because, here, *logos* and reason flourish only afterward—then it must at the same time be said that, as an incision, the date is the date of a *wound* [*herida*], and only thus and only therefore is the date an existence. Not only—but indeed always—a cut [*cisura*] or an ulcer [*llaga*] in bodily flesh, but also the wound as a radical rupture in culture, community, and language, the wound in the body of memory (and one, of course, is never entirely distinguishable from the other), the excision of a "we" that was never given through the possession of an identity and bloodless relation.[21] The word "wound" (*Wunde*) is extremely frequent in Celan's poetry and, wherever one finds traces of it, it seems to say the following: there is no relation to the other or to oneself if not on the basis of the wound. And I think that this is also legible in a series of paradoxical propositions in *The Meridian* that redouble the "I" and at the same time specify it through the "like" or "as" (*wie* or *als*), the details of which the reader can check for him- or herself. The "like" operates here like a wound, like the trace of a blow that, if it certainly could not have preceded existence, is one with existence, one with its occurrence, with its incidence.

Trauma: this would be a key for thinking the date and, more precisely, what I earlier called the *datum* of the date. With the wound dated by the date comes reality. Trauma is the blow that splits the "at the same time" and, by inscribing the *momentum*—the unrepeatable—in existence, "at the same time" gives it over to repetition, to the jolts of repetition.²²

> DEIN VOM WACHEN stößiger Traum.
> Mit der zwölfmal schrauben-
> förmig in sein
> Horn gekerbten
> Wortspur.
> (Celan, *Collected Later Poetry*, 12)

> YOUR DREAM, butting from the watch.
> With the wordspoor carved
> twelve times
> helically into its
> horn.
> (Celan, *Collected Later Poetry*, 13)

The dream (*Traum*) that assaults, the trauma as a trace of a rote word carved into the horn twelve times (hours, months, tribes?), and with the "last butt" (13) the ferry (*die Fähre*) that carries *Wundgelesenes* (what is read to the point of wounding and what is read in the wound or as a wound) over (*sie setzt / Wundgelesenes über*, which is not "to translate" since the wound is untranslatable, raw) to the other side: perhaps, as Derrida would have it, to the side of the other (Derrida, "Shibboleth," 54). Now, as the wound is the indelible trace of the real, the fissure, and the schism, it is also through trauma, through traumatic separation (which is also connection), that there is the other, that the other and the possibility of encounter are given, that a you is given as well as, for that very reason and only then, an I.

With the wound as the *datum* of reality, are we not near that which Celan designates in the Bremen speech as the condition of the poet today, his own condition, that is, the condition of those who, "exposed in an unsuspected, terrifying way [*auf das unheimlichste*], carry their existence into language, wounded by reality and in search of it [*wirklichkeitswund und wirklichkeitssuchend*]" (Celan, *Collected Prose*, 35; translation modified)?

Celan's poetry would be essentially traumatic, not because it elaborates the content or meaning of an event that exceeds the subject's capacities for comprehension and appropriation but, rather, because it inscribes the crisis of time, truth, and community in which trauma consists; the date is its mark. We can read this crisis in every pronoun recorded in Celan's poems, recorded as a passage to the other side. For the sake of the encounter, Celan thinks that the relation of the I and you is constitutive of lyrical poetry. This relation would be installed at the boundary of the I and you, in its very scission. By thinking the very possibility of the lyric in his poetry, he would no longer be a poet of the *re-ligatio* in any of the inherited modes for articulating the link—love, union, friendship, annunciation, hatred, reconciliation, or devotion. He would not be a poet of *Versammlung* or, of course, a poet of the "people" (*Volk*), as a notion of a community integrated on the basis of fundamental contents and meanings. The very essence of gathering and community is in radical crisis here and called into question; it is not gathering but rather encounter, not substantial community but rather reality of the encounter that, perhaps, is preserved in what is said. Preserved, perhaps, in the wound of the date: the poem is first of all for Celan the inscription, the incision of the date—one time, only one time, but replete with destiny. As Celan says in a short text on bilingualism in poetry: "Poetry is by the fateful uniqueness of language [*schicksalhafte Einmaligkeit der Sprache*]" (Celan, *Collected Prose*, 23; translation modified).[23] And that incision, to be sure, is the gesture of memory, "to remain mindful" (Celan, *Meridian*, 30a). *Denkmal*, in German, is the word for memorial, the monument erected to preserve the event. Without the imposing baggage that we tend to associate with it, we could use the word to describe Celan's writing. Memorial, poetry is *Denkmal* and *Wundmal*, a scar that is never done closing, a sign of a memory, a mark (*Mal*) that marks the temporal point (*Mal*) of existence, loaded with origination, filled with destiny. Its mouth (*Mund*) opens to recite the wound.

In contrast to the *Ort* that Heidegger speaks and thinks as the gathering of existence, language, and time, the date is the other place, the place of the other, the rise of the other [*el orto del otro*]. In contrast to the former, the latter does not lend itself to any foundation because it sinks further into itself, all the more so when snow covers it. The poetry of dates is not foundational: rather, it signals the abyss that (is) every date. A different task of poetry, a different zeal of the contemporary poem, another mission of the poet? *Was bleibet aber, stiften die Dichter*, we read at the end of Friedrich Hölderlin's poem "Andenken": "But what remains is founded by the poets." It is well known how Heidegger exploits this foundational motif—I mentioned this in passing in a note—over the course of a meditation on the essence of language that, in poetry, happens *as* language and in such a way that, in this event, the originary link between language and history becomes manifest. But the Heideggerian reading of the poem and Hölderlin's motif is *strong*. He emphasizes the *Stiftung*, which certainly does not have the evident and thundering vigor of a *fiat*, but it does have the positive latency of an origin, of a recuperation (and, as such, an institution of the origin); he emphasizes *was bleibet*, what remains as what endures, what entails the strength of historical duration inasmuch as it is purely and before all an opening: a date without date [*una data sin fecha*], a date that prolongs itself beyond itself, preserving its originariness in its latency and as latency, anticipating for that very reason its return, retaining its return as the possibility it always contains. But these verses also admit a weak reading. *Was bleibet aber, stiften die Dichter*: "But what remains is inscribed by the poets." *Was bleibet*: not that which does not abandon place to preserve it but, rather, that which remains as a remnant, as a small remnant, a remnant of life (*Leben*), of body (*Leib*).[24] And *stiften*, which could point toward a point, the extremity of a *Stift*, a trembling point for inscribing.[25] What remains, if it does, remains in silence. "*The rest is silence*."[26] But a singable remnant.

SINGBARER REST—der Umriß
dessen, der durch
die Sichelschrift lautlos hindurchbrach,
abseits, am Schneeort.
(Celan, *Collected Later Poetry*, 20)

SINGABLE REMNANT—the outline
of him, who through
the sicklescript broke through unvoiced,
apart, at the snowplace.
(Celan, *Collected Later Poetry*, 21)[27]

3

"Art"

At first sight, *The Meridian* energetically contrasts "art" and "poetry." The sense of this contrast would lie in a total strangeness separating poetry from art, a strangeness that one would have to affirm in order to keep poetry loyal to its own unstable possibility: today. Nevertheless, upon closer, more attentive, and more refined inspection, the contrast of art and poetry in Paul Celan is unsteady, "breathless."

To be sure, Celan rigorously and loyally follows in Georg Büchner's footsteps here; he has made the duty arising from the circumstances—by virtue of the prize instituted in Büchner's name—an occasion to essay an essential thought concerning the situation of the poem today.[1] This thought, guided by Büchner, appears to stir up anew the very old dispute concerning the untraversable—and always only falsifiable—distance between nature and art. It *appears*, then, and everything here, as in other similar cases, depends on whether one can slice the thin and translucent film of appearance. I would say that, despite appearances, it is not a question of opposing poetry to art categorically, as if poetry were the reliable gesture of human existence or the "personal" (like, put bluntly, Emmanuel Levinas does[2]) and art the extrahuman or that which is impassively absorbed in its own looking glass; slightly displacing the coordinates, one would perhaps have the right to think that the opposition takes place between a "testimonial" poetry and an "artistic" poetry, but these labels would be premature and, for the same reason, would conceal more than they reveal. Nor is it, I would say, a question of confronting art as a species of the artificial—artifact, mechanical offspring, technological supplement—with spontaneous and "creatural" nature. The text unequivocally suggests that such differends belong to what I will henceforth call the *discourse of art*; why and how, although in a slightly more restricted relation to this last opposition, will become clear later.

In spite of these precautions, one thing should remain clear: in no way, I believe, does Celan conceive a *continuous* relation between art and poetry. To say this in the register that I have been sounding: Celan could not in good conscience subscribe to the thesis that Martin Heidegger establishes in "The Origin of the Work of Art" according to which "the essence of art is poetry" (Heidegger, *Off the Beaten Track*, 47).[3] This thesis, of course, does not suppose a *mere* continuity between art and poetry: it does not posit that both are interchangeable magnitudes. Quite the contrary, Heidegger's sentence carries art back from its possible and eventual and visible deviations, from its uprootings and eccentricities,[4] toward the place of its origin and thus conceives, precisely in the mode of originarity and provenance in the pure event of truth, a determined inherence of poetry and art: of poetry *in* art, to be sure, as its *archē* and its decisive place, but also of art *in* poetry as the measure for the valid erection of that which we call and poorly conceive under the title of "art." And *this* inherence, this *double* inherence, is that to which Celan could not subscribe if, indeed, I have read him well. There is no room for it in his argument, not even in the most "authentic" (the most "appropriate") mode of art. This, however, does not mean mere disconnection. Between art and poetry, Celan installs a zone of acute friction, a schism, that accounts at the same time for their irreducible difference and for the complex imbrication of their destinies. Art and poetry, in the first and last instance, are foreign to each other but not, without further ado, mutually exclusive; there is a relation between them, a profound relation of mutual foreignness, a relation that begins and unfolds in the space of strangeness: of what, with a charged word, Celan calls *Unheimlichkeit*.

But these first strokes are too bare and unilateral. It is possible to make them more precise and, in so doing, to recognize the hidden complexity of the links they imply only if I begin by warning of the respective dimensions that *The Meridian*, a partitioning line, assigns to art and to poetry.

I say "dimensions" in view of what Celan indicates as the purpose he had in mind in approaching this text, which he prepared with patience and abundant care: to oppose a "'Lucilian' counterword" (Celan, *Meridian*, 42c) to the imperative of "enlargement" (the eighteenth-century dramaturg Louis-Sébastien Mercier's maxim *Elargissez l'art!*),[5] which demands the extension of art beyond its conventional forms and themes—the sacred space of verisimilitude—toward concrete individual existence neither stylized nor cosmeticized, without touchup or artifice, but rather "natural":

Enlarge art?
No. To the contrary: go with art into your innermost narrows [*allereigenste Enge*]. And set yourself free. (42e)

Enlarging and narrowing, then, are the respective, fundamental *dimensions* of art and poetry. Will enlarging belong to art in general and in every case? Perhaps not; perhaps not *immediately*. And will narrowing belong to poetry in general and to it alone? Perhaps not; perhaps not *simply*. In any case, however, both dimensions stand explicitly accused when poetry and art seek to take charge of existence, of its concrete singularity, of Dasein in the apex of its irreducible individualization, of its definitive fragility, of its own forgetting.

But why does Celan reject Mercier's maxim? What is rejected in and with this maxim? How does this discussion and the "contradictory" will that animates it link to Celan's confrontation with Büchner, in whom he nevertheless heralds the eruption of a "radical calling-into-question" of art indispensable for "all of today's poetry" (Celan, *Meridian*, 19)?

I think we should grasp precisely the latter sign—the "radical calling-into-question" and its necessity—in order to achieve the outline of an answer.

What, in Celan's reading of it, does Mercier's maxim say? Despite the fact that the evolution signaled by Celan himself, which links Reinhold Lenz, Büchner, and Gerhart Hauptmann after Mercier, emphasizes the filiation of literary naturalism in the German language and thus, without omitting all its importance, seems to recognize a specific scope for it, it seems to me that the meaning Celan attributes to the maxim is much greater and, for reasons that will soon appear, it would perhaps not be wrong to say "absolute." One needs only to keep reading in line with the same "sign":

> With other, perhaps too hasty words: may we, as happens in many places these days, start from art as something given and absolutely unconditional, should we before all, to put it most concretely, think—let's say—Mallarmé through to the end?" (*Meridian*, 19)

The "absolutely unconditional" presupposition of art—with which the "oh, art!" that Büchner puts in Camille's mouth continues to resonate[6]—is in truth the key. Read from this perspective, the maxim covers the general, absolute meaning of which I was speaking: one hears within it the murmur of expansive and uncontainable movement, which is the very regime of its meaning. Thus read, then, the maxim presents itself as the imperative to absolutize art, which maintains all its vigor and validity even despite—and even through—the intentions of its champions and adherents, even despite—and even through—the naturalism that has sought to remove the inherited foundation of art in order to save a difference (life, one would say, in its rawness) in the face of art itself.

The truth of the phrase *Elargissez l'art* would thus be art's irrepressible tendency toward its unconditionality. In Celan's reading, jealously seeking not to lose sight of that truth, the phrase would concentrate the essential momentum of art in the past two centuries, that is (I must immediately add), in the epoch of the "death of art." For thus one would have to affirm the following without objecting or haggling: art in the epoch of the "death of art" is governed by the will to the unconditionality of art itself. Anyone that suspects a paradox here will see that it is only apparent. Art's apotheosis is, at the same time, its suppression. According to Hegel, art consumes itself when it has exhausted the expression of spirit's contents, when it now only retains itself—and only wants itself—as its only possible content. This will seeks itself and represents itself to itself in the "system of art" and in the "absolute work"; it articulates itself and formulates itself in the "discourse of art." The wink in the preceding citation of Celan inscribes Mallarmé's name in the fiber of this will.

But what is the condition from which art frees itself and that is to be presupposed unconditionally? Do we not know it? It is the condition of art itself, of art as such, which the tradition has modulated in two fundamental ways: the real and existence. And both forms coincide in the single trait of *distance*. Unconditioned art eliminates the distance that made art possible; art eliminates this distance by incorporating it (this is, dialectically, its *Aufhebung*), and thus indifferentiates itself, absolutizes itself, unidimensionalizes itself. What I said earlier about Celan reiterating the old discussion concerning the untraversable distance between nature and art now shows its exact face: no, what Celan conceives and interrogates here is precisely the transit, the *trans* that eliminates distance. Hegel's phrase concerning the "death of art" is not a death certificate; it is a prognosis concerning an expansion of art as never before seen.

Celan's critique of Mercier's maxim, then, would be a critique directed toward the dynamic nucleus of so-called modern art.

An objection here: is this the only generality to which this exhortation alludes or, as if densely codified, that it implies? Philippe Lacoue-Labarthe takes it further: "In its most general sense, torn from historical inscription and context, *Elargissez l'art* tells the very secret of art; it indicates art's movement—and the obscure will presiding over this movement, or animating it from within. Art wants to expand itself; it clamors to be expanded" (*Poetry as Experience*, 46). I would tend to concede Lacoue-Labarthe's observation but with a double reservation. The first: is it not true that something has dictated, in the intimacy of the determination of art, the *containment* of the expansive movement that would be its "secret"? Would there not have been concern for what I earlier described as its condition? Would there not be, then, two "secrets" of art, and would the even more hidden dialogue between the two not be the principle of what we call the "history of art"? And the second: weighty, I think, is the affirmation that the "most general sense" of art is accomplished, fully exteriorized, only in what could be called the "epoch of the death of art," that is, upon the emergence and predominance of so-called modern art. One will rightly say that Plato was already aware of this and had glimpsed it upon condemning mimesis, which is the inveterate name of the movement of enlargement. But one should also admit that the condemnation unveils for the first time the condition the knowledge of which will make possible, in the end, the unconditional affirmation of art. The dynamic of art in the epoch of its death presupposes a dialectic, which indiscernibly unites containment, suppression, and unlimited expansion. Artistic modernity—to speak only of it for now—is the splendid sprout of this dialectic, of this death.

I advance a bit more with Lacoue-Labarthe's commentary (he says something else here that seems indispensable to me):

> Art wants to expand itself; it clamors to be expanded. It wants its difference from the things and beings of nature effaced. In a way, that which is art's own, "proper" to art (to the *Unheimliche*), is the tendency to mitigate differentiation, and in so doing invade and contaminate everything. Or mediate everything, according to Lenz-Büchner's dialectical formulation (nature is only nature by means of art). Thus, to "dis-own" everything. Art is, if the word can be risked, generalized, never-ending "estrangement"—the Medusa's head, the robots, the speeches—without end. (*Poetry as Experience*, 46–47)

I think there is reason to link Mercier's maxim with the theme of radical estrangement; I only want to give this understanding a slight twist, one that at various points crosses with what Lacoue-Labarthe argues here and elsewhere in his essay. I place this twist under an epigraph: Mercier's exhortation is in its most succinct and loaded formulation, in its historical opportunity, that which I called the "discourse of art." On the basis Mercier's exhortation, art and discourse would begin to fulfill the mandate of their inseparability.[7]

Elargissez l'art, then, would be the *unheimlich* imperative of art, the *mot d'ordre* that declares the fundamental estrangement of art, that impels art to exteriorize its essence absolutely, breaking even the barriers of its own containment. The "absolutely unconditional" presupposition that encloses this imperative is one of the eminent acceptations that *Unheimlichkeit* has in Celan's speech. The uneasiness of the imperative defines "modern art" and does so doubly: it defines the modernity of an art that survives its "death" ("art lives on," *die Kunst lebt fort* [Celan, *Meridian*, 42g]), and it also characterizes, at the same time, modernity itself as the product of art and its *Unheimlichkeit*; modernity is the uneasiness of historical time. That modernity is the epoch of radical estrangement—as Friedrich Hölderlin, Edgar Allan Poe, Charles Baudelaire, Friedrich Nietzsche, Georg Trakl, and Franz Kafka thought and said—is therefore not due in the first instance to a putative process of secularization governed by rationality (which could be proclaimed "instrumental," moreover, to the pleasure of many) but rather to the fact that in it and with it is realized, without reserve or continence, the essence of what the Occident has known, experienced, cultivated, and fomented in the name of "art" (*technē*, *ars*, *Kunst*); rationality itself would be nothing more than a moment of "art" thus conceived. If Mercier's maxim directly expresses the *unheimlich* essence of occidental art, its other side suggests that art itself is the essence of the Occident, the *Abendland* that Trakl poetized and, in dialogue with him, that Heidegger thought. What we call "modernity" is the epoch of art's consummation, the epoch of the *Unheimlichkeit* latent from the beginning of the "occidental."[8]

So far, and above all upon attending to these indications, one might think that Celan and Heidegger share the same historical diagnosis: *technē*, in its double face of art and technology, would carry the course of the Occident's destiny to the point of bordering its crisis and extenuation. I do not think it feasible to ignore the echoes of the Heideggerian meditation on the "essence of technology" in these phrases from *The Meridian*:

> Nobody can tell how long the breath pause—the testing and the thought [*das Verhoffen und der Gedanke*]—will last. The "swift [*Geschwinde*]," which has always been "outside," has gained speed . . . (31f)

The tense compliment between the thinking that saves and the speed that rules as an imperative and imposing urgency (it would be necessary to understand the Heideggerian *Gestell* in this way), it seems to me, is an equivocal warning of the proximity between one approach to the problem and another.

And the proximity can become completely deceiving.

On 28 May 1960, a few months before he wrote *The Meridian*, the letter that Celan sent to Hans Bender in response to the question "How are poems made?" includes fascinating lines on the determination of the poem, its essential handicraft, the testament—in those hands—to a mortal and unrepeatable human existence ("and these hands must belong to *one* person, i.e., a unique, mortal soul searching for its way with its voice and its dumbness"), the useless appeal to an archaic character of "craft" that can no longer account for the peculiarity of the "handiwork" (*Handwerk*) of poetry today (Celan, *Collected Prose*, 26). "Don't come with *poiein* and the like," Celan writes (26). "I suspect that this word, with all its nearness and distance, meant something quite different from its current context" (26). There are exercises "in the *spiritual* sense," he goes on, and there are also playful experiments with "so-called word-material" (26). But poems, he insists, are also gifts that bear destiny. "Some years ago, I had the occasion to witness and, later, to watch from a certain distance how 'making' [*das 'Machen'*] turns by and by into 'making it' [*die Mache*] and thence into machinations [*Machenschaft*]. Yes, there is *this*, too. Perhaps you know about it. It does not happen by accident" (26). Under the "dark skies" of the present day, there are few human beings, few poems, and the need "to hold on to what remains" (26).[9]

In all, a reservation must be admitted: in Heidegger there still persists for art—for *technē* and for *Kunst*—a remainder of "positive" meaning or, if you will (and it will be better to put it succinctly like this), a remainder of meaning, of irreducible truth, a safe place (the origin) on the most extreme edge of danger in which it can be saved from its total immersion in technology. Let us read, as a test, a few of the final words from "The Question Concerning Technology":

> Because the essence of technology is nothing technological, essential reflection upon technology and decisive confrontation with it must happen in a realm that is, on the one hand, akin to the essence of technology and, on the other, fundamentally different from it.

> Such a realm is art. But certainly only if reflection on art, for its part, does not shut its eyes to the constellation of truth after which we are *questioning*.

And then this, which is separated from the preceding paragraph by a space in the text:

> Thus questioning, we bear witness to the crisis that in our sheer preoccupation with technology we do not yet experience the coming to presence of technology, that in our sheer aesthetic-mindedness we no longer guard and preserve the coming to presence of art. Yet the more questioningly we ponder the essence of technology, the more mysterious the essence of art becomes.
>
> The closer we come to the danger, the more brightly do the ways into the saving power begin to shine and the more questioning we become. For questioning is the piety of thought.[10] (Heidegger, *Question Concerning Technology*, 35)

How does truth configure this devotion and this piety (the *Frömmigkeit* that would be proper to genuine questioning and that once, for a "brief but magnificent time" [Heidegger, *Question Concerning Technology*, 34], belonged to the determination of art with the simple denomination of *technē*)? In Heidegger, art is certainly *unheimlich* but in a way that, I would venture to say, relates to the sacrificial.[11] The preparation of a human inhabiting, the clearing of a lot for Dasein eminently entrusted to poets and thinkers, demands that they face the abrupt and the inhospitable, the savage, leads them to make the fatally violent gesture of aperture and foundation (a violence that manifests above all in the relation to language and the essence of language, "the most dangerous of goods" [Heidegger, *Elucidations*, 51]), and dictates, finally, that they should succumb because of that ineluctable *hubris*. The "remainder" of which I spoke is thus a certain memory preserved in art—in its essence and from its origin—a memory of tragicness, so to speak; the illumination of meaning (of truth) in the fire of suffering, in the conflagration of *pathos*, is a fundamental piece of the Heideggerian creed.

In Heidegger, then, would persist a determined, expiatory force of poetry, an inveterate resistance to the "artistic" (*das Artistische*) and, therefore, to the "technological." From Celan's experience, the claim to affirm art's resistance to technology would have no way out. Art and technology bear the same stamp; resistance can only be reinforcement, acceleration. But to technological acceleration, artistico-technological, Celan opposes another acceleration, that of poetry, which *brûle nos étapes* and is also the acceleration of existence, which incinerates meaning.[12]

Momentarily diverting attention from this incineration, the difficulties of which are not minor, will one nevertheless think that Celan's persistence in this trance of radical individuation, which I just called the "acceleration of existence," is truly that which separates him from Heidegger? Of course not; this is obvious. It suffices to recall a few introductory statements from *Being and Time*, brief but convincing, concerning individuation and transcendence in order to convince oneself that this cannot in anyway be the case. There, is the trance not precisely a step of existence's absolute acceleration into the place of its extreme narrowness (*Enge*) that is anxiety (*Angst*), which manifests the originary hiatus in which temporality consists? Or might one still suppose that there is here not one but rather two perhaps definitively irreconcilable thoughts of individuation? In the meantime, the question remains open.

I was speaking of the proximity of Celan and Heidegger, a proximity that might become, I held, entirely deceptive. If one does not wish to be held captive by some mirage, it should be kept in mind that this proximity itself lacks locality: it has no where. Hence, a proximity given in an incommensurable space—*a* space, the space of *a* language, experienced in radically different modes—itself has the character of the *Unheimliche*. It is not possible to construct a home or homeland (neither *Herd* nor *Heim* nor *Heimat*) for such a proximity, not only because of "what happened,"[13] but also because what happened reveals that a home has never been constructed, that there have only been façades and model homes, and the language that stirs therein, folding again and again upon itself, has always been bifid, irrecoverably double. But this would not necessarily have to lead to the supposition that somewhere there is, in truth, such a thing—a home; it would lead, rather, to accepting that one never achieves anything more than the simulation of a home there where one thinks to be in possession of the fire that nourishes and maintains it. The human never possess fire, in the final analysis, precisely because the human is given from it.

The arrogation of this possession lies at the root of what has been called *technē*, art, *Kunst*: it lies, then, in the very principle of *Unheimlichkeit*.

Yet, what is properly *unheimlich* in art according to the terms of *The Meridian*? A quick review and inventory of the passages in which Celan speaks directly of art clarifies the "operations" and "characteristics" that he considers essential in art: its constant return, its lethal and at the same time metamorphic and ubiquitous efficacy, the persistence of its life. These operations and characteristics are all marks of a *duplicity* that cannot be eliminated, a regime of double inscription that counts as that in which, earlier, the originary nature of art and its unsettling power were recognized.

So, in effect, we are here in the immediate vicinity of the mimetic determination of art. Mercier's exhortation rhymes with it on an extensive plane. *L'élargissement de l'art* is, indeed, the norm of its primordial and predestined *Unheimlichkeit*, whether mimesis—that is, the logic of mimesis—plays at mimicry and the parasitic adaptability of the allegedly "real" or projects the unlimited and generalized assimilation of everything into its dominion: into its unique dimension.[14] As fundamental quantities of art, the double and the one only apparently quarrel and, of course, this appearance is constitutive of the artistic effect; their secret connivance always, underhandedly, lies in the zone of the "unique dimension."

Precisely this unidimensionality lies at the bottom of that species of reverential fear that has laminated the aura of art, a deaf mistrust before its lethal force or its fixating power, a fascinating anxiety that suspects a nonhuman knowledge of death in the work's fundament. But one should not believe that this alone is in question. Art is not limited to being *unheimlich—deinon*, in Plato's phrasing (*Republic*, 59c)—because it rigs a copy of life that, upon inspection, proves inert. It is also *unheimlich* in the form of a vivifying power, a conjuration of universal animation. What is surprising about art—what provokes wonder and discomfort in it—consists in its *transfiguring* capacity, which opens an unlimited passage between life and death. It opens and installs the "trans."[15]

Consequently, this unique dimension continues to double, continues to redouble in itself. For lack of a better name—for lack of others or in summary of all those other names—"life" and "death" are the terms that would designate that constitutive duplicity of art's unidimensionality; they keep the irreconcilable poles united and in mutual reference to each other in their tension. This tension is portrayed in the operation of the "Medusa's head" (Celan, *Meridian*, 16a), a species of which the "artist" desires to be, as "one" (in the impersonality or, if you will, in the suprapersonality of the German word *man*) and not as "I" (vortex of attention),

> in order to . . . grasp the natural as the natural with the help of art [*das Natürliche als das Natürliche mittels der Kunst zu erfassen*]! (16a)

Art is art if it has mediation in its power, if it has the power of mediation and projects itself as the mediation that makes possible and institutes the "as" of "the natural as the natural." This mediation is and is not dialectical mediation: it is not, if one thereby understands only the reflective exposition of mediation itself, which makes the transit of the "as" explicit in the light of reason (in "reasoned light"); it is, if one at the same time conceives it as the erasure of mediation. At stake here is the *Unheimliche*. Does the latter consist, then, in erasure? No. It could be neither reason in its apex of autoexposition and unfolding, infinitely aware of its condition, nor the cosmetic or simulating fold that smooths over the *rictus* of finitude; both are, in truth, strategies of familiarity. *Unheimlich* is the "as" as such, which always returns to itself and sustains everything that is, insofar as it is, in the unlimited movement of this return. Reason attempts to rationalize it but remains forever enchanted by its enigma, which is the enigma to which reason is itself due; art wishes to capture it in the image, to approximate it in the poem or work's "images and tropes" (Celan, *Meridian*, 37b) that nevertheless return, uncertain and intangible, to their initial source: the abyss. The "as"—that abyss—is the *unheimlich* place, *Unheimlichkeit* as place. Art's "radical calling-into-question" that Celan proclaims and promotes would thus be the calling-into-question of this "as" from which perhaps would open a distinct relation to *Unheimlichkeit*, no longer articulated in terms of power—power of discourse or power of image—but rather mumbled in terms of memory: perceptive attention [*atención*] to and pensive pause [*detención*] on the efficacy of a few dates that bear witness to the literal excess of experience.

A patient rereading of Celan's work will verify that the syntax of comparison beats a hasty retreat very early on, but his reticence before the "as" does not weigh in favor of metaphor's revelatory force. His youthful proximity to surrealism—the program of which rests entirely upon that force—must be its own measure: without dazzle [*deslumbre*] or glimmer [*vislumbre*], Celan's "metaphors" prevail from the beginning like blind gropings that do not superimpose the opacity of the given with their radiant evidence or restore it to the initial vigor of its being but, rather, "search for reality" (Celan, *Collected Prose*, 35; translation modified). And his youthful proximity to surrealism, furthermore, must be measured against his highly mature poems and the last poems in which, isolated unto their most austere presence or encrusted or amalgamated with each other, words are now only ciphers of experiences that stubbornly continue to search for their center, already free of all "beauty," desiring only "truth."

Celan's reticence—and Heidegger's? Yes, indeed, revocation of the *analogical* structure of the "as," sustained on the certainty—no matter the nature or style—of something primordially given that can still be restituted, with no succinctly peremptory need to ask after the gift.[16] Here, too, the poem—in its knot [*nudo*] that is the word—is stripped [*se desnuda*] of the ligament of every image, trope, and especially metaphor. *Bildloses Denken*—thought without image—is not only a crucial maxim of *Denken* itself "beyond" metaphysics but also an index of the poem's destiny at the extreme limit of its pressured survival out in the elements of its "forced light." Walter Benjamin, to whom Celan relates in many ways, opens an emergency exit here by pointing to a speech emptied of images, now absorbed only in the Name, in the unapproachability of the Name.[17] Have Celan and Heidegger (and Benjamin)—in solidarity—thought in that direction? As if in the direction of a common vanishing point [*punto de fuga*]? Or does the disruption of the "between" prevail here as well? And even if this were the case, it would be necessary to measure the *tempo* of the vanishing. Because the vanishing takes place here, precisely here, between Celan and Heidegger: *die Fuge*, that which decides: that which divides.

That which decides, that which divides: I conclude here, without closing, by merely sounding out a fugacious and equivocal articulation in this third attempt. Right here, then, and with the stamp of the "as" that has—I believe—proven to be a mark of the *unheimlich* place of the "dialogue": a mark of the "between" that the latter nevertheless, in its vehement and vertiginous (bilateral) friction, ignites and incinerates. In Heidegger's meditation, the "as" sinks abyssally toward the depths that make it possible and that, if it—as pure and strict singularity—no longer allows strategies of comparison and ontological stratification, still conserves that incontrovertible aftertaste of articulating force and that peculiar strangeness of the return. In the Celanian experience of the *trans*, the "as" has begun to lose all its occult, secret, and tacit power (the power of transfiguration) nourished in the final analysis by articulation and return.[18] If it is necessary to indicate a border here—that is, in Celan's poetry—it would be necessary to say that with "Todesfuge," with "Death Fugue," the absolute limit of the transfigurable was traced (was written). There is no password for passage because every mouth that could have pronounced it is, irrevocably, a dead mouth. True, that limit still preserves, with an irony not exempt from rancor (and proper to limits), the name of art—the "art of the fugue [*la fuga*]"—but it is a fact that has definitively declined its own mastery.[19]

4

"Language"

Paul Celan's susceptibility and reserve with respect to what we call "art" extend—and this is even more arduous—toward "language." Another zone of extreme, intolerable friction between what Celan says in this regard and what Martin Heidegger thinks.

As an objection Celan directs to himself, this reserve—in *The Meridian*—is expressed in an interjection and takes issue with the notion of the poem it outlines:

But the poem does speak!
Aber das Gedicht spricht ja! (31a)

Precisely here, one line prior, Celan indicated what we should literally understand as the poem's destiny: loyalty to dates, the tenacious work of memory that, in mourning attire, persists in remembrance of them. That the poem nevertheless speaks, that it belongs to the system of language, that it is a verbal object implies an opposition to this destiny. The poem

stays mindful of its dates, but—it speaks. (31a)

How is language thought here such that this "but" should be erected with the force that we necessarily note in it? The references to Georg Büchner with which *The Meridian* begins have left a clear path for responding to this question. Three instances there: Valerio's stridency or, better, the stridency of his discourse that proclaims the appearance of art, the spectacle of art; the rosary of "word upon word" (4b) that Camille and Danton thread when it comes to speaking—abundantly—about art; and the plethora of "words, many artful words" (6b) (and we also hear: artificial words) that the condemned utter at that last tribunal and on that proscenium provided to them, the time of death having come, by the scaffold of Terror.[1] Here, as one sees, language always appears linked to art. The link, as I will try to show, is neither random nor particular. It is not a question only of the "discourse of art"—the discourse that deals enthusiastically with art and the discourse that purifies the enthusiasm in words on the basis of the matrix of art itself—or solely of its linguistic peculiarity. Or, rather, it is a question of the "discourse of art" on condition that one not take it as a separate domain enclosed in the general space of discourse. Thus, just as between art and discourse there is, for art, an essential relation (discourse, *its* discourse, does not *overtake* art as something foreign but, rather, shares its origin, even in those arts that do not possess an explicit discursive body), so too there subsists between discourse *in general* and art an indissociable ligament: in a certain sense, which is probably the most originary sense, all discourse is "artistic." To formulate this another way: all discourse is coined on the basis of the principle of *articulation*, the power of which is precisely that which we call "art" and which also prevails in those discourses that are not motivated by an expressly artistic purpose.[2]

Between art and discourse, then, a *system* fastens. This system is "language." How does "language" speak or how is it spoken [*se habla el "lenguaje"*]?

In *The Meridian*, Celan evokes another Büchnerian *locus*, "the—episodic—conversation" held "at table" and in which Lenz, in good spirits and confident, "spoke for a long time" concerning "questions about art" (20a–b). Celan underlines the phrase that seals that conversation: "He had completely forgotten himself" (20b). And he insists: "*He*, he himself" (20c). For the moment, this forgetting is the condition for speaking about art, for entering the space of the "discourse of art," which is none other than the space of art itself:

> He who has art before his eyes and on his mind . . . forgets himself. Art creates I-distance. Art here demands in a certain direction a certain distance, a certain route. (20d)

Art, says Celan, procures remoteness, distance: of the I. "Procures" is probably a feeble translation: the German *schafft* brings resonances of the creative and configurative vocation of art, and it is an energetic, industrious, imposing word. And Celan does not say that art relegates the I to remote confines (*l'art déporte le Moi au plus lointain*, as André de Bouchet translates it [Celan, *Le méridien*, 19]) or that art merely alienates the I without first and foremost having *created* remoteness, having *posited* distance as a condition (this is its demand, its *Forderung*) for the relation of the I to itself in the predicament of art. What is this forgetting, this I-distance (*Ichferne*), this remoteness from self that art demands of anyone concerned with and interested in it? "Uncanniness" (*Unheimlichkeit*) and "strangeness" (*Fremde*) are the terms that Celan chooses to name—paradoxically—the dimension in which art "seem[s] to be at home" (*Meridian*, 17a), the same dimension that the "I," the individual, the "figure," the "person" (24f) cannot inhabit without self-alienation or self-forgetting. This dimension, in which forgetting, distance, and uncanniness prevail, is perhaps language. Language that speaks or is spoken [*se habla*].

Let us preserve the ambiguity of this phrase—language that speaks or is spoken: the language that each and every one of us speaks, that anyone speaks, indistinctly, without the change in speaker marking a difference; the language that, indifferent to who speaks it, in truth speaks to itself, that is to say, utters to itself and at the same time—through "us"—addresses the word to itself. Confronted with this double [*doblete*], the *poem* would be the interruption of and the flagrant exception to the regime of *se* [itself], whether we understand it as the fundamental anonymity of everyday chatting or as the pure unfolding of language as such. It would be tempting to suppose that Heidegger implies the latter—that is to say, a certain erasure of "personality"—in the sentence *die Sprache spricht* and that, to the dictatorship of chatter (*Gerede*) so finely discerned in *Being and Time*, he opposes the even more tyrannical authority of *Sprache* itself; in fact, this vision sprouts in many of the critical interpretations of Heideggerian philosophy.[3] But let's not precipitate. The erasure of the "personal" does not take place in Heidegger so coarsely; nor does Celan suppose a simple exception to this regime in any of its forms. What matters for now is to recognize the regime, the legality that sustains it. I advance a hypothesis: such legality is *eloquence*, the "art of speaking." No one speaks without having subscribed to the pact of that eloquence; no one speaks—no one *can* speak—without having become skilled, in one way or another and even minimally, in that art.

I collect here, *in extenso*, a few of Philippe Lacoue-Labarthe's observations bearing upon this point and what is associated with it, beginning with that which is—one might say—life in art, let's say, "drama":

> But in reality, eloquence precedes dramatization and provides a reason for it: theater and threatricalized existence only *are* because there is discourse. Or rather, discoursing [*le discourir*]. This means that the *Unheimliche* is essentially a matter of language. Or that language is the locus of the *Unheimliche*, if indeed such a locus exists. In other words, language is what "estranges" the human. Not because it is the loss or forgetting of the singular, since by definition language embraces generality . . . ; but because to speak, to let oneself be caught up and swept away by speech, to trust language, or even, at the limit, to be content to borrow it or submit to it, is to "forget oneself." Language *is* not the *Unheimliche*, though only language contains the possibility of the *Unheimliche*. But the *Unheimliche* appears, or rather, sets in (and no doubt it is always, already there)—something turns in man and displaces the human, something in man even overturns, perhaps, or turns around, expelling him from the human—along with a certain posture in language: the "artistic" posture, if you will, or the mimetic. That is, the most "natural" posture in language, as long as one thinks or pre-understands language as a mimeme. In the infinite cross-purposes of the "artistic" and the "natural," in linguistic misprision, the *Unheimliche* is, finally, forgetfulness: forgetting who speaks when I speak, which clearly goes with forgetting to whom I speak when I speak, and who listens when I am spoken to. And, always thus prompted, forgetting what is spoken of. (*Poetry as Experience*, 48–49; translation modified)

I have preferred to cite the passage extensively to let several themes that interest me resonate, although my theme will not necessarily vibrate on the same chord. I will for the moment ignore the allusion to Friedrich Hölderlin contained in these lines, but it touches upon the decisive issue, and I will at least have to touch upon it very soon.[4] I want to remain with eloquence, understood as the law that governs language speaking itself [*el hablarse del lenguaje*], the law of *se* [itself]. Which is, definitively, an *unheimlich* law.[5] It demands "self-forgetting," "self-distance," as its own condition. It modifies, then, the relation to the self [*sí*], to the I (which is not the same), but it does so *originarily*; consequently, it prescribes the mode in which everyone relates to him- or herself, "to self," and it prescribes the "self" (as the premise of its forgetting, which immediately begins to govern) precisely in the place where that which I utter, without experiencing it, as "I" should happen. And the modification occurs imperceptibly because it is given with language itself, because it is the condition of my entry into language. So, if the "law" of *se* demands as its condition "self-forgetting," it is because it implants the system of what I will henceforth call the *speaking-beyond-oneself* [*hablar-más-allá-de-sí-mismo*]. In it, I find the *universal essence of language*. Eloquence would not be a determined, discursive *capacity* but, rather, the essence of discourse itself. *In* eloquence, without fail, self-forgetting occurs.

And it will perhaps not be inappropriate to link this system—the system of language as the system of speaking-beyond-oneself—with what Celan himself qualifies as "language itself [*die Sprache selbst*]" and "language as such [*die Sprache schlechthin*]" on two significant occasions (one in response to the Flinker bookstore in 1958 [*Collected Prose*, 16]; the other in *The Meridian* [33a]). To the latter he opposes—as the poem's peculiar language—the "actualized" language (*aktualisierte Sprache*) of an I that "speaks under the angle of inclination [*Neigungswinkel*] of his Being," language "set free under the sign of a radical individuation that at the same time, however, remains mindful of the borders language draws and of the possibilities language opens up for it" (*Meridian*, 33b–c). I think, however, one must not suppose that "forgetting" can be countered by an act of memory that makes present that "angle of inclination," that is to say, the historical conditions that determine it. Celanian poetry does not confer curative, regenerative, or redeeming powers to anamnesis insofar as it can only take place in the space of language, and language itself has been intimately and indelibly damaged by some conditions that have a universal scope and make their terrible weight felt in every word. The "enrichment" of language that crossed the ineffable certainly does not constitute a capital that the poet can "put to work" freely in the gestation of new literary undertakings. Quite the contrary:

Welches der Worte du sprichst—
du dankst
dem Verderben.
(Celan, *Threshold*, 84)[6]

Whichever word you speak—
you thank
corruption.
(Celan, *Threshold*, 85)

Thus, as no date is "innocent," no word is either: a general contamination infects words and dates alike. As I already insinuated in passing in my first note, the "system of language" concerns relations not only to nature but also to history. The *Unheimlichkeit* of language and the power of forgetting that art puts to work also entail a sort of usurpation of the very ground of history, a radical condition of estrangement of that ground or, to put it another way, a condition of appropriation of experience through the tacit imperative to omit its irreducible singularity. The *Unheimlichkeit* of language is consummated in the joint dominion over nature and history, made possible by what in general we could call the citational capacity of language; thanks to this capacity, language repeats (mediates) both nature and history, with the tendency to blind its depth in the mirror of the figures that the citation forges such that, by virtue thereof, language itself tends to absorb (to model) both in its process, in its mediation. But the polished surface might be scratched: by the word, by the step, by the voice without a message, by silence itself.[7] The poem as counterword [*contra-palabra*] and as the inscription of dates runs counter [*a contrapelo*] to that tendency, turning the repetitive *vis* of language against [*contra*] itself. Certainly, there is no absolute outside-of-language, but it is indeed possible to encrust an outside within; this is perhaps one of the essential operations of Celanian poetry.

There is a poem in *No One's Rose*—it bears the title "Tübingen, Jänner"—the beginning of which clearly marks, I think, what I am trying to say; it is one of the fundamental poems for calibrating Celan's relation to Hölderlin:

> Zur Blindheit über-
> redete Augen.
> (*No One's Rose*, 48)

> Eyes persuaded
> to be blind.
> (*No One's Rose*, 49)

The German could also be translated as "To blindness eyes over- / come by speech." *Überreden* is to persuade the other, to convince him or her, that is to say, to prevail over him or her (to tie and subordinate his or her will or opinion to one's own) by means of discourse. But such a version not only eschews the cut that, by suspending it in the first verse's cornice, highlights the principle of the power of discourse (of *Rede*); it also makes discourse the instrument of a determined will. But the instrumentality of language is not stated here. The very operation of *Rede* is named;[8] in this operation one recognizes its essential output: the excess or overflow that buries every alleged "subject" beneath the alluvial stream. The essence of *Rede*—this would be written here—is *Überredung*, this speech beyond (*über*) oneself and over (*über*) that about which one speaks and to whom one speaks, on the condition that one conceives it as being prior to all difference between the "logical" configuration and the "rhetorical" configuration of discourse into which—along the oppositions between reason and will, reality and appearance, power and knowledge—the occidental experience of language splinters earlier on.

Furthermore, the ineluctably reiterative but never consummate persistence of stuttering, of babbling, as the only language—language in caesura—that "a man [. . .] with / the shining beard of / patriarchs" would speak "if he spoke / about these / times":

[. . .] er
dürfte
nur lallen und lallen,
immer-, immer-
zuzu.
(*No One's Rose*, 48)

[. . .] he
would only go on to
babble, babble,
ever-, ever-,
moremore.
(*No One's Rose*, 49)

A language, a speaking, that sinks abyssally into nonsense:

("Pallaksch. Pallaksch.")
(*No One's Rose*, 48–49)

Thus, the poem concludes with a citation in parentheses (and what do these parentheses *say*, if they say something?): a word muttered twice by Hölderlin, time and again, in the night of his madness, a word that sometimes meant "no" and sometimes "yes" without one ever being able to prescribe the occasion each "time."⁹ In that locution—if one can call such a babbling that seems to swallow the word barely sketched out in its very possibility a "locution" (and ultimately one cannot)—the abyssal caesura opens, and language submerges totally in it.¹⁰

It submerges and splits open, renouncing its primacy, its "anteriority," in favor of—it can perhaps still be said—the possibility of the poem. A strictly marginal, fragilely borderline possibility—for that very reason not distinct from the impossibility—of the edge: the poem "stands fast" at the edge of itself and "calls and brings itself, in order to be able to exist, ceaselessly back from its already-no-longer into its always-still" (*Meridian*, 32b).

We know it, we have read it, we read it right here: on the verge of tumbling from the edge of itself, standing on its head, and suspended in a trice of abolition, this *Behauptung*—this "extreme" affirmation (32b)—belongs to one and the same bold movement that pushes Celan's dissertation through the "breathturn" (29b), through the double "strangeness" (42g), through "dates," through the prevalence of "language," through the problematic obstinacy of hope and mere expectation, under the pressure of "acceleration," in the difficulty of the word and the "tendency to fall silent" (32a), en route in only one direction, in the direction of—an *encounter*, the encounter with an *other*. And precisely this exit, this step, this liberation here defines or clears the "place of poetry" (21). An exit, then, an incommensurable step—a peculiar, an absolutely peculiar mode of the "beyond"? Another mode, an entirely distinct but perhaps not distant mode of the "beyond" that governs the eloquent essence of language and, in its own and powerful movement, places every other in its dominion? Not "speaking beyond oneself," then, but perhaps rather the listening "beyond itself and the words [*über sich and die Worte*]" (48c) that Celan mentions in the uneasy figure of the little hare's ears at the end of *The Meridian*, the listening to which earlier he also gives the name "attention [*Aufmerksamkeit*]" as that "concentration that remains mindful of all our dates" (35c), of the moments of drastic opening to the other, of the irruption of the other. Perhaps a "beyond" language *in language*, as "language actualized," as "one person's language-become-shape [*gestaltgewordene Sprache eines Einzelnen*]" (33d), presence and present of an encounter, of *"the mystery of the encounter"* (34b), in the intimation of whose occurrence the poem opens to the time of the other and in whose caesura and disjunctive punctuality one time and another make a date in their difference (a difference that language does not fill but rather marks) without pattern or established form. This place—pure fracture, imminence of a you—is the place of the poem.

Considered from this perspective, however, from the place of this absolute irruption, of this radical breathturn, what would the poem be?

The poem?
The poem with its images and tropes?
Ladies and gentlemen, what am I actually speaking about, when I speak from *this* direction, in *this* direction, with *these* words about poetry—no, about *the* poem?
For I am talking about a poem which does not exist!
The absolute poem—no, that certainly does not exist, cannot exist!
But there is indeed in each real poem, even in the most unassuming poem, this irreducible question, this outrageous claim. (37a–38d)

The "poem which does not exist"—the "absolute poem." The figure has been known explicitly at least since early romanticism. Formulated in Celan's terms, what does this figure mean?

In no case can *the* poem be understood as the *idea* of the poem or its *ideal*. When thought in that way, each "real poem" is a refraction, a more or less pure splinter or shred of the poem: its image, if you will, one trope among many, a mode—among so many others—of saying the poem in its reserve. Between the instance and the idea subsists an allusive relation that the tradition with Greek and Latin roots, oriented by the values of *poiesis* and "making," has conceived as mimesis and emulation. There is also that other mode of understanding that relation, which comes from another tradition and which in the language of the Kabbalah (which interested Celan, who admired Gershom Scholem and knew his studies well) is forged in the figure of the broken vessel.[11] At this point, it is already evident that Celan's poetic differs essentially from the "productivist" matrix—the onto-teleology of production, as I have thought opportune to call it elsewhere[12]—in which the ideality of the poetic in the Occident has gestated. One might feel tempted, then, to barter one provenance for another and to believe that *the* poem of which Celan speaks has that force of nihilating concentration. I have reserves in this respect, given that Celan's diction is difficult and never—especially not here—bears univocal fixity.[13]

No doubt, the characterization of "images" (*Bilder*) that, as if defining the frame for its insertion, both immediately precedes and immediately follows the reference to the "absolute poem"—"and then, what would the images be?" (39a)—belongs to the argument refusing mimesis and its link, which continues for long stretches of *The Meridian*. Whatever the images might be, precisely this is a crucial point; it is, in a certain sense, the point where the loosening of the Celanian poem from the form and dominant format of poetry in the occidental tradition is decided. The images would be

> what is perceived and is to be perceived once and always again once, and only here and now. (39b)[14]

The abnormal grammar of these lines forces the plural "images" to pass through the gorge of an absolute singularization. The latter comes marked and governed by the "once," the only one time (*einmal*), which establishes the condition for that which is called "perception" here, for its temporality. Punctual and in itself unrepeatable, the *einmal* nevertheless returns "always again" (*immer wieder*), always another time, but it is precisely "other" as "once." Other, that is to say, "only here and now": we already know this precipitation, this synthesis-of-difference. One should not think that the "once" has a formal character, a vacuous and identical schema capable of indefinite application, while the "perceiving" contributes the content, that is, the difference and the material of what is. Indissociable from the perceived, not split into a here and a there or into a now and a then, the perceiving itself is also inseparably "once." Perceiving is the *absolute contact* of the perceiver with *his or her* time, as the "once" of a total irruption: *his or her* time as the coming without arrival of the time of the other.[15] That *einmal* registers as difference, on the basis of its incommensurability.[16] Precisely by virtue of that *einmal*, furthermore, the image is essentially subtracted from the *fundamental nexus of commensurability* and *similarity* in which the occidental mimetic tradition has cultivated it; for the same reason, it is uprooted from its cultivation and implementation [*implantación*] in the garden of rhetoric.[17]

Uprooted from its pertinence to the metaphorical regime of occidental language. Is metaphor not the axis of that which I thought inadequate to call the system of "speaking-beyond-oneself"? So, in an extensive acceptation that is indeed metaphorically conditioned, meta-phor is, on the one hand, a vehicular agency that permits one to go—to take oneself—beyond oneself, "to communicate oneself." Linking the entire space of dispersed languages in an annular movement (but not that of the meridian!), making its profound relative sensible, and congregating a determined diversity of ethnicities in the familiarity of that feeling, metaphor is the condition under which, in the circle of occidental languages, the possibility of the relation to the other has been established, predefining that relation as communication: it is, therefore, the solution to the problem of transmitting experiences.[18] Yet, on the other hand, metaphor is conceived specifically and punctually, in a sense that prevails throughout the whole dimension that we call the "Occident," as the "speaking-beyond-oneself" of language as such, metaphor being understood as the latter's manifesting power. Aristotle established the rule for this conception: metaphor places what happens before one's eyes by presenting it in the movement of its actualization. Language thereby achieves the *summum* of clarity, which is its most inherent demand: evidence (*energeia*), the transparency of what is [*es*] insofar as it is being [*está siendo*].

Celan brings the metaphorical contexture of language into crisis.[19] From the "black milk" (Celan, *Poems*, 30–33), which tautens the structure of metaphor to the most extreme point of tolerance, to the last poems in which images are consumed in their own incandescence, Celan destroys the metaphorical.[20]

And the poem? What happens with the poem by virtue of uprooting the image from its instituted nourishing soil and its reinsertion into the primary and punctual experience of perceiving?

> Hence the poem would be the place where all tropes and metaphors want to be carried ad absurdum. (*Meridian*, 39b)

Tropes and metaphors specify the order of the "imaginal." They remain valid in the poem—the "possibilities" and "borders" (33b) that language fixes no doubt still and interminably prevail in the poem—but they "want to be carried ad absurdum"; with a renunciatory will, so to speak, they "want" to renounce the power that has forged them and that continues to confirm itself in them. With this will that the poem—but which poem?—induces in them, tropes and metaphors want the "absurd": not disorder or confusion, not mere unreason or deformity. No, they want *truth*, the undeniable—because witnessed—truth of perception.[21] The absurd, then: the truth. Yet, to be sure: not *the* truth, in its restful universality, but rather the truth of the unrepeatable, *das Einmalige*, not re-presented truth but rather truth experienced in its "once," its "one time," "only here and now." It is the vertigo of truth, and truth as vertigo.[22] Previously, Celan spoke of "the absurd" and, even more emphatically, of "the majesty of the absurd" (majesty here as a power without power) with respect to Lucile's "counterword" in *The Death of Danton* as a witness for the presence—for the present (*die Gegenwart*)—of the human (7b, 8c). Unre-presentable present, a present that escapes the play of re-presentation (as eloquent discourse, trope, and metaphor), a present that has the sole character of testimony. Hence, the *Gegen-wart* is responsibility for the encounter, but not as the "correspondence" that smooths the encounter over or negotiates it, that makes it commensurable on the basis of the word, but rather responsibility *toward* the encounter: a wait that holds and holds on for (*warten*)—and thus affirms—the very possibility of the encounter (*Begegnung*) in an affirmation that can only be achieved with the present itself, the being there (*da sein*).[23] This testimony—like "one person's language-becoming-shape" (33d)—*is the poem*.[24]

Which poem? I asked. The question persists. *The* poem—"the absolute poem" that is not given to us, that certainly and absolutely does not exist (*das es nicht gibt*), or "each real poem"? Not the latter, however, in any case not simply, not in its closure that—when complete—is its rapture and beauty. Not simply but, rather, in its *truth*. So, "each real poem," even the most unassuming and least ambitious (*anspruchslosesten*), should be understood not as an image or emanation of *the* poem but rather as an "irreducible question [*unabweisbare Frage*]," as an "outrageous claim [*unerhörter Anspruch*]" (38d). Gestures *of* language, certainly, questions and claims take place *in* language, but they point toward a beyond (or before) of language. Just as language cannot constitute itself in rejection or refusal (*Abweisung*) before *this* question that confronts it absolutely and fissures it from one end to another; just as the claim that overflows language resounds in it, inaudible for all hearing that might want to understand; just as the claim resounds there ab-surdly; so, too, the "language" in which such fissuring and such resonance occur must not be confused with that "speaking beyond" that persists in language's closure upon itself (the closure of rejection that circumscribes the dominion of understanding, of meaning, by gathering unto it everything that is). Rather, it has the open character of a place without place, that is to say, of u-topia. Which is the poem as place, as place opened and free, clearing of the encounter: the beyond (or before) language that, nevertheless, only persists in language.

Which poem, then? Which poem is *that* poem in which prevail the unavoidable question and the claim (*Anspruch*, which also means "interpellation") that Celan in all strictness calls "unheard-of," *unerhört*, resistant to the ear's habits, to the auditory regime governed by the expectation of meaning, the claim that is therefore inevitably discordant, outlandish, *ab-surd*?

The poem that does not exist, the absolute poem,[25] would be the poem freed from this circle, from this enchantment, from the spell of commensurability and similarity (of meaning). Here, in these terms, a radical and absolute change in poetry would be named. The absolute poem is the poem that does not *yet* exist but that, upon *arriving* (upon coming from its "yet" and eliminating it), also eliminates the poem; it is no longer a poem in any of the forms or senses in which we know it. (But can it arrive? Can it not, at most, "exist, ceaselessly back from its already-no-longer into its always still" [Celan, *Meridian*, 32b]?) Would this be the language without image, *bildlos*, of which Heidegger and Benjamin speak?

> Topos research?
> Certainly! But in light of what is to be searched for: in light of u-topia.
> And the human being? And the creature?
> In this light.
> What questions! What claims!
> It is time to turn back. (Celan, *Meridian*, 40a–41b)

Another light: what light, which light, would this light of u-topia be?

In what I have named the regime of eloquence (the occidental law of language), there prevails a light, a certain light, a law of light that forces clarity: *Lichtzwang*. This is the title of the book of poems published immediately after Celan's death in 1970; Celan had sent it to the printer, having already completed the task of correcting it. In the poem that gives the volume its title, a "we" speaks of having laid deep in the "Macchia," the thicket, a word that became synonymous with the partisans of the Resistance in Italy and France (*maquis*). In the poem, there is one who "finally crept along," but darkening over (*hinüberdunkeln*) toward him or her was not possible:

> es herrschte
> Lichtzwang.
> (Celan, *Collected Later Poetry*, 242)

> there reigned
> lightduress.
> (Celan, *Collected Later Poetry*, 243)

The reason for this poem, the reason for the impossibility of and impotence for welcoming the other—"you"—in the safekeeping of the hiding place, sanctions the relation between light and dominion (*Herrschaft*), purified in the coercive and compulsive rule of light, in the "pressure of light." The question is: What light is this? What experience of light is expressed here? With the expansion of its resonating meaning, the poem bespeaks the condition of history: the compulsion of light is a whole history in which no shelter is found; the poem speaks the wrong way around, but not in order to offer or arrange a refuge, which might be only a simulacrum. The poem speaks beneath the rule of light's compulsion, which it does not ignore but rather knows as what has become its own historical condition, in preparation for radical *exposition*: one will recall the apothegm "la poésie ne s'impose plus, elle s'expose."[26] And under such pressure, indeed, which is the darkness that cannot be cast over toward the other? Is it a question of darkness as a shelter, as protection? A requirement of darkness, of *shade*, installed itself early in Celan's poetry:

> Sprich —
> Doch scheide das Nein nicht vom Ja.
> Gib deinem Spruch auch den Sinn:
> gib ihm den Schatten.
> (Celan, *Threshold*, 96)

> Speak —
> but never split No off from Yes.
> Give your word a meaning:
> give it the shade.
> (Celan, *Threshold*, 97)

Shade and meaning coincide here: shade *is* meaning. But shade, as the No inseparable from the Yes, is the truth of this inseparability. Shade-meaning is truth immediately. The sentence, the *Spruch*, cannot be an affirmation. Or: in every affirmation the nonaffirmable—negation—must be said. This is the condition of the truth of saying, the condition on which anyone—a someone, *wer*—truly exercises language: to speak shade(s). "Whoever speaks shade speaks truth [*Wahr spricht, wer Schatten spricht*]!" (96–97). The penumbra thus belongs to Celan's poetics essentially, and it remains throughout his work with a rigorous tenacity, as the solidary tenor of a couple of poems from *Lightduress* shows. The first urges one to knock or beat wedges of light away because

> das schwimmende Wort
> hat der Dämmer.
> (Celan, *Collected Later Poetry*, 264)

dusk has
the swimming word.
(Celan, *Collected Later Poetry*, 265)

In the second poem, webbed words have a swamp or slough as their "timehalo":

Graugrätiges hinter
dem Leuchtschopf
Bedeutung.
(Celan, *Collected Later Poetry*, 286)

graycrestedness behind
the lightmane
meaning.
(Celan, *Collected Later Poetry*, 287)

And yet, one must also affirm another mode of light. It is the light of u-topia, of the *absurd* place. And it is the light—this word would have to be said—the light of salvation. Thus, in the poem that closes *Breathturn* and stands out for being the only poem in the sixth part of the volume, one reads about an uncertain God ("him") who "once" (and only once seems to be implied) "did wash the world":

Eins und Unendlich,
vernichtet,
ichten,

Licht war. Rettung.
(Celan, *Collected Later Poetry*, 106)

One and unending,
annihilated,
I'ed.

Light was. Salvation.
(Celan, *Collected Later Poetry*, 107)

Once: the "one time" governs here in the past, in an absolute past filled with event, a past in which there governs that indeterminate "him" that the name "God" would define or, *mutatis mutandis*, that would be left over excessively, that "him" and his secret and constant ablution. I evoke the "sprouting Never" named in "Pain, the syllable" (Celan, *No One's Rose*, 139), which will concern me later. I think, however, one need not think in a past that has been superseded by times and times again; the absolute past is absolute insofar as it is immediate, in the fashion of an *a priori* validated only in its negation, which is the same negation that constitutes me as the singular existent that I am: the negation and the annihilation (*nicht* and *Vernichtung*) that in their heart preserve the trace of the I (*ich*) rescued by the light in its truth (*Licht war: Licht wahr*).

We always arrive late to language, but *we arrive*. What lies in this arriving? What happens in it and with it? *From whence* do we arrive? And can this question even be formulated? Would there be, perhaps, an *outside of language*? And can this even be thought? Yet, why do we have *to learn* to speak and to write? Why can we remain speechless? Why do we stutter or stammer? How is it *in general* that quivering, dumbfounding, and vacillating govern our state in language, as if we always remained at the threshold of arriving?

5

Pain

"Language actualized," "angle of inclination of his Being," "one person's language-become-shape" (Celan, *Meridian*, 33b–d): individualized language, hence, inevitably embodied language since it speaks—in that punctual actuality, in that angle of inclination and incidence, in that figure—from a body, from a body's trepidation. The body thus seems to speak; my body thus speaks before I utter a word; thus, it has already spoken. It has spoken—before. Perhaps all anteriority of language, perhaps all ahumanity of language (one would have to recall a few warnings here),[1] takes root nowhere other than precisely in this always prior persistence of the body, of a body that speaks, of a body that has spoken as a body: before, in a past the distance of which cannot be measured chronologically, an immemorial past, no doubt, but a past that ceaselessly passes each moment, resumed each moment, forgotten again and again, a past that ceaselessly announces itself deafly, slipping the threat of sudden shock beneath my entrusted constancy. A past that has passed, alas, now. My body has spoken, at each moment, by its mere presence, which is the presence of an imminent past.[2]

Perhaps this is what the perceiver in *The Meridian* perceives, what Lucile's swaying hearing hears (a hearing that "sees," that "sees . . . speak" [Celan, *Meridian*, 5b], at the margin of all possible synesthesia, no doubt, due to a rare metathesis of the senses that could indicate something to us about the contexture *of* sense), the hearing of the little hare's ears (48c) that, in its trepidation, lies open to the trembling of the existent, open in its total attention to "the 'life of the smallest,' the 'twitches,' the 'intimations,' the 'whole fine, nearly unnoticed pantomime,'" open to "what is natural and creaturely" (14c). Perhaps the perceiver perceives this: the incidence, the corporal incident of an existence, the clinamen of a body as the "language and shape, and also . . . breath, that is, direction and destiny" (5b).

I cannot imagine a more corporal poetry than that of Paul Celan. Perhaps, among us, it would be necessary to mention César Vallejo and a certain Gabriela Mistral. In Celan, that corporality is molded and inscribed in the poem as the persistent attention (*Aufmerksamkeit*) that the poem itself "tries to pay to everything it encounters," to every other, an attention sustained in the poem through "its sharper sense of detail, outline, structure, color, but also of the 'tremors' and 'hints,'" and attention is certainly not an intention or intentionality that could procure the coming of the other or what is other but, rather, "a concentration that remains mindful of all our dates" (35c). Hence, an attention that demands attention: attention to each of its marks (I will not say signs: parentheses, hiatuses, dashes, colons, semicolons, ellipses, *blanks*, perhaps *blanks* above all . . .) that transcribe the body's every trembling and panting, its faltering temporality, in the body of the poem. A writing that demands to be read, a writing read by de-writing itself and de-reading itself in the poem, as the body's un-writing [*in-escritura*], as exscription [*excripción*].[3] Nonwritten corporality, painfully exscribed in the poem as—this is how I previously attempted to formulate it—the date of a wound.

Not written, my body has spoken—already. My body—my wound. My pain.

But does pain speak? The question apparently amounts to this other: can we speak *pain*? Not to speak *of* pain, for example, the pain I feel or have felt, by attempting to describe it, to pinpoint its locale, its intensity, as I might before a doctor so that he or she can form a picture of the possible illness afflicting me. Nor to speak *about* pain, which might happen, for instance, in a clinical or a philosophical treatise . . . We groan: thus, it seems, we say pain. But we do not really *say* it, not only because the groan tends to be almost inarticulate, a vowel or a consonant protractedly and gruelingly exhaled, but also because we seek to exteriorize pain by groaning, as if the lament could place outside of us that which in the most undeniable intimacy constitutes us in the absolute narrows of *this* time and *this* space. Should pain speak, should pain speak *as* pain, this does not occur without making the whole system of language collapse, without inflicting upon it—at least in one point (and this would be the *punctum* of language)—an *absolute* interruption: pain speaks in silence, as silence, *pain speaks silence*. In *this* silence, which we will not confuse with reticence or reserve (the inhibition a speaker inflicts upon his or her discourse), the body is exscribed as a memento and a moment of mortality.⁴ It is the silence of trembling, of pulsing, suspense *between* life and death, neither life nor death, time without time of the return of the imminent past of the body as relentless finitude's strictness or narrowness.⁵ And the poem transcribes the caesura. Would the poem, the Celanian poem, not be precisely a language of pain? In Celan, let it be said tentatively, pain lies in the middle of the poem like a wound of reality, a deaf and absurd pain that divides and disperses. To speak of pain, if it is possible *to speak of pain*, with designs on loyalty to the language of pain itself is, perhaps, to speak of the *between*, of the diabolical—and mute—place. It remains to be seen if *this* silence, this caesura, is perhaps the secret fold in which language now communicates only with itself beyond or before human languages and in which, for that very reason, it no longer communicates anything (or communicates *nothing*).

On pain (and in the direction of questions like the one recently posed), it would be necessary to read what Martin Heidegger says in the essay that opens *Unterwegs zur Sprache*. Concisely called "Language [*Die Sprache*],"⁶ the essay is dedicated to the interpretation of only one poem by Georg Trakl, which bears the title "A Winter Evening [*Ein Winterabend*]" (second version). On Heidegger's *reading*, the entire poem gravitates toward the second verse in the last of three stanzas, which speak of pain and its work.

> Wanderer tritt still herein;
> Schmerz versteinerte die Schwelle.
> Da erglänzt in reiner Helle
> Auf dem Tische Brot und Wein.
> (Cited in Heidegger, *Unterwegs*, 15)

> Wandering quietly steps within;
> Pain has petrified the threshold.
> There lie, in limpid brightness shown,
> Upon the table bread and wine.
> (Cited in Heidegger, *Poetry*, 192–93; translation modified)

In the *project* of that reading, pain and its work are magnetized in turn by the unfolding of language itself in the poem. Once again, one will note the *dictum* of language: language speaks, *die Sprache spricht*. Language speaks: in what is spoken and, before all, in what is spoken purely, in the pure spoken—in the poem, in *this* poem. And in this poem pain speaks. An essential, radical, originary relation between language and pain, between pain and language. It is a question now of interrogating this relation, this "between." And Heidegger interprets pain (*Schmerz*)—literally—from the Between, planting one foot in the poem's axial verse:

> Schmerz versteinerte die Schwelle.
> Pain has petrified the threshold.

One will note the article's elision, which is not unusual in German; it tends to be employed in poetry for greater emphasis and gives the word *Schmerz* the look of a proper name. There is certainly no talk here of *a* pain or of *the* pain either, of a putative universal essence of pain, of its *eidos*. The pain that breaks and divides, in its rifting *vis*, has neither *eidos* nor essence. And yet, it is not a mere fact shut away in the untransferable stronghold of a particular sensibility or private consciousness; pain shows essence above all. Let this all be said abundantly of Heidegger's commentary and, from a certain distance, in anticipation of what is said therein.

This verse's importance in the Heideggerian reading of Trakl is well known: the concentration of the poem in its primordial place or in the originary source from which it flows occurs in this precise verse (one should recall what was said in the second chapter; I will inevitably take up again a few of the things recorded there). In this verse, *die Sprache spricht*. For that very reason, the verse lies *alone* in the poem, *einsam*, gathering the poem around itself as though around its essential unity.[7] "This verse speaks all by itself [*einsam*] in what is spoken in the whole poem" (Heidegger, *Poetry*, 201). Its loneliness is not isolation but rather unity: if, as Heidegger says upon summarizing his examination of the two previous stanzas, the first stanza calls to things that—in being things—gestate the world (gathering sky and earth, mortals and gods), if the second stanza calls to the world that—in being world—dispenses things, if the first calls things to come to the world and the second calls the world to come to things and thus convokes the intimate unity—certainly not homogeneous or juxtaposed but rather *in difference*—*between* the two to its unfolding, then the third stanza calls to this dif-ference (*Unter-Schied*) as that which ap-propriates world and thing from the middle.[8]

I will soon have the opportunity to consider that which is called "dif-ference" here. Meanwhile, it is necessary to heed Heidegger's warning with respect to the word "petrified" and its tense: "This is the only word in the poem that speaks in the past tense. Even so, it does not name something past, something that no longer presences [*anwest*]. It names something that persists [*Wesendes*] and that has already persisted [*gewesen*]. The threshold first presences in the having been of petrifying [*Gewese des Versteinerns*]" (Heidegger, *Poetry*, 201; translation modified). We could also add: the expression "petrified" does not *refer* to a past but rather *opens (names) the past as such*; in this sense it *calls* the past to unfold as past: the past stands out, governs, and remains in force as petrification. The latter is the *work* of pain. At this point, how can one avoid evoking that other transformation into stone that, as the desire of the fundamental work of the artist and his or her art (both erected into Medusa heads), Georg Büchner sketches in Lenz's story? It is not improbable to think that this evocation touches upon what, at a crucial point in *The Meridian*, Celan calls "two strangenesses—close together, and in one and the same direction" (Celan, *Meridian*, 28): artistic strangeness and poetic strangeness. It is not improbable because the same proximity of the two petrifications allows one to recognize the differences between the two strangenesses. Perhaps the two principal ones: on the one hand, the Medusa of art governs in the present, in a present that could be called perennial to the extent that it erases the traces of its own coming and installs itself in the actuality of the spectacle;[9] on the other hand, the status of its governance is mediation, that is to say, the fact of the "as" that, assimilating difference (the "between"), makes the gesture of restituting the natural to the natural in order to institute it as the essential plunder of its capture. The petrification of pain, by contrast, gravitates as what is indelible of a past that, for that very reason, is reluctant toward and resistant to all mediation: from its muteness, it intimates our finitude. In this sense, the second essay that Heidegger writes on Trakl indicates the identity of the work of pain and its petrified "image": "The old stones are pain itself, for pain looks earthily upon mortals" (Heidegger, *On the Way*, 182).

As stone, which is "pain itself," the past stands out, governs, and remains in force: at the threshold. Where I pause.

On the threshold and its bordering condition—threshold or lintel, *Schwelle*, "the ground-beam that bears the doorway as a whole"—Heidegger says: "The threshold bears the Between" (*Poetry*, 201; translation modified), which holds sway between outside and inside. The secure support of the threshold, which adjusts and de-cides the Between, must be persistent and hard; it is such through the work of petrifying pain, which nevertheless does not thereby end up coagulated or congealed once and for all. "The pain presences unflagging in the threshold, as pain" (201). The specifications are directed toward establishing the very condition of pain in terms of the "between" that finds its neuralgic figure in the threshold.

Immediately, we read the fundamental passage on pain:

> But what is pain? Pain rends [*reißt*]. It is the rift [*Riß*]. But it does not tear apart into dispersive fragments. Pain indeed tears asunder, it separates [*scheidet*], yet so that at the same time it draws everything to itself, gathers it to itself [*in sich versammelt*]. Its rending, as a separating that gathers, is at the same time that drawing which, like the pen-drawing of a plan or sketch [*Vorriß und Aufriß*], draws and joins together what is held apart in separation. Pain is the joining agent in the rending that divides and gathers. Pain is the joining [*die Fuge*] of the rift. The joining is the threshold. It settles the between, the middle of the two that are separated in it. Pain joins the rift of the difference. Pain is the dif-ference [*Unter-Schied*, ex-cision] itself. (*Poetry*, 201–2)

One must wonder how, definitively, pain is being conceived here. Proper to it, we are told, is the rift. Yet, warned as we are against referring it to a sensibility or to the sphere of the subjective, we must understand that this "rift," without being a metaphor, is of a nature very distinct from the nature that spontaneously imposes itself upon us through the "lived experience" of pain. Heidegger understands—and clarifies it thus in the other text aforementioned—that the poetic thought of pain he reads in Trakl demands abandoning every biological, organic, physiological, and also psychological ground of explication; he establishes this fundamental admonition in which we must recognize the polemical, negative key of his own elucidation in the following way: "Its essence [*Wesen*] remains closed to any opinion [*Meinen*] that understands pain in terms of sensitivity" (*On the Way*, 181; translation modified). To that extent, we cannot open ourselves to that essence on the basis of a conception of life, whatever that conception might be; pain, rather, shows us what and how life is: "Everything that is alive, is painful" (181).[10] The concept of pain promoted here is properly ontological, prehuman, insofar as it is a primitive determination of Dasein as pure finite opening and therefore the passion of finitude, and it is in this precise sense that Heidegger characterizes pain as dif-ference. With such a title, pain—ontologically considered—divides and de-cides world and thing by referring one to the other and vice versa on the basis of their originary difference that, by virtue of this reciprocal reference, is at the same time their unity. Therefore, what is decisive in this text—de-cisive—is that it *assigns pain a gathering character*.[11] Beyond contesting the metaphysical perspectives that scan his argument, this assignation is the axis of the Heideggerian conception of pain. By conceiving it on the basis of gathering, Heidegger *refers pain essentially to logos*. Such is the joint pertinence that the essay premeditates between pain and language. The *purity* wishing to be expressed in the sentence *die Sprache spricht*, which is therefore the purity of the *logos* that rests on itself alone, depends upon this referral, upon this interpretation. If, in what follows in the text, the previously prepared theme of *intimacy* (*Innigkeit*) appears in immediate relation to pain ("then would the intimacy of the dif-ference for world and thing be pain?" [Heidegger, *Poetry*, 202]), if at that point we are to take precautions against understanding pain "anthropologically as a sensation that makes us feel afflicted" and against understanding intimacy "psychologically as the sort in which sentimentality makes a nest for itself" (202), if pain and intimacy are inseparable here (they are, at the same time, the passion of dif-ference), it is because *intimacy determines nothing other than the cobelonging of pain and logos*: *logos is due* to dif-ference; pain hatches in *logos*.[12] This is also how it can happen that, as the stone *speaks* or upon *speaking* the stone [*al* hablar *la piedra*], "pain itself has the word," and from its long silence it says with evangelical resonance: "Truly! I shall forever be with you" (*On the Way*, 182).[13]

Pain and word, pain and *logos*, hence, pain and meaning. This thought of pain, this thought that thinks and weighs pain as gathering in the rift and as articulation of what its own work separates, this thought that thus recuperates an originary principle of unity in the very unfolding of the dispersive potential of pain must be linked, I think, with Heidegger's understanding of the structure of the poem's meaning, which is to say, the "plurivocity [*Mehrdeutigkeit*]" that he says is proper to the poem (Heidegger, *On the Way*, 192; translation modified). In "Language in the Poem," the second of the essays dedicated to Trakl that I continue to cite, we find the following observations:

> The poetic work speaks out of an ambiguous ambiguousness [*zweideutigen Zweideutigkeit*]. Yet this multiple plurivocity of the poetic saying does not scatter in vague equivocations. The ambiguous tone of Trakl's poetry arises out of a gathering [*Versammlung*], that is, out of a unison which, meant for itself alone, always remains unsayable. The plurivocity of this poetic saying is not lax imprecision [*Ungenaue des Lässigen*], but rather the rigor of him who leaves what is as it is [*des Lassenden*], who becomes involved [*sich . . . eingelassen hat*] with the care

[*Sorgfalte*] of "righteous vision" and submits to it. (*On the Way*, 192; translation modified)

The poem's plurivocity is not dispersion (dissemination, if you will) but rather gathering—consonance [*consonancia*] and, earlier still, unisonance [*unisonancia*]—which remains unsayable. *The sense of sense is gathering*: *there is* sense on the basis of gathering; gathering—primordially—gives sense.[14] Yet, for that very reason, this sense (*Sinn*) does not have the character of signification (*Bedeutung*) but, rather, that of the concentration of Dasein in its most originary possibility, and this concentration—precisely this concentration—is shown to Dasein through pain. Pain understood, as we already know, prior to the metaphysical division between the sensible (sensible sense) and the intelligible (spiritual sense). Heidegger names *that* concentration *Be-sinnung*, in which we would have to read the originary unity of thinking-and-poeticizing.

Unity (in difference, no doubt) that is unity of silence, the mode (Heidegger plays with the double sense of *die Weise*, mode and melody) in which language speaks, letting the thing in the world and the world in the thing be still (another play: *stillen*, to calm and to silence). "When the dif-ference gathers world and things into the simple onefold of the pain of intimacy, it bids the two to come into their very essence" (Heidegger, *Poetry*, 204; translation modified). The *Stille* is the regathering and the recollection of sense—and, certainly, of *the* senses—that grounds the "plurivocity" of poetic saying, as well as the reconcentrated and thoughtful hearing that can hear and think only what is said in that saying if it itself lets itself be convoked by the call of silence. The notion of *Stille* is, certainly, the decisive complement of the sentence *die Sprache spricht* advanced in the essay's preamble; it completes the sentence insofar as it brings it to rest in the essential operation that it names: "*Language speaks as the peal of stillness* [Die Sprache spricht als das Geläut der Stille]" (205).[15] Yet, the important factor of this issue lies in the fact that, certainly, Heidegger does not resolve pain (dif-ference) in language: "Only the third stanza gathers the bidding [*Heißen*] of things and the bidding of world. For the third stanza calls [*ruft*] primally out of the simplicity of the intimate bidding which calls the dif-ference by leaving it unspoken [*ungesprochen*]" (203). Pain, then, remains unspoken in its pure intimacy; language cannot assume it, cannot incorporate it into its dominion. But this does not mean that pain belongs to the dimension of the nonlinguistic. On the contrary, the originarity of language—before what is human, which happens only from that originarity—consists in that it welcomes dif-ference insofar as it lets it happen in what is proper to it: stillness. "Stillness stills by the carrying out, the bearing and enduring, of world and things in their presence. The carrying out of world and thing in the manner of stilling is the appropriative taking place of the dif-ference. Language, the peal of stillness, is, inasmuch as the dif-ference takes place. Language goes on as the taking place or occurring of the dif-ference for world and things" (205).

Keeping these determinations in mind (determinations that, of course, will have to be withdrawn from their precarity), how will we understand the question of pain in Celan? I said at the beginning that the body—my body, the body of each individual, the body that *is* each individual—has spoken before, has spoken *already*. It has spoken through its reticence to incorporation in discourse, thus denying that a body takes place only on the basis of a discourse and like a flower of language. The body has spoken before: for that very reason it cannot be said. It has spoken, painfully, by exscribing itself. It has spoken from its wound, mark of finitude, root of reality.

> IN DER LUFT, da bleibt deine Wurzel, da,
> in der Luft.
> Wo sich das Irdische ballt, erdig,
> Atem-und-Lehm.
> (Celan, *No One's Rose*, 158)

> IN THE AIR, your root still hovers, there,
> in the air.
> Where the Earth balls itself, earthy,
> breath-and-clay.
> (Celan, *No One's Rose*, 159)

And:

> STEHEN, im Schatten
> des Wundenmals in der Luft.
>
> Für-niemand-und-nichts-Stehn.
> Unerkannt,
> für dich
> allein.
> (Celan, *Collected Later Poetry*, 10–12)

> TO STAND, in the shadow
> of the stigma in the air.
>
> Standing-for-no-one-and-nothing.
> Unrecognized,
> for you
> alone.
> (Celan, *Collected Later Poetry*, 11–13)

For the moment, let us venture the following: in Celan, distinctly from the way in which it occurs in Heidegger, *the wound has (been) thought before* [la herida (se) ha pensado antes]. Would the wound's "having (been) thought before" (which would make gathering impossible but—perhaps—the encounter possible) be the raw? Or, rather, the thought of the raw, knowledge of the raw? That which resists that which gathers, that which resists the *Be-sinnung*? In Heidegger, everything that could be conceived as wound is referred to pain and not the inverse: there is wound on the basis of pain (the proper of which is the rift that separates and divides); this referral is essential for the Heideggerian understanding of pain as the articulation of gathering and separation, and the basis of this understanding is certainly clear: Heidegger interprets the wound on the basis of its sense, that is to say, on the basis of its primordial incorporation into language. Would it be the case that, in Celan, there is an indelible anteriority of the wound that marks all experience with the trace of its division?

It has (been) thought before; we could also say, perhaps, that it has already occurred *behind*. This "behind" is sung in both beginnings of two poems in *Breathturn*, poems of raw love, which insist upon division: "Ashglory" and "Cello-entry."

> ASCHENGLORIE hinter
> deinen erschüttert-verknoteten
> Händen am Dreiweg.
> (Celan, *Collected Later Poetry*, 62)

> ASHGLORY behind
> your shaken-knotted
> hands at the threeway.
> (Celan, *Collected Later Poetry*, 63)

CELLO-EINSATZ
von hinter dem Schmerz:
(Celan, *Collected Later Poetry*, 66)

CELLO-ENTRY
from behind pain:
(Celan, *Collected Later Poetry*, 67)

In both poems, duality: "two painknots" (65); "she, black- / biled, drinks / the blackbiled's seed" (69).

Reading the poem "Pain, the syllable [*Die Silbe Schmerz*]," contained in the fourth—and final—section of *No One's Rose*, might possibly offer orientation in this matter. The word "pain" has been inscribed only in the title and precisely in such a way that it warns us that it is not a question of a "word": pain is a "syllable," something that remains halfway between mere sound and the articulation and regathering unity of *logos*. We must understand that the entire poem speaks of pain, that it speaks of pain as what breaks and crushes language, or rather that pain unfolds in the poem from the very origin of everything (of language as well) and as that origin. The intelligible key for what the title calls "syllable" appears only at the end in that crippled reading of the "carnival-eyed brood" or "litter" (*Brut* can be read equally in the singular and in the plural), in the stuttering and hobbling—"buch-, buch-, buch- / stabierte, stabierte" ("Buch," book; "Stab," rod, pole, word-syllable-letter, the book's *Inbegriff*) [Celan, *No One's Rose*, 138–41].

As happens in many other poems by Celan, one notes in this poem the genetic, cosmogonic, primordial breath blowing in a swirling movement that recalls the Democritean passage of the "Hurricanes, part- / icle storms" in "Stretto" (Celan, *Language Behind Bars*, 97). And, as in so many other poems, comprehension oscillates between the processes of a putative reality to which the text appears to refer, here with its narrative diction of embryonic beginnings and events with epic resonance, and that which one would have to describe as the pure linguistic fact that takes place only in the poem. This itself permits one to think—or even brings one to think—that what the title calls "pain" is first of all an event of language, that is, something that happens to language as such, to language itself. A trance [*trance*], a chance [*lance*] first unleashes the process, and mention of it marks in language the incidence not of the word, not of the name, but rather of the pronominal, of the prenominal: "It gave itself into Thy hand, / a Thou, deathless, / at which all that was *I* came to itself" (Celan, *No One's Rose*, 139). It is, one might say, the incidence or the incident of individuation on the basis of duality, of alterity; Celanian poetry insists thereon. *This* event gives place to primordial and material chaos—of "Voices, / wordless, . . . empty forms" (139)—into which everything enters in a syncopated rhythm of mixtures and separations and mixtures. Its entire dimension is that immense and oceanic "sprouting Never [*keimendes Niemal*]" in which the second stanza ends and, along with it, the "description" of the Origin in the first moment of the poem. The Numberless, that singular-plural (and the singular-dual first of all: the wound) which is—if anything can be—the "subject" of Celanian poetry, provides the key to that movement first of all. The second moment is the trip, the mad Columbian navigation ("Columbus, / his eye on the saffron crocus, / the mother-flower, / murdered masts and sails" [139]) that flows into "a blind // L e t t h e r e b e [*ein blindes // Es sei*]," the only word in Celan's poetic written in letterspacing (what the Germans imaginatively call *Sperrdruck*, writing or printing between bars),[16] which is nevertheless a knot: "a / knot / (and counter- and over- and yet- and double- and thou- / sand-knot" (140–41). Pain as a knot, then: in pain, the "brood" book-stalls, and what it book-stalls, with "carnival" eyes looking blindly, is precisely that l e t t h e r e b e. The origination of the world "related" by this poem spills apocalyptically into a *fiat* that does not create or gestate, does not gather or compose but, rather, erodes the totality by painfully returning it to its elements, its *stoicheia*. Insofar as the grille of the l e t t h e r e b e measures the "sprouting Never" with its three temporal tenses (present imperative, future optative, and present subjunctive), "the pain syllable"—a title tensed between the (im)possibility of the word or its plenitude (its force of creative nomination) and the blind materiality of the letter—is a poem that bespeaks the catastrophe of language, what we could perhaps call its *unworldly filth* [*in-mundicia*].[17]

In "Words [*Das Wort*]," the penultimate essay in *On the Way to Language* and dedicated to the examination of Stefan George's eponymous poem, it is also a question of a "sei" that has been inscribed in the final distich of the piece, which is composed of seven stanzas each of two verses:

So lernt ich traurig den verzicht:
Kein ding sei wo das wort gebricht.
(Cited in Heidegger, *Unterwegs*, 208)

So I renounced and sadly see:
Where word breaks off no thing may be.
(Cited in Heidegger, *On the Way*, 140).

Heidegger understands—and this is the core of his attempt—that the "renunciation" neither supposes nor is a simple self-denial, more so still if in its doubly negating form the last verse contains a decisive affirmation: a thing *is* there where the word is protected. The renunciation, Heidegger holds, pertains to the poetic claim of the word's sovereignty in its force of nomination insofar as the latter lies in its capacity to present and represent the thing. But this renunciation opens and concedes in turn a more originary relation of word and thing, a higher power of the word itself, which in the poet's diction remains shielded in mystery. Heidegger names that relation with an old German word: *Bedingnis* ("bethinging"). This must not be understood in the sense of "condition" (*Bedingung*), as a being's ground and reason of being, a ground that is also in turn a being and, for that very reason, obeys the principle of reason; it must be understood, rather, as letting the thing presence as thing.

> Self-denial—which appears to be only refusal and self-withdrawal—is in truth nondenial of self: to the mystery of the word. This nondenial of self can speak in this way only, that it says: "may there be." From now on may the word be: the bethinging of the thing. This "may there be" lets be the relation of word and thing, what and how it really *is*. Without the word, no thing is. [. . .] In this nondenial of self, renunciation says itself as that kind of Saying which owes itself wholly [*sich ganz . . . verdankt*] to the mystery of the word. (Heidegger, *On the Way*, 151–52)

The renunciation, this stage of the reading ultimately says, in truth is not a revocation or a loss but rather (a gesture of) gratitude.

The immediately following stage returns to the previous verse and inquires after the sadness that the poet declares, the sadness that accompanies the apprenticeship in renunciation. Naturally, if Heidegger's intention has been, so to speak, to read the final distich positively, this sadness seems to return us to something like a defeat or failure assumed in resignation. But that appearance is superficial: the timbre of happiness likewise lies in the sadness; a poem that has the timbre and tone of happiness and the last word of which is "melancholy" helps to understand that profound link. The poet's "sadness" is explained as the reciprocal play that tempers joy (*Freude*) and sadness (*Trauer*). "The play itself which attunes the two by letting the remote be near and the near be remote is pain. This is why both, highest joy and deepest sadness, are painful each in its way. But pain so touches [*mutet*] the spirit of mortals that the spirit receives its gravity [*Schwergewicht*] from pain. That gravity keeps mortals with all their wavering at rest in their being. The spirit which answers to pain, the spirit attuned by pain and to pain, is melancholy" (Heidegger, *On the Way*, 153). Pain, it must be said in conformity with this play, tempers the spirit of mortals in the weight—the load—of their own being: of their mortal being. Such is the nature of *Schwermut*, melancholia. This same connection should help to advance what follows in the text, especially with respect to the Heideggerian concept of *Bedingnis* in distinction from the principle of reason. What lies between pain and the principle of sufficient reason?

Nevertheless, Heidegger does not *ask* himself in what the word's break (*Bruch*) consists. The patient and subtle reading, which begins by emphasizing precisely the last verse, provisionally equates the break, the rupture, and the interruption with lack such that the verse would say: there where the word lacks, no thing is. Questions follow this temporary warning, "questions upon questions" (Heidegger, *On the Way*, 141), questions directed to the word, to the thing, to being. The interpretation of the break as lack is not taken up or debated again in the essay, and yet it determines the explication of that which lies in the marrow of the negation's self-denial: "The treasure which never graced the poet's land is the word for the essence [*Wesen*] of language. [. . .] But the word for the essence [*Wesen*] of the word is not granted" (154; translation modified). The word, then, lacks for the word: the apprenticeship of renunciation would be the experience of this lack. But that same word glints in the other poem that Heidegger cites; the word stands out with its capital in a writing that, breaking the rule, does not begin nouns with capitals: the word *Sage* (of *sagen*, "to say," with an acceptation of the legendary, as in "saga" or "fable"). Near the conclusion, we read:

> The word's rule springs to light as that which makes the thing be a thing [*als die Bedingnis des Dinges zum Ding*]. The word begins to shine as the gathering which first brings what presences to it presence.
>
> The oldest word for the rule of the word thus thought, for Saying, is *logos*: Saying which, in showing, lets beings appear in their "it is" [*er ist*].

> The same word, however, the word for Saying, is also the word for *Being*, that is, for the presencing of beings. Saying and Being, word and thing, belong to each other in a veiled way, a way which has hardly been thought and is not to be thought out to the end. (Heidegger, *On the Way*, 155)

Must it be said? Could one think the rule of the word that gathers in Celan's poetry? Or is the essential experience of this poetry not the word's literally unheard-of break, an unsayable break in any of the modes in which saying is—still—possible? A break that does not permit the thread that ties thing, word, and world in the word *is* (*es ist*)? A break that in the "blind / Let there be" lets pain, pain itself, speak as originary dispersion?

6

Doit

We always arrive late to language, as I said previously. We arrive late, but *we arrive*. Who are we who arrive? From whence do we arrive? Would perhaps there therefore be an "outside of language," entirely other, another *Unheimlichkeit* to be discerned with precision and in distinction from the *Unheimlichkeit* constructed by art and language ("perhaps there are two strangenesses—close together, and in one and the same direction" [Celan, *Meridian*, 28])?[1] Another radical strangeness (*Fremde*), then, that would be the place of an other, the nonplace from which an other comes to the encounter? An "outside" that announces its arrival by faltering "I," an "outside" invoked in the "you"—perhaps a pro-nominal, pre-nominal "outside"? This would be, for the moment, the experience in Paul Celan with respect to the relation with language: *the "I" would be the trace of "something"—an intensity, a direction—that comes from outside language and that, through language (in speech and inscription), addresses a "you," interpellating and calling it, opening (even desperately) the space of an encounter.* It is in this sense that I have spoken of "a word coming from outside language": such would be the *poem*, the poem as *experience*.

(I do not wish to interpret; nor do I wish to imagine. Here, gradually, we enter the district of the absolutely unrepresentable, where "all tropes and metaphors want to be carried ad absurdum" [Celan, *Meridian*, 39b]; we waver on the threshold of the poem's "one, unique, momentary present" [36b]. But I still retain—I project—one last image. The most archaic landscape, a phosphorescent ground sown with pockmarks, night-and-night traversed with meteors. Language precedes us, to be sure, we arrive late to language, to dwelling in the dimension of the *Unheimliche*, but something irrupts there, something opens a path, something leads through a narrow path: a meteoric word that falls, acceleratingly, and upon entering "our" atmosphere—meaning as the air that we breathe in language—incandesces and incinerates but leaves a crater as a trace—language as writing, as inscription. A meteor-word that falls *acceleratingly*: "La poésie, elle aussi, brûle nos étapes" [22d]. Soon, it will be necessary to inquire into this acceleration and ask if there is only one species of acceleration.)

The "I" would be the trace, I said, of "something" that comes from outside language. But what "something"? Where does the pronoun point? Where does it point, indeed, because indication—*deixis*—is in question. "I" is not merely a position; it is a deictic of existence. Existence that persists "outside language" and is in no way full, consummated, or rounded off in itself because it can only announce itself in language—by saying "I"—and can only take place there in relation to the other from which it is—is it accurate to employ this word?—constituted. For that very reason, in addition, existence that as such is nothing. *This* which arrives and says (stammers) "I"—*ich*, a splinter encrusted in *dicht, Gedicht*, and *nicht*, in *Nichts*—is certainly a *nothing*. Do we have a sign of this nothing? Let us attempt one path.

This poem from *Timestead*,[2] the first stanza of which can still be read in the mode of an ars poetica, occupies a decisive place here:

> ICH TRINK WEIN aus zwei Gläsern
> und zackere an
> der Königszäsur
> wie Jener
> am Pindar,
> (Celan, *Collected Later Poetry*, 442)

> I DRINK WINE from two glasses
> and harrow
> the king's caesura
> like that other
> does Pindar,
> (Celan, *Collected Later Poetry*, 443)[3]

Inevitably, as I have already said, the reflection "between Celan and Heidegger"—the work of this "Between"—must take into account the relation of both Celan and Martin Heidegger to Friedrich Hölderlin, to "that other" who, this poem says, "harrows" like Pindar.[4] In this relation, in this obstinate connection, the poem "Tübingen, Jänner"—upon which I touched previously—also has an essential gravitation. There is a tight connection, I believe, between the two poems, which I want to localize here between the "harrowing" or the "tiptoeing" (*zackern*) of which the present poem speaks and the only language possible—the stuttering babble—for speaking of "this time." Let us recall the third stanza of this poem, which I quoted above: "if there came a man to the world today, with / the shining beard of / patriarchs . . . he / would only go on to / babble, babble, / ever-, ever-, / moremore" (Celan, *No One's Rose*, 49). For there seems to be a relation between *lallen* ("babble") and *zackern* ("harrow," "tiptoe"), a relation that would have to be inscribed in the general mode in which language unfolds in Celanian poetry on the basis of an *essential mutation of language that from eloquence to babble, to the edge of going mute, carries a historical mutation that is also at the same time a mutation of history itself as destiny.*

(Babbling is the speech of the time of acceleration, of *our* time. "The 'swift [*Geschwinde*],' " Celan says, "which has always been 'outside,' has gained speed; the poem knows this, but heads straight for that 'other' " [*Meridian*, 31f]. The relation that links Celan to Hölderlin, the experience in which they relate, is the experience of "lean time [*dürftiger Zeit*]" (Hölderlin, *Poems and Fragments*, 251; translation modified) as the time of acceleration. This was the essential trait that Hölderlin recognized in "modern" times, which made the alternation of tones radically unstable and uncertain, threatening to destitute the poem—that is to say, human existence itself—on the basis of the principle of its possibility, and it imposed the obsessive—and even desperate—search for measure [*Maß*].[5] In this sense, Celan not only seems to interpret Hölderlin's mad speech [*Pallaksch, Pallaksch*], the babbling speech, as the only speech in which one can speak of "this time"; he also offers his own clarification of the question of measure. To which I now turn.)

And, certainly, it is ultimately a question of destiny, fate, and "lot" in the poem from *Zeitgehöft*. In *this* poem, then, I attend especially to the last word (and one would have to ponder the weight, the deaf gravitation of every "last word" in all of Celan's poems, each of which is spoken, literally, as the last of all words, as a tatter on the edge of the abyss: of a radical falling silent).

aus der Lostrommel fällt
unser Deut.
(Celan, *Collected Later Poetry*, 442)

> from the lottery drum falls
> our doit.
> (Celan, *Collected Later Poetry*, 443)

I attend to the word *Deut*, infinitely dense in its smallness. I transcribe—I translate—the corresponding entry in the *Etymologisches Wörterbuch des Deutschen*:

> **Deut** masculine. Now only in the fixed combinations with *no* or *not a Deut*, "not at all." *Deut* (since the 17th century in High German texts) is originally the designation for a small copper coin in Holland and the Lower Rhine, which circulated until the 19th century; Middle Dutch *duit, doyt, deuit, deyt*, Dutch *duit*, thereafter Middle Low German *deut, doyt*, English *doit*, related to Old Norse *þveiti* "coin, a measure of butter," properly "the cut off, the punched off piece," to the Old Norse *þvita* "to hit, to beat, to punch," and to the Old English *þwītan* "to cut, to cut off." Along with livestock as the most common measure of value at the beginning of trade relations (before the introduction of minted money), pieces of broken or chopped off precious metal are a valid means of payment. From the second half of the 18th century on, *Deut* stands for a "small sum of money," above all in the abovementioned relations. (Pfeifer, *Etymologisches Wörterbuch*, 218)

Deut is probably a *crucial* word—if one can call it a word at all—or a word of *crossings* and in this sense what, reading Celan, Jacques Derrida would call a *shibboleth*. *Deut*, on the one hand, points toward the domain of the semantic and the symbolic, of interpretation and signification: toward *Deutung* and *Bedeutung*. It points, but at the same time and first of all it persists in the crossing, at the threshold of meaning, as the apex of insignificance lodged in all signification, as that which is definitive and essentially uninterpretable, as that which cannot be brought to the *dominion* of language but is, at the same time, that *deutlich* uniqueness the clarity or *evidence* of which repeals and places in crisis all interpretation, all attribution of meaning, that is to say, all attribution of *importance*. (And here, perhaps, one could not refer the term "evidence" primarily to the visual field because, even if *Deutlichkeit* is effectively a quality of perception and not that of the significant word, it is not a quality of mere seeing either: let us not forget that eyes have been "persuaded / to be blind" [Celan, *No One's Rose*, 49]; the clarity of perception is the trembling of the existence that opens to another existence and thus, I believe, should be understood along the lines of witnessing and testimony: I will return to this.) *Deut* is *that which has no im-port at all*, that which im-ports (contraband) only to itself. This currency of insignificant value, circulating without exchange value, would seem to define the element and principle of an an-economy in which one would perhaps have to recognize the essential relation of poetry and existence, of poetry and reality.

And, on the other hand, an allusion to what is "German," to *Deutsch*, is not far off: *deuten* and *bedeuten*, from the same root, mean to make manifest for the people. (The reader will remember my initial musings on the play of this word in "Todtnauberg.")

Also nearby, however, is the beginning of Hölderlin's sketch for "Mnemosyne," in which resound questions of interpretation, signification, and the insignificant, that which resists interpretation and, to that extent, lacks meaning (*deutungslos*):

Ein Zeichen sind wir, deutungslos
Schmerzlos sind wir und haben fast
die Sprache in der Fremde verloren.
(Hölderlin, *Hymns*, 116)

A sign we are, without meaning
Without pain we are and nearly have
Lost our language in foreign lands.
(Hölderlin, *Hymns*, 117)

It would take a long time to meditate on the experience defined by these first three verses, unfathomably deep, and on the relations between sign, interpretation, pain, language, and the foreign. The only thing I wish to insinuate here is that such a meditation—together with the examination of the hymns' poetic—should bring us into the vicinity of the Celanian experience, which probes its own relation to language in secret audience to Hölderlin's poetry and in the intermittent persistence—of stammering—in that "almost [*fast*]" in which, announcing a *Deut*, the second verse remains suspended.[6]

What, then, is the *Deut* in Celan? The *Deut* is *nothing*, to be sure, nothing as lot, fortune, or destiny—of each individual: nothing as Dasein, but Dasein as witness, as *Zeuge*. We thus return to the theme of "a word coming from outside language." What does this word "I" *say*? What does it *mean*? Does the coming of a saying occur with its irruption? Yes, no doubt, but not a saying rooted in the said. Rooted, rather, in what comes in and with the said, that is to say, in the incommensurability of experience as an event of freedom in the world. This coming, in any case, should be related to the *Enge*, to the *narrowness*, to the *straitness*: one will recall the link between narrowness [*angostura*] and anxiety [*angustia*], between *Enge* and *Angst*. In Celan, *Enge* would be existence: Da-sein, being-there, testimony.

What arrives and says "I," that the coming of which the "I" addresses as a "you," is a nothing, *nothing-of-being*, and not (being as) a *nothing-of-beings*: it is the *Deut*, the doit, the insignificant, the "trifle," the valueless hidden at the same time from all ontology and all axiology, Dasein. *To speak, to write, is to incise this nothing in language* (a wound, therefore). And if I previously defined the essence of language as "speaking-beyond-oneself," it becomes clear here that the fundamental conflict lies between such *Überreden* (which blinds perception and, with it, the opening to the present) and *saying a word against language—a Gegenwort—*that indelibly inscribes the present (*Gegenwart*). But the latter, perhaps, can happen only as stammering or by falling silent in the narrow throat in which the word is cut.

It is necessary, then, to examine the grand poem "Stretto [*Engführung*]," which closes *Language Behind Bars*, and to confront—to that end—Peter Szondi's interpretation, which has long remained the fundamental attempt to offer an interpretation of the poem in its entirety. It is also no doubt necessary to examine those interpretations that object to the point of view of Szondi's reading with respect to, above all, the idea that the poem demands an exegesis closed upon itself, as if it contained the principles of and keys to its own reading.[7] The term with which Celan titles his most extensive poem is, as is well known, a technical musical term—*stretto*—that designates the execution of a movement in quick time, especially a piece's final movement in which, an artifice peculiar to the composition of fugues, the theme and the figure superpose. Needless to say, this implies a peculiar reference to "Death Fugue," in which one could read the already inscribed theme of narrowness, to which I have given special weight in the Celanian poetic. Inscribed, that is, in that promise or that condemnable seduction of the Master Death: "we dig a grave in the breezes there one lies unconfined [*da liegt man nicht eng*]" (Celan, *Poems*, 31–32). But that reference is not reiterative: we can understand it as a self-critical revision of that first grand poem of the Holocaust. The sense of this self-critique could be stated thus: renouncing the lyricism of the "Fugue," its haughty melodic structure, and emphasizing ellipsis as an essential operation of poetic articulation (the sense for which—the same sense as "the faster fall of syntax," as Celan says in *The Meridian* [32a]—is more awake in today's poetry), "Engführung" persists in the *step* or the *trance* (not a *trans*, neither a "like" nor a "beyond") that refuses to be linguistically administered to the same extent that it entails the index of a forcing, a fate, that the beginning of the poem stipulates.

*

VERBRACHT ins
Gelände
mit der untrüglichen Spur:
(Celan, *Language Behind Bars*, 88)

*

BROUGHT forcibly to
the terrain with
the unmistakable trace:
(Celan, *Language Behind Bars*, 89)[8]

The poem's opening—I say this as a first approach—is not absolute: the poem is not established in its own jurisdiction and its full locutionary present; something has already happened, something or someone has been "displaced"—who?—to a terrain or territory (*Gelände*) in which the trace (*Spur*) prevails, the unequivocal vestige (of what? of whom?), the mark of a past that maintains its validity and its irrevocable truth. A terrain: "Grass, written asunder," "stones, white," "the shadows of grassblades" (89), which also unequivocally means a demolished extermination camp where everything—total annihilation—has already befallen not merely as a registerable fact but, rather, as an event that cannot belong to any present and that, in its exhaustive dispersion, cannot be conjured in the present by any word either. Preceded and made abyssal by a writing—of grass, of stones, of shadows—indecipherable through merely linguistic means (of substitution and equivalence), the impotence of language is betrayed here: there is no name for what happened (*das, was geschah*, in the succinct formulation of the "Speech at Bremen" [Celan, *Collected Prose*, 34]). The word that "came through the night," the word that "wanted to glow," is consumed in its very incandescence, and now only "Ashes. / Ashes, ashes" prevail as a painful litany (Celan, *Language Behind Bars*, 93). In the empire of "Night. / Night-and-night" (93). The night, without stars, is the night of disaster. Someone—a "you"—is exhorted not to read but to watch, and not to watch but to walk:

> Lies nicht mehr—schau!
> Schau nicht mehr—geh!
> (88)

> Read no more—watch!
> Watch no more—go!
> (89)

Someone is exhorted to follow the order for (and of) displacement through the terrain to the slow and deaf rhythm of the "hour" that "has no sisters" (89), the definitive hour, as Szondi notes (the hour of death, he says [*Celan Studies*, 32], but the same could also be said of birth). From the first moment, the poem stipulates a temporality marked by ruptures.

But the terrain or territory is also, indiscernibly, at the same time the poem, *this* poem. I say "at the same time" to emphasize that the very construction of the text radically resists being decided in terms of the appeal to a "reality," whether that of the historical world or that of the poem as such. If so, then the exhortation (or the command) that I just mentioned could no longer be understood simply in accordance with the difference between a poetic (and semantic) interiority and a real (and factical) exteriority. The sequence read-watch-go characterizes the essential movement of displacement conceived as a relation to a writing that, as I said, cannot be resolved by exclusively linguistic means: an *other* reading, then, that the poem demands for itself and for what has been inscribed and exscribed at the same time in it; an *other* reading that is delivered to the poem's evidence ("watch!"), that is to say, to its own movement ("go!").[9]

As various commentators have already observed, a similar resistance can be examined in light of the concept of caesura that Hölderlin proposes as one of the keys for his poetological reflections on tragedy. In his "Notes to *Oedipus*," the concept belongs to the explication of "tragic transport," and it would not be out of place to mention that Hölderlin employs the word "transport" (*Transport*) in the colloquial sense of the Greek term for metaphor: "displacement." With that word, Hölderlin designates the dynamic proper to tragedy, which the preceding paragraph in the "Notes" characterizes with the formulation "more a matter of weighting and balance than of pure sequence" (Hölderlin, *Sophocles*, 63). Established time and again between the antagonistic forces that violently collide in tragedy, this balance by its very nature destroys all determined content in which that conflict could be synthesized, resulting each time in a ceaselessly aggravated "emptiness" and inexorably clearing the path to catastrophe. Hölderlin signals:

> For that reason in the rhythmical succession of scenes in which *the transport* is made manifest, it becomes necessary to have *what in prosody is known as a caesura*; the pure word, the counter-rhythmical interruption [*gegenrhythmische Unterbrechung*], is needed, so as to confront the pull of the succession [*reißenden Wechsel*] of scenes at its height and in such a fashion that instead of facets of a manifestation there comes manifestation itself. (63)

The theory of the caesura (*Cäsur*, the meaning of which should not be confused simply with the rupture or articulation of the verse's metric structure, to which Hölderlin himself alludes here) identifies the caesura with the point at which the tragic catastrophe is produced, the moment of tense balance in the rhythm of the manifestations, the action's upheaval, as the march of destiny that, Hölderlin will say, drags the human into "the eccentric zone of the dead" (64): the wrenching time and impossibility for beginning and end or anteriority and posteriority to rhyme. And precisely in tragedy "the god, in the shape of death, is present" (116). The "manifestation itself [*die Vorstellung selbst*]" of which the passage speaks has the absolute peculiarity of lacking all content and possessing an absolutely indeterminable content. It is, if one wishes to express it thus, empty as an infinite relation.[10] And it is thus "the pure word [*das reine Wort*]," the cut in the temporal succession that scans the manifestations, the incommensurable and incalculable *momentum* that no longer *says* anything, no longer *signifies* or *expresses*, but rather only maintains and holds itself within its suspensive incidence.[11]

I think it perfectly probable that the aforementioned resistance, with the repercussion of exigency that it entails and that could be connected to the Hölderlinian caesura, brings us very close to what Celan calls testimony insofar as the latter does not obtain credit from what it gives or what it says about the *content* of what it gives or says but, rather, settles its truth in the very act of witnessing, the abyssal act that has no other ground than its own *performance*:[12]

> Niemand
> zeugt für den
> Zeugen.
> (Celan, *Collected Later Poetry*, 64)

> No one
> bears witness for the
> witness.
> (Celan, *Collected Later Poetry*, 65)

This is the form of what Celan calls the "counterword" in *The Meridian*, which entails precisely the trait of the caesura, that is to say, of the "breath-turn." In one instance, Celan says, it is Lucile's "Long live the king!" that, an "act of freedom" and a "step," "cuts the 'string'" (*Meridian*, 7a) and makes the *continuum* of discourse on art and history fall; like the "majesty of the absurd," it serves as a "witness for the presence of the human" (8c).[13] In another instance, Lenz's annoyance at being unable to "walk on his head" (25b) is his step (*Schritt*): "He who walks on his head, ladies and gentlemen—he who walks on his head, has the sky beneath himself as an abyss" (26b). Here as well, Celan's comment evokes Hölderlin, who warns that falling can also be falling toward the sky.[14] The abyssal step of the "counterword" demands a "counter-reading": a reading of the trace or the remainder, a reading of the "doit," one might also say a testimonial reading. And the form of the testimonial would be the irruption of the estranged and alienated I that is only "for itself," for its doit, "even without / language" (Celan, *Collected Later Poetry*, 13).[15] Irruption, to be sure, but not position and not a subjective act subjected to its place, appropriating it; I can be "for myself" only insofar as I am estranged from myself, not forgotten but rather magnetized by the coming without arrival of the other. Testimony, then, is also the form of the encounter. Encounter *toward* which it is "even without / language." Or spurred on by a language that—precisely so—erosively frees in and beneath language itself the absolute and unrepeatable instance of testimony: of existence.

> WEGGEBEIZT vom
> Strahlenwind deiner Sprache
> das bunte Gerede des An-
> erlebten—das hundert-
> züngige Mein-
> gedicht, das Genicht.
> (Celan, *Collected Later Poetry*, 18)
>
> ERODED by
> the beamwind of your speech
> the gaudy chatter of the pseudo-

experienced—the hundred-
tongued perjury-
poem, the noem.
(Celan, *Collected Later Poetry*, 19)

In *Remnants of Song*, Ulrich Baer makes this poem—of which I have quoted the first stanza—one of the central pieces and exemplars of his interpretation of Celan as "the last modern poet" (together with Charles Baudelaire as the first, a double characteristic to which I also tend to subscribe), and he dedicates considerable attention to it (182 ff.). Baer indicates that the first stanza is constructed upon a triple citation of Antonin Artaud (his exasperated effort to liberate the force subsisting beneath the petrification of what has been transmitted to us), Heidegger (the rabble of inauthentic everydayness), and Benjamin (the emptying of experience into mere "lived experience [*Erlebnis*]," which is also—it is worth recalling—a Heideggerian theme). The erosion of *your* speech cancels the multifarious prattle of secondhand lived experiences and, with it, the poem in which the "I" gives free expression to that chatter, a my-poem that is mere "opinion" (*das . . . Mein-Gedicht*, which would therefore also be the *Gedicht* as *Meinung*),[16] and thus a "noem," a *Genicht* that in its negation (*nicht*) cancels the "you" (*du, dich*) in the interpellation and imminence of which, nevertheless, it should be constituted.

Beyond the differend of the readings and the theoretico-critical paradigms with which the aforementioned readings work, the complexity of which, of course, should be recognized, what is required (in favor of that *other* reading, that of the "doit") is the construction of the model of the relation between the poem and the real that this Celanian composition demands. That there in any case subsists, in the margin of the mimetic investment it rejects, an indifference determinant for the poem itself, that there is an exteriority with respect to the poem that leaves traces in it, all of this is emphasized by what I earlier called the impotence of language, which is certainly double: not merely impotence due to the impossibility of naming—through any thinkable tropic recourse—that which has no name, not because one cannot say or signify that which is conserved as a vestige and, therefore, as "objective" memory in the name itself, but rather because all of language's powers—rhetorical and semiotic—inexorably bury the vestiges. By virtue of its most originary strength—repetition—language is at the same time the medium of memory *and* of forgetting or, to say this another way, it is for us not only the medium of every possible search for the real but also that which, through its very mediating condition, irremediably separates us from the real. So, as I already affirmed, there is always a remainder; there is always an irreducible remainder charged with the valence of the "real" or, to put it with an emphasis that would seem indispensable at this point, of the real of the "real."[17] "Deep / in the timecrevasse, / in the / honeycomb-ice / waits, a breathcrystal, / your unalterable / testimony" (Celan, *Collected Later Poetry*, 19). The task of the poem is to preserve that remainder in its own body, to give it value as the abyss of the name, if I might put it thus. The ellipsis, understood as the form and operation that govern Celanian poetry insofar as it is determined with increasing insistence by that law, is one of the essential modes of such preservation.

But what, then, is that law? The model of which I spoke should clarify it for us. The notion of the caesura seems to be indispensable in this regard. But the notion of chiasmus should be heeded, as well. Fioretos, who also appeals to the Hölderlinian theory of the caesura, argues for the importance of this other figure in "Engführung" by referring to the passage between the fourth and fifth stanzas (the fifth stanza forming the middle in the poem's enneadic structure, which Szondi conceives as "the very center of the composition" [Szondi, *Celan Studies*, 36] and which Fioretos also stresses as the turning point marked by the abrupt temporal change in which time now rules only as a breach, hence, as a moment of caesura) and to the inversion of a question without answer:

                        Bin es noch immer—

Jahre.
Jahre, Jahre, ein Finger
tastet hinab und hinan, tastet
umher:
Nahtstellen, fühlbar, hier
klafft es weit auseinander, hier
wuchs es wieder zusammen—wer
deckte es zu?

*

                        Deckte es
                            zu—wer?

Kam, kam.
Kam ein Wort, kam,

kam durch die Nacht,
wollt leuchten, wollt leuchten.

Asche.
Asche, Asche.
Nacht.
Nacht-und-Nacht.—Zum
Aug geh, zum feuchten.
(Celan, *Language Behind Bars*, 92)

                                                I'm still the same—

Years.
Years, years, a finger
fumbles up and down, fumbles
around:
seams, palpable, here
it's split wide open, here
it grew together again—who
covered it up?

*

                                        Covered it
                                            up—who?

Came, came.
A word came, came,
came through the night,
wanted to glow, wanted to glow.

Ashes.
Ashes, ashes.
Night.
Night-and-night.—Go
to the eye, the wet one.
(Celan, *Language Behind Bars*, 93)

With respect to the inversion of the question, Fioretos notes that the "chiasmus marks the tropological movement over an abyss which cannot be endowed with meaning. This abyss gapes open, grows together again, but lacks the meaningful ground that could answer the chiasmatically arranged questions. Open but not accessible, veiled but not sealed, this is the 'abyss' out of which Celan's poem seems to speak" (Fioretos, "Nothing," 328). Fioretos's insistence concerns the impossibility of naming—and also, to the same extent, the renunciation of naming—"that which cannot be named, a refusal to utter that which resists articulation" (328). But the truly important thing in Fioretos's proposed reading of the poem is the comprehension of this resistance as one that opposes a "nothing." Szondi, Fioretos says, clearly perceives this resistance and the poet's renunciation of all capacity for naming, and yet something is lost in his admirable reading: "strictly speaking, *nothing* is lost" (328). This is what the poem says in its penultimate section:

> Also
> stehen noch Tempel. Ein
> Stern[18]
> hat wohl noch Licht.
> Nichts,
> nichts ist verloren.
> (Celan, *Language Behind Bars*, 100)

> Thus
> temples still stand. A
> star
> surely has light.
> Nothing,
> Nothing is lost.
> (Celan, *Language Behind Bars*, 101)

Nichts, / nichts ist verloren: this phrase—and Celan's very insistence on the word "nothing"—bears two alternative readings. Once in the tone of hope, let's say, which resounds so audibly in this section and, despite the annihilating moment of the "youngest rejection" (and this *jüngste Verwerfung* [Celan, *Language Behind Bars*, 100–1] certainly evokes *das jüngste Gericht*, the Final Judgment), affirms the living persistence of the condemned population, its temples, its hymns, its star. A tone of restitution, then. Then again, however, in a different tone: *nothing* is lost (in the mode that Fioretos emphasizes), that is, *there is* loss, loss governs, and it governs as the most unfathomable of all losses because it is loss that sinks into itself, as if the loss of *nothing* were the loss of *everything* and as if it were possible to harbor hope only by virtue of the loss of loss. The *other* reading demanded by "Engführung" would thus accord with that of the trace, of the remainder, of the "doit," the reading of this "nothing" inscribed and at the same time exscribed in the poem, trace of the real, reality of the real that only persists poetically but, by persisting, also opens the poem to the real, that is to say, to its time, to time as the breach of the real.[19]

What nothing? One would perhaps have to say it thus: the human condition itself, persistent in its own abolition, just as it is sung in "Psalm," which measures the relation between God—"No one," *Niemand*—and "us":

Ein Nichts
waren wir, sind wir, werden
wir bleiben, blühend:
die Nichts-, die
Niemandsrose.
(Celan, *No One's Rose*, 46)

We were
a Nothing, we are, we
will remain, blooming:
the Nothing-, the
No one's–rose.
(Celan, *No One's Rose*, 47)

And perhaps Rabbi Loew is exhorted to write the same "living / nothingness [*Nichts*]" in the heart of the "twittering creature," the miserable creature kneaded by obscure operations that evoke the golem, in "To one who stood at the door" from *No One's Rose* (78–79). Thus, made into a noun and of a stature raised (or fallen) to the desolate heavens, "Nothing" or "nothingness" is a recidivist word in Celan. It would be necessary to investigate the grammar of "nothing," of "Nothing" and "No one," in Celanian poetry. A grammar, I say, and not a rhetoric because all eloquence meets its end therein. Perhaps an allegorical grammar, provided that we conceive allegory not as a figure or a trope in the traditional sense, which presupposes the constancy of a truth and a code of figuration, but rather—more in the vein of Benjamin, in a nonintentional key—as the evidence of an irreducible fracture of totality, the denunciation of totality and the ex-position of the existence previously recognized therein due to a historical disaster that is the disaster of history itself. Perhaps this is the reduction of every image and every trope ad absurdum. The Celanian allegory would thus be a figure *of* language, not the master stratagem of an incorporation of the other into the circle of what is sayable, but rather the remission or the *duction*—through the gorge of narrowness—of language itself to the *allos*, to the *alter*, "outside itself," in a "when" without measure for its present or without other measure than the doit of existence.[20] Meanwhile, it remains only for us to return to narrowness. I cite the last stanza of "So many constellations [*Soviel Gestirne*]":

> ich weiß,
> ich weiß und du weißt, wir wußten,
> wir wußten nicht, wir
> waren ja da und nicht dort,
> und zuweilen, wenn
> nur das Nichts zwischen uns stand, fanden
> wir ganz zueinander.
> (*No One's Rose*, 30)

> I know,
> I know and you know, we knew,
> we didn't know, since we
> were here and not there,
> and sometimes, when
> only nothingness stood between us, we
> found our way to one another.
> (*No One's Rose*, 31)

7

"Dialogue"

Back to the beginning, to the question of "dialogue." I would like to believe that the preceding chapters will have inclined the reader to concede: that this question is not of minor importance in the attempt to read and understand Paul Celan and that his relation to the thought, text, and figure of Martin Heidegger has particular gravitation for understanding him; that this relation is not simple or the result of an expeditious sanction but, rather, worked from within by an incessant tension [*tirantez*] and turning [*tironeo*] with surprising feints of proximity and brusque separations; that it is possible to establish a protocol for the tense relation in what could be described as a series of knots that, each designated as a trail marker (and without any claim to exhaustion), form the itinerary that I have invited the reader to follow; that perhaps all of the foregoing justify the quotation marks I inflict upon the term "dialogue." One might think I expect too much of my reader. But the truth is that much of what I just enumerated has already been prolifically debated and demonstrated by the literature registering this issue. It would therefore be legitimate for the reader to retort by demanding to know what, in the final analysis, I have tried to add to this copious literature. I will say only that this has been an effort to show what I believe to be the—to my mind decisive—singularity of Celan's poetry and poetic thought, which becomes all the more patent, it seems to me, the more one attends to the tension of which I was speaking.

Therefore, the problem here is not to show how a "dialogue" between Celan and Heidegger can be conceived and, so to speak, staged. The reserved character of that relation—the silence (the dense humidity: "Feuchtes, / viel" [Celan, *Collected Later Poetry*, 256]) into which it essentially plunges—cannot be substituted by any crafty articulation of motives and themes; nor is it possible to supplant the names implicated and imbricated here with the feigned *partners* of an eloquent exchange.[1] Nor is it a question of offering, at the last moment, a Heideggerian reading of Celan or of counteracting Heidegger with supposed Celanian theses. *The problem pertains to the very possibility of thinking the poem—the poem, today, in the indelible dating in which Celan's poetry is inscribed—in accordance with the matrix defined by the concept of dialogue.* And, of course, this is the grand matrix that has been established by Heidegger's thought of the poem, by the relations between poem and thought that Heidegger has minted. Does Celan not present, in a *certain* sense, an absolute resistance to this matrix?

The mere formulation of this problem invites the inscription of a double epigraph, the internal connection of which was first spotted by Beda Allemann.[2] A double epigraph, the first text of which contains *in nuce* the Heideggerian elaboration of the dialogic matrix. It belongs to Friedrich Hölderlin, and I take it here from the version that Heidegger prefers:

> Viel hat erfahren der Mensch.
> Der Himmlischen viele genannt,
> Seit ein Gespräch wir sind
> Und hören können voneinander.
> (Cited in Heidegger, *Erläuterungen*, 33)

> Much has man experienced.
> Named many of the heavenly ones,
> Since we have been a conversation
> And able to hear from one another.
> (Cited in Heidegger, *Elucidations*, 51)

Taken from a draft, these verses are the third guidewords (*Leitworte*) that Heidegger chooses to carry out his inquiry into the "essence of poetry" from Hölderlin's hand.[3]

Five of these "guidewords" scan this inquiry. This passage occupies the exact middle, and such a location—which is certainly demanded by the argument—is in no way innocuous. Just as the prefix *Ge-* of *Gespräch*, of dialogue, of *con*versation signals, the fundamental movement that links language and poetry and the historical dwelling of humans as a people meet in this middle.

From Celan, the second epigraph is an envoi to Bertolt Brecht. It is a brief poem in the posthumous *Snowpart* (*Schneepart*), which is at the same time a kind of dedication and offering, the offering of a leaf (or a sheet, "ein Blatt") separated from the tree to which it should belong:

Was sind das für Zeiten,
wo ein Gespräch
beinah ein Verbrechen ist,
weil es soviel Gesagtes
mit einschließt?
(Celan, *Collected Later Poetry*, 368)

What times are these
when a conversation
is nearly a crime,
because it includes so much
that's already been said.
(Celan, *Collected Later Poetry*, 369)[4]

Like Hölderlin's, Celan's poem is an *essentially political* poem. This quality of the poem does not come only from the Brecht connection, from the contagion of a name that, in the contemporary context, marks a decisive site of the relation between poetry and politics. Not only *this* poem is political; rather, *the political* is a principal key for all Celanian poetry: it is political poetry in the highest and most radical sense. Precisely the style and mode in which it is political, however, bring crucial consequences for the occidental form of the poem and above all for that form which, unfolding between the cycle's "morning" and "evening," begins with Hölderlin and casts its shadow beyond, covering the post-Mallarméan poem as well.

The form begins with Hölderlin, indeed, because "*the poet's poet*"—as Heidegger calls him (*Elucidations*, 52), making use of a formula that evokes the romantic motif of the "poetry of poetry" (Friedrich Schlegel, Novalis)[5]— is also first of all a poet that takes to its maximum elevation the question concerning the relation between the poet and the people, its historical community, and concerning the essential political possibility of the latter.[6]

The question takes root here of knowing whether Celanian "political poetry" can be referred to the same model to which Heidegger refers Hölderlin's poetry. On this issue, one thing appears clear in principle: the universal community of the human, the universal common-being that is still an essential concern for Hölderlin ("notwithstanding the differences of the times and of the political systems" [Hölderlin, *Sophocles*, 63]), the same common-being that brings Hölderlin to announce the eschatological promise (as Allemann puts it) that "soon we shall be song"[7] (a "song" that, according to the same Allemann, is a consumed and "heightened dialogue" [Allemann, "Paul Celan," 445]), a common-being that Heidegger does not take up (this is not the version he privileges, but it is also a promise that introduces an imbalanced tension in "lean years [*dürftiger Zeit*]" [Hölderlin, *Poems and Fragments*, 251]), the *universal* common-being of the human, in short, is no longer an experience for Celan. To put this another way: if dialogue is the constructive principle of community in Hölderlin (and the community's fabric is thus essentially linguistic), it should be clear that his experience lies in the fact that, in the modern world, community has become radically problematic, and the possibility of founding a community is entrusted to poetry—to a poetry of balance desperate for measure. Yet, if community is already problematic for Hölderlin, it has become impossible for Celan: essentially open to history, experience has been radicalized from the beginning; it has in itself plunged into the abyss through the work of history itself unfolding beneath the predominance of excess. It should no doubt be conceded that this impossibility does not imply an absolute closure or a species of poetico-political pessimism. In the envoi to Brecht, we read that dialogue in these times (of indigence steeped in horror) encloses what has "already been said" (Celan, *Collected Later Poetry*, 369); we read that it is not actual and authentic saying; we read that—channeled into the place (the mass grave) of trivialized discourses and contaminated by "murderous speech" (Celan, *Collected Prose*, 34)—dialogue therefore does not form a community but, rather, breaks it (*Verbrechen*, "crime," contains *brechen*—"to break"). Yet, as I already insinuated, the memory of a different possibility of dialogue is conserved here, and *The Meridian* insists on it: "language actualized" (Celan, *Meridian*, 33b), "interpellation of the other" (see 35a and 36a–b), even if it is desperate. The "nearly [*beinah*]" (Celan, *Collected Later Poetry*, 369) that modulates the crime is also the narrow opening to that same possibility's future. The political of Celan's poetry proposes a hard and inexpugnable nucleus, an *aporia of dialogue*, the latter being understood precisely as the dynamic, constitutive, and constructive principle of that common-being and its free universality.

This aporia defines a determined impossibility of reconciling the Celanian poem with what we could call the Greco-Germanic matrix of dialogue, if the latter is an appropriate name for the prestigious paradigm that Heidegger manufactures in his interpretation of Hölderlin. It is true, in any case, that this paradigm suits a certain Hölderlin, and one should take into account that the Celanian "aporia" also supposes a reading of Hölderlin—incorporated in his poem thematically—and thus also of an "other Hölderlin."

Could this irreconcilable relation be delimited on the basis of an *other* paradigm, that is to say, on the basis of the efficacy of an *other* paradigm that, actual and actually expressed in the Celanian poem, would be—how to deny it?—the *Jewish* paradigm?

With no room for doubt, there might be a lot of material to nourish the temptation to understand things in this way. I nevertheless remain wary of affirming this without reserve. Further still: it seems to me that an understanding of this nature would undermine a possible reading of the Celanian poem with which the latter explicitly reckons and labors. To keep this prevention within view, one would perhaps have to add a new epigraph, a third, which would be a sort of modified Joyce:

Jewgreek is greekjew?
Extremes hardly meet.[8]

Beneath this epigraph, which I will almost call a mantra, I resume what I have sketched: one might certainly think that, in the trance of the pure aporia of dialogue, appealing to a *Judaic theory of the poem* would provide a way out.

There are two dissimilar indices in this respect. The first comes from John Felstiner's brilliant biography of Celan, *Paul Celan: Poet, Survivor, Jew*. Although his work makes no theoretical claims, it is entirely organized around a fundamental thesis. This thesis is that of the *Name*. This hypothesis seems to find strong support in Celan's declaration to Allemann that "words become names [*Worte werden Namen*]" (Allemann, "Paul Celan," 440) and in his justification of his verbal production—registered by Clemens Podewils and already cited above—through his interest in "get[ting] free of words as mere designations" and in "hear[ing] again in words the *names* of things" (Podewils, "Namen," 69; cited in Felstiner, *Paul Celan*, 324n17). Here, however, everything depends upon the modulations and emphases. If they are heightened, then "to Judaize" Celan's poetry radically would amount to supposing that *there is* the Name, that *there is* the Sacred Language, and that the latter is Hebrew.[9] Felstiner reads Celan's increasing proximity to Hebraic words in his poetry precisely in this direction. To which, furthermore, one can add that, with such proximity, Celan is making a historical passage [*paso*]—a passing through [*pasaje*]—from German to Hebrew, a symmetrical passage with respect to the one Heidegger takes from German to Greek (or, rather, inversely). It would be necessary to argue, moreover, that this passage is realized by what many commentators might feel inclined to consider an active principle of Celan's poetry, namely *revenge*, because repressed and "unconscious" or in any case untamed zones of the German language awaken with this passage, zones that refer to the process of coining language that Martin Luther undertook upon translating the Sacred Scripture.[10]

As I already said, however, everything depends upon the modulations and emphases. The authority of the Name in Celan's poetry is, I believe, indelible. But it seems to me that it is more a question of the Name in a sense similar to the one that Benjamin conceives, as the asymptotic relation of languages among themselves, as the trace legible only in the originary and inextirpable fracture. It is a question of the Name, then, more in the Babelic scene than in the paradisiacal or Pentecostal or eschatological scene. What Celan accomplishes for German—depropriating it, uprooting it from itself, converting it into the place through which a plurivocity passes, a Babelic plurivocity, in order to root it in an unnamable other (the Name, then, as essentially unnamable)—holds for all language. If this is to be conceived as "revenge," then it will be necessary to define a distinct concept of "revenge" grounded no longer in the interest of an assaulted or in-dignant subjectivity but, rather, in the opening to an unforeseeable coming.

In the context of this first option, which I call a "Judaic theory of the poem," Allemann makes an important observation in "Paul Celan" concerning "Wan-voiced [*Fahlstimmig*]," a poem from *Lichtzwang*, wherein a voice gives of itself "not a word, not a thing, / and of both the single name, / . . . sore gain / of a world" (Celan, *Collected Later Poetry*, 294–95). Allemann refers to the relations between word, thing, and name (and world) and also stresses the aforementioned "becoming-names of words": "We should not reassure ourselves with the fact that, with the lyrical concept of 'name,' a position is named . . . that solves the problem of language. The 'gain / of a world' does not result from its postulation, and the poem would be a doubtful image if it were exhausted in this postulate" (Allemann, "Paul Celan," 443). To emphasize the precaution—completely legitimate to my mind—expressed in these terms, one must note the bifid word that qualifies the "gain": *wunder, wunder Gewinn*. To translate the word *wunder* as "sore" or "wounded" is to lose that ambivalence, a loss that must perforce take place here.[11] *Wunder* designates the "wounded" as an adjective, but it indicates a "miracle," a "wonder," a "marvel" as a noun.[12] Felstiner, who also mentions this duplicity, eagerly listens to the animated tones in this poem: "It takes a moment to hear Psalm 130 in this voice from the depths. Then another moment to see that the Hebrew *davar*, meaning both 'word' (sacred and secular) and 'thing,' must be that single name" (Felstiner, *Paul Celan*, 247).[13] But this reading seems to insinuate that, as the unique name, the Hebraic word *davar* entails the reparation, healing, and finally erasure of the wound in the splendor of the miracle, of the wonder of the gain. Nevertheless, the calembour of *Wunde* and *Wunder* (wound and wonder), with its compulsive synthesis, has strength and efficacy only if the irrepressible tension in that synthesis increases (and does not soften), along with the untraversable hiatus of the two antithetical terms. In a certain sense, at the same time discrete and brimming with eloquence due to its excess of signification (an excess before which the word, as calembour, remains neutral and indifferent), this same word documents [*rubrica*] the unapproachability of the Name, of the "single name."

Felstiner's, as I said, is the first index of what I called the "Judaic theory of the poem." Jacques Derrida delivers the other fundamental index with his reflection on the shibboleth. This notion is clearly more precise, more radical, more astute (if one might put it thus) than the appeal to the originary nature of the Name and the Sacred Language. In addition, it has the virtue of situating us in a political and essential, a politico-bellicose, a politico-Babelic scene that marks at the same time the aporia of dialogue and the impossibility of constituting the human community in a universal sense. It is worth citing *in extenso* the pertinent passage in which Derrida refers to the issue, which occurs with respect to the poem "In one [*In eins*]" from *No One's Rose* and, in particular, with respect to a "second language" that, already in the "second line," "arises in the 'heart's mouth' " with "an apparently Hebrew word":

> This second language could well be a first language, the language of the morning, the language of origin speaking of the heart, from the heart, and from the East.
>
> (One will note the lucid warning concerning the possibility of an "archaizing" interpretation of this appeal to Hebrew, the appeal to a dawn that is certainly distinct from the one Hölderlin recalls.)
>
> "Language" in Hebrew is "lip," rather than "tongue," and does not Celan elsewhere (we will come to it) call words

circumcised, as one speaks of the "circumcised heart"? For the moment, let this be. *Shibboleth*, this word I have called Hebrew, is found, as you know, in a whole family of languages, Phoenician, Judeo-Aramaic, Syriac. It is traversed by a multiplicity of meanings: river, stream, ear of grain, olive twig. But beyond these meanings, it has acquired the value of a password. It was used during or after war, at the crossing of a border under watch. The meaning of the word was less important than the way in which it was pronounced. The relation to the meaning or to the thing was suspended, neutralized, bracketed: the opposite, one might say, of a phenomenological *epochē*, which preserves, above all, the meaning. The Ephraimites had been defeated by the army of Jephthah; in order to keep their soldiers from escaping across the river (*shibboleth* also means "river," of course, but that is not necessarily the reason it was chosen), each person was required to say *shibboleth*. Now the Ephraimites were known for their inability to pronounce correctly the *shi* of *shibboleth*, which became for them, in consequence, an *unpronounceable name*.[14]

They said *sibboleth*, and, at the invisible border between *shi* and *si*, betrayed themselves to the sentinel at the risk of their life. They betrayed their difference by showing themselves indifferent to the diacritical difference between *shi* and *si*; they marked themselves with their inability to re-mark a mark thus coded. (Derrida, "Shibboleth," 22–23)

This passage's phrasing, the careful selection of terms and turns, would merit a patient commentary. The interest here, in any case, lies in the suggestive characterization of Celanian poetry—put to the test in the *shibboleth*—as poetry of passage, of the border, of the indecisive and undecidable zone of transfer, of translation, of trans-position (*Über-tragung, Über-setzung*), which is also, to be sure, the "place" of the date; the date is the passage in the strict sense defined by *The Meridian*, as slippage in the directionality of writing—of existence—in the date: "But don't we all write ourselves from such dates? And toward what dates do we write ourselves?" (Celan, *Meridian*, 30b). Therefore, Celan's is not poetry that versifies "about" passage, that makes passage its theme; it is not poetry that seeks to experiment with passage; rather, it is poetry that is positioned and exposed—transposed—in the untamable situation of passage. In this situation, which is the sharpest trance of discrimination and the *crisis* of poetry itself as it takes our breath away, a rhythm caesura, and a word circumcision, the task—the only task of poetry—is to give (to find) the word: Which word will secure passage? Which will be the watchword [*santo y seña*], the *shibboleth*?

Yet, of course, as Derrida suggests, the *shibboleth* key consists in the fact that it itself is not a "word" in the way in which we are accustomed to recognizing, as a nucleus of meaning; put another way, the *shibboleth* key lies in the fact that it is an insignificant word. A quasiword or, to express it with the exact term of *The Meridian*, a counterword, a *Gegenwort* that is now only testimony, the sign of a presence, or even a nonword, an *Aberwort* that would refuse the vocation of enlargement, of significance, at the very heart of the word. The *shibboleth* is the *Deut*, the doit, which is not a word but rather, as I said, an existence.

In any case, the complexity of Derrida's exposition does not annul the proposal for a Judaic theory of the poem, which is inscribed here with the mantra that Celan takes from Marina Tsvetayeva as an epigraph for his poem "And with the book from Tarussa [*Und mit dem Buch aus Tarussa*]": "*All poets are Yids*" (Celan, *No One's Rose*, 152–53; translation modified).[15] A theory aware that it is necessary to avoid taking the "Jewish" for granted as an essential claim, a theory aware of its obligation to construct itself with the feeble support of quotation marks. This suspicion accompanies the question of circumcision in the Derridean text and the question of the circumcised word. Thus, in relation to what concerns us here, the end of "Shibboleth" reads:

> *By the same stroke*, as it were, the circumcised word grants access to the community, to the covenant or alliance, to the partaking of a language, in a language. And in the Jewish language as poetic language, if all poetic language is, like all poets according to the epigraph, Jewish in essence; but this essence promises itself only through dis-identification, that expropriation in the nothing of the non-essence of which we have spoken. The Germanic language, like any other, but here with what privilege, must be circumcised by a rabbi, and the rabbi becomes then a poet, reveals the poet in him. How can the German language receive circumcision at this poem's date, that is to say, following the holocaust, the solution, the final cremation, the ash of everything? How is one to bless ashes in German? (Derrida, "Shibboleth," 62–63)

Derrida ends his reflection by appealing to the impossibility of situating the word's circumcision, to its prehistoricity that, as the word's opening to the other, is also the inauguration of "history and the poem and philosophy and hermeneutics and religion" (Derrida, "Shibboleth," 64), and by *situating* the Jewish (what we could call, literally, the *Jewish operation*: circumcision) precisely in this *other* dawn.

What passage plays out here? Is it the passage of languages, of regions, of times, of histories? And what measure would be entailed by that passage, which would be in itself incommensurable and immense?

Without detriment to this passage, without detriment to everything pertinent in Derrida's reading, I confess that I do not feel inclined to validate *his* "Jewish theory of the poem." Just as Celan, *in* the Jewish and its im-propriety, persists between the "small" and the "large,"[16] it would be a question of persisting, I believe, *between* the Germanic and the Jewish, as well as between the *Greek* and the *Jew*; it would be a question, then, of persisting in a *failed encounter* [desencuentro] *of extremes*—including with themselves.[17]

What is the law—if we could call it a law—of this failed encounter? What is the law that a "poem of the encounter" (as Celan's would be) *should* always take into account?

I will not claim to respond to this question that, I believe, in principle exceeds every possible response that is not the one that the poem, each poem, contributes. I will make use, then, of signs emitted from two poems in order to insist on the question. Nothing more.

In what concerns the first poem, I will let myself be guided by Peter Szondi's observation with respect to the analysis that he dedicates to it: the poem is "You lie [*Du liegst*]," the second in *Snowpart* (*Schneepart*), the last volume that Celan left completely corrected and the publication of which was posthumous.[18] As is known, Szondi's book was left unfinished because of his suicide in 1971, a year after Celan leapt into the Seine. Yet, despite its unfinished status, the book preserves a sort of exemplary value that has incited multiple commentaries and, among them, one from Hans-Georg Gadamer.[19] I cite part of the poem first of all:

DU LIEGST im großen Gelausche,
umbuscht, umflockt.
(Celan, *Collected Later Poetry*, 322)

YOU LIE in the great listening,
ambushed, snowed in.
(Celan, *Collected Later Poetry*, 323)

The poem was written during Celan's only visit to Berlin, on Christmas Eve in 1967, and published the next year in a book paying homage to Peter Huchel. Szondi accompanied the poet during this visit, bore direct witness to various details that the poem records with stenographic brevity—as is characteristic of most texts after *Breathturn*—and was aided by the documentary book *Der Mord an Rosa Luxemburg und Karl Liebknecht*. All the particularities are minutely, scrupulously registered in the unfinished essay: the Spree and Havel Rivers; the butcher hooks of the Plötzensee Prison, where three thousand people were murdered under the Nazi regime; the red apples on a wreath from the Christmas market; the Eden apartment building that ominously preserves the name of the hotel where Rosa Luxemburg and Karl Liebknecht briefly had to stay on the eve of their assassination by police agents, their bodies thrown into the Landwehrkanal in January 1919 ("The Landwehr canal will not roar. / Nothing /   stalls" [Celan, *Collected Later Poetry*, 323]). The illuminating effect of Szondi's protocol is surprising, so surprising—or even unsettling—that he himself has to pose the decisive question (something that, incidentally, lies in the properly *theoretical* nerve of his discussion): "To what extent does understanding the poem depend on a knowledge of the biographical/historical framework? Or, in more general terms, to what extent is the poem determined by things external to it, and this determination from without invalidated by the poem's own internal logic?" (Szondi, *Celan Studies*, 88). This is the question that Gadamer is quick to endorse and take up in his own account, the double question concerning the necessity of information and the poem's internal determination or its (exclusive) "knowledge," and he himself emphasizes that Szondi rejects recourse to material from empirical references as a betrayal. Gadamer's intention is to resolve the question canonically—according to the canon of a hermeneutic that conceives its task as the constant restitution of meaning's universality—by way of the distinction between the essential and the accessory: "One need not know anything private and ephemeral. Even if one does, one must forget it and concentrate only on what the poem knows. The poem, for its part, wants us to know, learn, and experience everything that it knows—and never to forget it" (Gadamer, *Gadamer on Celan*, 142). But this resolution is, it seems to me, distinct from the resolution that Szondi's text sketches in reconstructing the logic of the poem, the unfinished status of which Gadamer laments.

Let us say, in the first place, that the issue of "betrayal" refers not so much to the absolute impertinence of all "information" as to its use as an "interpretational refuge" (Szondi, *Celan Studies*, 89) and for its "tranquilizing effect." If indeed Szondi stipulates that the poem, to be a poem, must give its own justification, that it "transcend its empirical premise" (and this is inherent to Szondi's own hermeneutical convocation), he suggests at the same time that the poem reinscribes this same premise on the basis of a more profound reality "that cannot be reduced to subjective happenstance" (89–90). Whatever this "reality" might be, he believes he discerns it sheltered in the ambiguity of the poem's two central verses and, especially, in the word "Eden," the old name of the hotel in which the two communist leaders lived their last and atrocious hours, a name that a modern and luxurious building scandalously preserves: "conjoining of paradise and purgatory" (91). Lucidly warned of the irreducible character of this "dialectic" (which he so names) and of Celan's idiosyncratic perception (for whom "contradictions were not contradictory" [90]), Szondi establishes his essential thesis:

> The indifference of history and human beings that let the place where Rosa Luxemburg and Karl Liebknecht spent their final hours be named for that paradisiacal pleasure garden and let the luxury apartment building erected on the same site be named for the hotel turned purgatory—this impassivity can only have confirmed Celan's basic experience of an *in-difference*. This is why he was struck by the indifference here and made it the core of his poem. (91)

The "experience of indifference": would this not perhaps be a capital key, I will not say for only this poem in particular, but rather for all of Celan's poetry? Is it not the *punctum* of this poetry? Human history's indifference, Szondi says, but perhaps these attributions are pacifying; perhaps they guard us from the abyss that one glimpses in that primary formula, because they assign to indifference something like an agent, a subject, the focus of a responsibility that, of course, can never be omitted or excused but perhaps obeys something more radical than the crime of human negligence, a basic structure of temporality and existence: the iterative logic of the date would pertain to that structure. No, the experience of indifference accounts for the latter as the eye of the hurricane of history: the undesignatable center in which all differences meet, in which they remain united in their very dispersion, in their general conflagration. Indifference is—"a sprouting Never" (Celan, *No One's Rose*, 139) or "one of Time's fissures" (Celan, *Threshold*, 53)—in/difference.

Celan would write on the basis of this experience, and in that experience he wagers for a breathturn, for the caesura that would open in its heart the possibility of what is other [*lo otro*], the coming of the other [*el otro*]. As an ethico-politics—a po-ethics—that has at its root the singular existent submitted to the most implacable exposition. A short text responding to a survey in the magazine *Der Spiegel*, motivated by a declaration from Hans Magnus Enzensberger in 1968, contains one of Celan's rare public pronouncements on political issues. In it, the anarchistic aftertaste makes itself felt:

> I still hope, and not only in regard to the Federal Republic and Germany, for change, for transformation. Substitute systems will not bring it about, and revolution—a social and at the same time anti-authoritarian one—can only be conceived with change as its basis. It begins, in Germany, here, today, with the individual. [*Sie fängt, in Deutschland, hier und heute, beim Einzelnen an.*] May we be spared a fourth possibility.[20] (Celan, *Collected Prose*, 27)

Not a fourth possibility but, rather, the possibility of possibility would remain harbored in in/difference, that possibility which Celan calls u-topia in *The Meridian*.

In view of which, then, the second poem, the very poem upon which Derrida comments in the long citation that I took from "Shibboleth," the poem titled "In one [*In eins*]":

> Dreizehnter Feber. Im Herzmund
> erwachtes Schibboleth. Mit dir,
> Peuple
> de Paris. *No pasarán.*
> (Celan, *No One's Rose*, 120)

> February 13th. In the heart's mouth
> a shibboleth is roused. With you,
> people
> of Paris. "*No pasarán.*"
> (Celan, *No One's Rose*, 121)

The entire time of an interpretation—and it is known that every interpretation is interminable because its condition, the condition that disposes it and destines it from the very nucleus of its command, is that which will always remain to be interpreted—all the time of interpretation would be required in order to trace the unity of this poem that convokes multiple languages and dialects interwoven together Babel-like (four speak in the first stanza), multiple localities of language and of land, dates, experiences and citations, experiences and citations of experience. All the time, and nevertheless: that other universality is univocal (of only one voice and one mouth, the painful mouth into which all exiles crowd, all "those not forgotten" [121] who were displaced from universal memory and, for that very reason, clamor deafly—absurdly—not to be forgotten); the political universality of this poem preserves, without erasing or reconciling it, the dispersed provenance of so many marks. Political universality, which would be to say, the universality of exile, of u-topia. "*Peace to the cottages* [Friede den Hütten]!" (120–21). But Celan does not speak for this universality or promise a return; rather, he opens his word to the disjunctive crossroads of hope for a word—to come. Crisis of the poet-prophet, then, whether we conceive this figure under the tutelage of Judaic theory or, as Heidegger understands Hölderlin, under the tutelage of Germanic theory.[21]

Celan remains between one theory and the other in the (non) place of in/difference.

It is time to turn back.

Mindful of its dates, open to the other, headed toward the other, in search of reality, the poem, Celan notes, "becomes conversation—often a desperate conversation": *verzweifeltes Gespräch* (Celan, *Meridian*, 36a). Of all the aching, faltering, orphaned, or frustrated dialogues that inexorably span throughout Celan's life and writings (and this inexorability is their sign and seal), there is perhaps none more pregnant with consequences for the lot of poetry and thought today, in the today of "the breath pause" (31), than the dialogue without protocol or register, maintained between the lines of "Todtnauberg," bogged down in the high marshes and at the same time buried beneath the mountain of death.

As a first epigraph in this chapter, I turned to a verse from the second version of Hölderlin's "Celebration of Peace," which remains—amplified—in the definitive version. The preparatory work for "Todtnauberg" contains that same verse under the protection—or visage—of a parenthesis:

(seit ein Gespräch wir sind,
an dem wir würgen{)},
an dem ich

würge)
(Celan, *Lichtzwang*, 49)

(since we have been a dialogue,
on which we choke{)},
on which I
choke)

Removing the parenthesis, another note expands the theme:

<u>*Seit ein Gespräch wir sind,*</u>
an dem
wir würgen,
an dem ich würge,
das mich
aus mir hinausstieß, {zw}dreimal, | viermal,
(Celan, *Lichtzwang*, 49)

<u>*Since we have been a dialogue,*</u>
on which
we choke,
on which I choke,
which expels me
from myself, {tw}three, | four times,

In the cabin, in the book, Celan wrote brief lines of hope. As we already know, three years later, on Holy Thursday 1970, he met with Heidegger again in Freiburg. Celan had come after reciting poems from *Lightduress* in Stuttgart on 21 March before an audience that had no ear for speech that was already posthumous. The summer having arrived, the old philosopher expressed his desire to take a walk with the poet. Days later, on 20 April, having returned to Paris, Celan leapt into the Seine from the Mirabeau Bridge. There were no witnesses. A fisherman found his body seven miles away on the first of May. Wilhelm Michel's biography of Hölderlin was found on the desk in Celan's frugal apartment. A passage that reproduces a warning from Clemens Brentano was underlined: "Sometimes this genius goes dark and sinks down into the bitter well of his heart" (quoted in Felstiner, *Paul Celan*, 287). The passage continues: "but mostly his apocalyptic star glitters wondrously" (287).

Notes

Notes to the Foreword

1. According to Hugo Friedrich, "Obscurity has become a dominant aesthetic principle," and, interestingly, "hermeticism in general has become a fixed concept of criticism" (Friedrich, *Struktur*, 178, 180; my translation).

2. Rosemarie Waldrop writes in her "Introduction" that "Celan's prose is a poet's prose" (Celan, *Collected Prose*, ix).

3. *Dichtung* is not literature but, rather, poetry. Unfortunately, Jerry Glenn's English translation of *The Meridian* consistently renders the German term by "literature." If Celan had meant to refer to literature, he would have used the German term *Literatur*.

4. Given that the sun reaches its highest point at midday, "meridian" is also used figuratively to speak of "a point or period of highest development, greatest prosperity, or the like" (*New Century Dictionary*, 1:1047).

5. In German, the term "Tropen" refers not only to the tropics and *topoi*, or commonplaces, but also to the turns or turnings of figures of speech or *tropoi*.

6. See also Pöggeler, "—Ach, die Kunst!," 93.

7. To be fair to Gadamer, it needs to be pointed out that, in *Who Am I and Who Are You?*, he raises the question of what "understanding" means in the context of reading Celan and acknowledges that, according to the speech about the meridian, *Ichvergessenheit* constitutes the very character of a poem (Gadamer, *Gadamer on Celan*, 118). As a result, a much more complex approach to Celan's work occurs in this text, in which reading begins to replace the earlier obsession with interpretation. Gadamer writes that Celan "insisted that a poem must be left to its own existence and detached from its creator. Whoever does not understand more than what the poet could have said without his poetry understands far too little" (133). Still, a reading aimed at what the text itself says, however attentive, is "one of the most pressing tasks" of establishing not its "unambiguousness of the meaning" but, rather, "the unity of meaning" that the poem represents as a formation of language (127).

8. For Celan's disappointment about the meeting, see Lacoue-Labarthe, *Poetry as Experience*, 38, and, especially, the remarkable essay by Werner Hamacher, "Wasen: Um Celans Todtnauberg," 35–83.

9. If, nonetheless, their meeting is of importance, it is for other than "epochal" reasons.

10. Walde adds: "Obscuritas becomes often necessary as a result of the complexity of difficulty of the subject matter in question with the result that the latter can become paradoxically more transparent and more precise compared to a 'false' pseudo-precision which is inappropriate to the subject matter because simplifying it" (Walde et al., "Obscuritas," 363).

11. I am referring here, of course, to Theodor W. Adorno's claim that "to write poetry after Auschwitz is barbaric" and "has become impossible" (Adorno, *Prisms*, 34), a statement he later recanted.

12. I note that the English translation of "Reading 'Engführung'" omits Szondi's reference in the original to "the idiom of the poem" (Szondi, "Durch die Enge geführt," 354).

13. In his forceful reading of "Todtnauburg," Werner Hamacher argues that "Celan's debate with Heidegger is first, and foremost, a debate with the latter's philosophy, with his question concerning Being and his thought regarding language and poetry, and only, therefore, also with his Nazi-Rektorat, and his silence about it." Yet, by qualifying Celan's response in the form of the poem "Todtnauberg" as philosophical, even though it is "the response of a *thinking poetry* in precisely a sense in which Heidegger could not understand it," Hamacher risks blurring the difference between thought, or philosophy, and poetry. By substituting the word *Wasen* for the Heideggerian *Wesen* and *entwo* for *Ort*, Celan is said not only to practice an *epokhe* of the subjectivity of the subject and of Being itself but also to put out of work even Being's onto-topological self-preservation (*Selbst-Verwahrung*). By doing so, Hamacher writes, Celan "radicalizes the de-essentializing of existence which Heidegger broached but did not pursue, and severs the uncanniness of Dasein from its being trapped in Being-in in which it occupies the abode of Dasein's dwelling" (Hamacher, "Wasen," 65).

14. See Oyarzun's discussion of Celan's poem "Lightduress [*Lichtzwang*]" (*Between Celan and Heidegger*, 57–58).

Notes to the Prologue

1. Very associatively, I call upon a piece from the 1970 collection of poems *Lightduress* (*Lichtzwang*). The first lines run:

DIE MIR HINTERLASSNE
balkengekreuzte

Eins:
(Celan, *Collected Later Poetry*, 278)

THE LEFT-TO-ME
beamcrossed
One:
(Celan, *Collected Later Poetry*, 279)

The poem concerns a riddle that the "I" of the poem ought to unravel, while an undetermined "you," dressed in sackcloth, "knit[s] at the secretstocking" (line 6). The "beamcrossed" distantly recalls the peculiar orthography that the late Heidegger inflicts upon the word "being" in order to signal the "fourfold" (*das Geviert*) of gods and mortals, earth and sky, in a Hölderlinian inspiration.

2. Philippe Lacoue-Labarthe recalls this characterization in his essay "Poetry, Philosophy, Politics" (*Heidegger*, 19). Lacoue-Labarthe refers explicitly to Badiou's expression, and his consideration of it is directed toward refuting his idea of an "age of the poets" that would reach its end precisely with Celan and with this meeting as an exemplary moment.

3. Parts of this book, written largely between 1996 and 1997, have been previously published: "Entre Celan y Heidegger" (which corresponds to the first chapter, "Dialogue") in *Seminarios de Filosofía* 9 (1996): 193–212; "Lugar" (the first third of the second chapter) in *El espíritu del valle* 4/5 (1998): 22–27; "Ah, el arte" (the third chapter) in *La filosofía como pasión: Homenaje a Jorge Eduardo Rivera Cruchaga en su 75 cumpleaños*, ed. Juan Pablo Brickle (Madrid: Trotta 2003), 275–90; and "Diálogo" (a fragment of the last chapter) in *Extremoccidente* 3 (2003): 73–75. The book served as the basis for a doctoral seminar at the Universidad de Chile in the first semester of 2003.

4. According to Rüdiger Safranski (*Martin Heidegger*, 423).

Notes to Chapter 1

1. Gerhard Baumann, who accompanied the two and was at that time preparing a doctoral thesis in literature, recorded the meeting's preambles, details, and aftereffects in *Erinnerung an Paul Celan* (58 ff.). Baumann had arranged a poetry reading on 24 July in Freiburg, in which Heidegger himself played a part by requiring the city's bookstores to keep the poet's work in adequate stock. Celan wrote the poem in Frankfurt am Main a week after his visit, 1 August of the same year, and sent Heidegger a signed copy of the special edition. A review of these details can be consulted in Walter Hoefler's article "Todtnauberg" (39–43), which in this respect is based upon works by Baumann, Otto Pöggeler ("Spur des Wortes"), and George Steiner (*Martin Heidegger*).

2. For the German text, see *Gedicht und Gespräch*. The essay treats the theme of its title through an analysis of a poem by Gottfried Benn ("Dann gliederten sich die Laute") and two poems by Celan ("Wirk nicht voraus" and "Todtnauberg"). Gadamer says that these authors are "the two great poets who, in the time after the Second World War, adequately expressed in poetry something of the German sense of life, the German fate—the uncertain position between belief and disbelief, between hope and despair" (Gadamer, "Under the Shadow," 111–12). Certainly, Gadamer qualifies Celan's work as "hermetic" and "cryptic" (116).

3. At the end of the first part of *Poetry as Experience* ("Two Poems by Paul Celan"), the author refers more extensively to "Todtnauberg," of which he also offers a properly French version. Later on, I will touch upon what he says there.

4. Later on, I will have to examine the temporality of the "always still," *Immernoch*, that in Celan's terms characterizes the poem: the poem today.

5. And I will soon encounter this *kommendes* once again in a different light. In the meantime, I confess that I find it impossible not to relate (but what is the link?) this "word / to come" with that other word that "came" in "Stretto [*Engführung*]," the great poem that closes the volume *Language Behind Bars* (1959). A word that "came," however, only to be consumed in its own unspeakable incandescence, in a lapse, in a silence that excludes all presential testimony:

> Kam, kam.
> Kam ein Wort, kam,
> kam durch die Nacht,
> wollt leuchten, wollt leuchten.
>
> Asche.
> Asche, Asche.
> Nacht.
> Nacht-und-Nacht.
> (Celan, *Language Behind Bars*, 92)
>
> Came, came.
> A word came, came,
> came through the night,
> wanted to glow, wanted to glow.
>
> Ashes.
> Ashes, ashes.
> Night.
> Night-and-night.
> (Celan, *Language Behind Bars*, 93)

I will address this poem in chapter 6.

6. I say "grandiose deafness" without an ounce of sarcasm. For, on the one hand, Gadamer's reading is indispensable to me because, in what I judge to be its abuse, it obliges one to pose the questions that I believe to be decisive and to sharpen the very choice of reading and render it more tenacious. And, on the other hand, as I previously indicated, at stake is precisely the difference between one mode of listening and another. Without claiming to clarify or refine these nomenclatures now, because I am not sure that they are entirely pertinent, I would speak of the difference between a hermeneutic listening and a testimonial listening, one that speaks with eloquence of meaning's unfolding in the ambit of ideality—willingly or not—and the other that only gives an account of being there, of having been there.

7. In English and italics in the original.—Translator.

8. What does *deutlich* mean? *Was bedeutet "deutlich"?* This question will make its obstinate gravity and, perhaps, its very impossibility felt throughout this essay. And for what touches upon the immediate: will it not be the case that this word concentrates the resistance that this poem and, in general, Celan's poetry opposes to hermeneutics and its essential project of reappropriating meaning?

9. Concerning the last stanza, Gadamer says: "What follows this is no longer an 'action,' but something like a result, which was drawn in the conversation of those riding back, i.e., the risks of this attempt to walk in the impassable" (Gadamer, "Under the Shadow," 123). And a little later, concerning the penultimate stanza: "It is a description of the risky paths of this thinker's thought—and again, a situation in which we all, as humans today, more or less consciously stand and which necessitates our thinking to travel risky paths" (123). It will still be necessary to interrogate this effect of expansion, of universal representation, that Gadamer attributes to the poem.

10. It is true that Lacoue-Labarthe ventures a hypothesis about this word. With recourse to the "Speech on the Occasion of Receiving the Literature Prize of the Free Hanseatic City of Bremen" (1958), in which Celan alludes to what might be called the indelible wound of language, Lacoue-Labarthe understands the poem to speak of "the language in which Auschwitz was pronounced, and which pronounced Auschwitz" (Lacoue-Labarthe, *Poetry*, 37), and "Todtnauberg" would be, in that connection, the poem of a disappointment or, rather, the poem of *the* disappointment of poetry. Disappointment due to a missing word that Heidegger leaves unpronounced, that he suppresses:

> A word about pain. From there, perhaps, all might still be possible. Not "life," which is always possible, which remained possible, as we know, even in Auschwitz, but existence, poetry, speech. Language. That is, relation to others. [. . .] I do not know what word Celan could have expected. What word he felt would have had enough force to wrench

him from the threat of aphasia or idiom (in-advent of the word), into which this poem, mumbled against silence, could only sink as if into a bog. What word could suddenly have constituted an *event*.

I do not know. Yet something tells me it is at once the humblest and most difficult word to say, the only that requires, precisely "a going out of the self." The word that the West, in its pathos of redemption, has never been able to say. The word it remains for us to learn to speak, lest we should sink ourselves. The word *pardon*. (Lacoue-Labarthe, *Poetry*, 38)

Lacoue-Labarthe's reading is simultaneously rigorous and delicate: respectful, I would say, toward the absolute singularity of that secret event that was Heidegger and Celan's encounter in the summer of 1967. He asks, as Derrida says, "the essential questions, the just one" (Derrida, "Shibboleth" 201, note to page 62). But in this respect I can only reiterate what I noted earlier: hope—and hope above all—cannot conjure up what it hopes for, nor can it do so—much less so—in the mode of representation; the word to come is not programmable as this or that word, and it is not even possible to know it beforehand as a word because the word, whatever it is, will be decided only by its coming.

11. This expression might sound extravagant. Today de-spairs? But can the today be hoped for precisely *today*, hoped for *as today*, today? Furthermore, does the desperation that I experience today not speak to the mere intolerability of this present, of the fact that its ghastly validity suppresses all hope and expectations? It appears to be—as I previously said—a purely verbal mirage. And yet, is the "today" not the deadline of my vigil? If so, then hope is not alien to it, cannot be alien to it, given that to be awake is essentially to be waiting, "on guard," vigilant. The today, in truth, is sustained in hoping. Only thus can it become intolerable. [The verb "to hope," in Spanish, is *esperar*. Oyarzun is capitalizing on the word's relation to "despair" (*desesperar*), which is lost in the English discrepancy between "hope" and "despair." In addition, *esperar* means "to expect," which is why Oyarzun weaves seamlessly between "expectation" and "hope."—Translator.]

12. Celan broaches the etymologically supported link between "to think" and "to thank," the link between *denken* and *danken* so dear to Heidegger, at the beginning of his "Speech" at Bremen: "The words 'denken' and 'danken,' to think and to thank, have the same root in our language. If we follow it to 'gedenken,' 'eingedenk sein,' 'Andenken' and 'Andacht' we enter the semantic fields of memory and devotion" (Celan, *Collected Prose*, 33).

13. The counterpoint with Mallarmé's poetic to which Gadamer alludes refers to *The Meridian* (*Der Meridian*), Celan's speech upon receiving the Büchner Prize in Darmstadt in 1960. That speech will be the center of my subsequent reflections on the relation between Celan and Heidegger.

14. And will Celan's poetry not be, in what most rigorously and insistently belongs to it, this "irruption of nothing"?

15. "Raw," from Latin *crudus*: flesh not yet cooked, which expands because it bleeds; and *cruor*: blood that flows abundantly from a wound.

16. There is *always* something that bleeds, that continues bleeding; there is *always* the irreducible raw. But this "always" *always* escapes the logic of the general and the universal: *it speaks to me immediately*. Those losses, those pains, and those nothings are not equations or symbols or metaphors for those that were inflicted upon me, but they speak to me immediately because I know of loss, of pain, and nothingness (and I know of them before they are even inflicted upon me; I know of them *a priori*, in the *a priori* of my facticity, to put it in Heideggerian terms).

17. See Martin Heidegger, "A Dialogue on Language between a Japanese and an Inquirer," in *On the Way to Language*.

18. The letter is dated 18 May 1960 and written in response to an invitation to participate in the anthology on which Bender was working, *Mein Gedicht ist mein Messer* (My poem is my knife).

19. See Celan, *Meridian*, 36b.

20. And a distance never entirely defined. I could not subscribe to the sudden observation that, evidently motivated by a refusal of Levinas's position, Lacoue-Labarthe makes in a note in "Remembering Dates," the second part of *Poetry as Experience*: "As for Celan's determination of the human, what would it be without relation to Being, that is . . . to time? Even if 'The Meridian' is, as we may plausibly allow, partially addressed to Heidegger, that is not sufficient reason to hastily read into it an 'ethical' response to 'ontology.' The human is in no way an 'ethical' category, and moreover, no category of this kind can resist the question of Being" (132n13).

21. How could I affirm it if "Todtnauberg" registers its unsaying? How could I deny it if Celan ceaselessly insists that the essence of the poem is dialogue, although the latter is, as *The Meridian* says, "often a desperate conversation" (Celan, *Meridian*, 36a)?

22. I cite the conclusion of *Leonce and Lena*:

> And I'll be Minister of State, and it shall be decreed that whoever gets calluses on his hands shall be placed in custody, that whoever works himself sick shall be criminally prosecuted, that anyone who boasts of eating his bread in the sweat of his face shall be declared insane and dangerous to human society, and then we'll lie in the shade and ask God for macaroni, melons, and figs, for musical voices, classical bodies, and a comfortable [*commode*] religion! (Büchner, *Complete Collected Works*, 171–72)

23. Celan is playing on the word *Gänsefüßchen*. *Gänsefüßchen* is the playful image with which a child learning German graphic conventions is introduced to the use of quotation marks, which look like little feet or footprints in language when it is a matter of citations or nicknames and allusive, imprecise, uncertain, and probably ironic forms of denomination.

Notes to Chapter 2

1. At the time, the novelist Hermann Kasack presided over the Academy. The poet Marie Luise Kaschnitz presented the *laudatio*.

2. Depending upon context, I have translated *discurso* as either "speech" or "discourse."—Translator.

3. On this point, see Christopher Fynsk's comments on the time of the poem and the temporal structure of the encounter in his essay "The Realities at Stake in a Poem" (especially 146 ff.). Fynsk holds that "the 'abyss' for Celan . . . lies in time itself" (Fynsk, *Language*, 153).

4. It is well known that Celan worked on his poems by patiently referring to lexicological and etymological dictionaries. The dictionary is also a map. And Celan's relation to language—to German—supposes one think this irrepressible *Unheimlichkeit* together with his declaration that it is only possible to write poetry in one's mother tongue (this declaration will have to be examined).

5. This is the "small four-line stanza" that Celan himself cites toward the end of *The Meridian* (45b–c), removing the italics from "voices" and adding them to the second verse, which he separates from the first with only a space.

6. Heidegger's original subtitle—"Eine Erörterung vom Gedicht Georg Trakls"—has been correctly rendered into English as "A Discussion on Georg Trakl's Poetic Work," but the etymological root of the German word for "discussion" (*Erörterung*) is "place" (*Ort*). Whence Oyarzun's formulation, "localizing discussion [*consideración localizadora*]."—Translator.

7. Heidegger offers an etymological justification for this motif:

> Originally the word "Ort [place]" names the point of a spear. In it everything gathers together. The *Ort* gathers unto itself, supremely and in the extreme. Its gathering power penetrates and pervades everything. The *Ort*, the gathering power, gathers in and preserves all it has gathered, not like an encapsulating shell but rather by penetrating with its light all it has gathered, and only thus releasing it into its own nature. (Heidegger, *On the Way*, 159–60; translation modified)

The gathering—and I will have to intervene on this point later—is also perhaps what makes it possible to say "us." Does the exploration of this possibility, that is, the refoundation of the "us" in the trance in which the stature of what has called itself "human" atrophies beneath the weight of its own determination, not belong to the most essential aspect of the Heideggerian meditation? "The dialogue of thinking with poetry aims to call forth the *nature* of language [*das* Wesen *der Sprache hervorzurufen*], so that mortals may learn again to live within language" (Heidegger, *On the Way*, 161).

8. The word "performance" is in English and italics in the original. —Translator.

9. This is perhaps the "doctrine," if I may say so, of a decisive poem in *From Threshold to Threshold* (*Von Schwelle zu Schwelle*), the title of which—"You too speak [*Sprich auch du*]"—reproduces the first verse. I quote the second and third stanzas:

Sprich—
Doch scheide das Nein nicht vom Ja.
Gib deinem Spruch auch den Sinn:
gib ihm den Schatten.

Gib ihm Schatten genug,
gib ihm so viel,
also du um dich verteilt weißt zwischen
Mittnacht und Mittag und Mittnacht.
(Celan, *Threshold*, 96)

Speak—
but never split No off from Yes.
Give your word a meaning:
give it the shade.

Give it enough shade,
give it as much shade
as you know is parceled around you
between midnight and noon and midnight.
(Celan, *Threshold*, 97)

This poem is one of place (and pure possibility: u-topia), of the *zwischen*, the "between" ("between midnight and midday and midnight"), that through vertiginous inversions speaks meaning as a shadow and shadow as the truth: life as No, an absurd, marginal, and peripheral obstinacy against reigning death. Labile, meaning (the absurd) hangs from this obstinacy; errant words slip beneath it ("the groundswell / of drifting words" [97]).

I will return to these relations later in chapter 4, "Language."

10. The truth is that it is ultimately too difficult, if not impossible, to withdraw from the necessity of choosing and thus enclosing in translation that which the original holds at the crossroads of meaning (only the threshold [*umbral*]) with abrupt indecision (only the *shadow* [umbra]). And, certainly, the poem speaks of crossroads, of the "threeway [*am Dreiweg*]," of hands wrought with pain and trembling there. In his commentary on this poem, Derrida discerns three directions for the syntax governed by the uncontrollable "für" (*für den / Zeugen*): to bear witness *for* or *in favor of* someone, to testify *in the place of* someone, and to testify *before* someone. (Derrida addresses the poem "Aschenglorie" in the conference "'A Self-Unsealing

Poetic Text': Poetics and Politics of Witnessing," one version of which was read at the Universidad Católica de Valparaíso in November of 1995.)

11. And here this "before" (let us recall what was just said concerning the preposition "für" in order to add yet another knot to its complicated weave) should also be understood in the sense of a "through," satisfying the designated operation. If I do not rightly say "through," it is because it operates as the demand to be constituted "before": "before the law" in its rigorous, Kafkan determination.

12. To think the singularity of the event has been the task of contemporary philosophy, its interminable debate with Hegel in the first instance, its infinite reticence regarding the thought of mediation, which forgets (in that profoundly ambiguous mode of forgetting that is the *Aufhebung*) the finitude of thought. This reticence remains in force there where the irrepressible vigor of repetition is recognized but maintained in relation to the unrepeatable, which occurs in the formulation used earlier. To repeat the event as unrepeatable is to resist the mediating power of repetition: to insist that there is, in the margin of the latter, an interruptive repetition. The Derridean discovery of the date in the wake of Paul Celan's poetic thought—and thoughtful poetry—seems to sharpen that debate precisely when it is on the cusp of faltering.

13. I think this, which I have said through the grammar of subjectivity, is also valid there where that grammar has been abolished: the *Stiftung* that Heidegger conceives in a Hölderlinian inspiration ("But what remains is inscribed by the poets"—I will return to this) also has an appropriating character; it appropriates beings to the truth of being to the extent that it converts beings into being's depository. [The line cited in parentheses comes from Hölderlin's poem "Remembrance [*Andenken*]." For Heidegger's eponymous commentary, see *Elucidations of Hölderlin's Poetry*, 101–74. The latter includes an English translation of Hölderlin's poem on pages 102–5. For a bilingual translation, see Hölderlin, *Poems and Fragments*, 488–91.—Translator.]

14. But for this very reason it is also the possibility of every institution's destitution.

15. This "toward" ("*toward* where he lived, how he lived *on*" [Celan, *Meridian*, 24c])—this *hin* in which Celan concentrates the whole theme of "direction [*Richtung*] and destiny [*Schicksal*]" broached early in *The Meridian* and linked to perception (hearing), the poem, and breath (5b)—would have to be interrogated in relation to the destinal character of dates.

16. It is true that, in his analysis of the date and in particular through the relation between date and ash, Derrida ventures to attribute generally and essentially the character of *that* event to the structure of the date: "There is certainly today the date of that holocaust we know, the hell of our memory; but there is a holocaust for every date, and somewhere in the world at every hour" (Derrida, "Shibboleth," 46).

17. Written in 1959, published for the first time in the *Neue Rundschau* in 1960, and included Celan's *Collected Prose*, the story to which Celan refers here is the "Conversation in the Mountains [*Gespräch im Gebirg*]." It narrates the encounter

between two Jews, Gross and Klein, whose casual chat sharpens their strangeness in the middle of the splendid and silent nature that surrounds them. The inspiration for this piece was a missed encounter—"not accidentally" missed, according to Celan himself (Felstiner, "Goodbye Silence," 33)—with Theodor W. Adorno in Sils-Maria, Zarathustra's "homeland." Adorno (Gross) had declared in 1955 that "to write poetry after Auschwitz is barbaric" (Adorno, *Prisms*, 34). Some suppose that this famous dictum from *Prisms*, which was published that year, alluded between the lines to Celan's "Death Fugue," which remains open to debate. In any case, Adorno himself later backtracked and—precisely in a chapter of *Negative Dialectics* (1966) titled "After Auschwitz"—admitted that "it may have been wrong to say that after Auschwitz you could no longer write poems" (Adorno, *Negative Dialectics*, 362).

18. Derrida insists upon this "at the same time" and relates it above all to the poem's dating and its paradoxical condition with respect to the poem's meaning, which Peter Szondi—in his commentary on "You lie [*Du liegst*]"—would be the first to recognize:

> How is one to give an account of this: concerning the circumstances in which the poem was written or, better, concerning those which it names, ciphers, disguises, or dates in its own body, concerning whose secrets it partakes, witnessing is *at the same time* [à la fois] indispensable, *essential* to the reading of the poem, to the partaking that it becomes in its turn, and, finally, *supplementary, nonessential*, merely the guarantee of an excess of intelligibility, which the poem can also forgo. *At the same time* essential and inessential. This *at the same time* stems—this is my hypothesis—from the structure of the date. (Derrida, "Shibboleth," 17; translation modified)

Concerning this structure, which he advances here hypothetically, Derrida later signals the following with respect to the legibility of the date: "And so what must be commemorated, *at the same time* gathered and repeated, is therefore, *at the same time*, the date's annihilation, a kind of nothing, or ash" (Derrida, "Shibboleth," 20). (This is another clause, then, in the *dossier* on the discussion with hermeneutics. As I have already had occasion to note in passing, Hans-Georg Gadamer contests the pertinence of knowing the real circumstances of a poem for the comprehension of its meaning, for what really matters and constitutes the poetic truth. In his essay "What Must the Reader Know [*Was muß der Leser wissen*]?," he addresses this point precisely in relation to Szondi's commentary. I will attempt to approach the problem in the final chapter below.)

19. This is how the German language names the present time: if the Latin *prae* of *praesens* designates "being in front of," the term *Gegenwart* indicates the perseverance, perception, and maintenance of what confronts, with emphasis on difference and on opposition. This "counter" (*gegen*) is an essential theme of *The Meridian*; it

resonates forcefully in the notion of the "encounter" (*Begegnung*) as an opening to the other in the place of the open, empty, and free (see Celan, *Meridian*, 36a–d).

20. This is the double acceptation of the word *Mal*: as its first meaning and according to a first etymology, point and limit of time, stipulated timeframe, which supposedly comes from the Indo-European root **me-*, the meaning of which is "to measure"; as its second meaning, sign, stain, mark, which is likely related to the root **mai-*, with the sense of "to stain," "to dirty." The Spanish term "vez" comes from the Latin *vicis*, "turn," "alternative," "revolve."

21. Reading "Death Fugue," Shoshana Felman notes:

> The wound within the culture opens up in the discrepancy, the muteness, the abrupt disjunction, not only between "Marguerite" and "Shulamith," but, primarily, between "*we drink*," "*we dig*" and "*he writes*." The open wound is marked within the language by the incapacity of "*we*" to *address*, precisely, in this poem of apostrophe and of address, the "*he*." It is in this radical disruption of address between the "*we*" . . . and the "*he*" . . . that Celan locates the very essence of the violence, and the very essence of the Holocaust. (Felman, "Education and Crisis," 39)

I point out here that the theme of the wound (which I will continue elaborating below) is continuous with the theme of the raw, just as "Art" (chapter 3) will treat the "like" by way of a suture.

22. I pull these lucid lines from Cathy Caruth:

> The pathology cannot be defined either by the event itself—which may or may not be catastrophic, and may not traumatize everyone equally—nor can it be defined in terms of a *distortion* of the event, achieving its haunting power as a result of distorting personal significances attached to it. The pathology consists, rather, solely in the *structure of its experience* or reception: the event is not assimilated or experienced fully at the time, but only belatedly, in its repeated *possession* of the one who experiences it. To be traumatized is precisely to be possessed by an image or event. And thus the traumatic symptom cannot be interpreted, simply, as a distortion of reality, nor as the lending of unconscious meaning to a reality it wishes to ignore, nor as the repression of what once was wished. (Caruth, "Trauma and Experience," 4–5)

Caruth also notes the attention that contemporary psychoanalysis pays to

> the surprising *literality* and nonsymbolic nature of traumatic dreams and flashbacks, which resist cure to the extent that they remain, precisely, literal. It is this literality and its insistent return which thus constitutes

trauma and points toward its enigmatic core: the delay or incompletion in knowing, or even in seeing, an overwhelming occurrence that then remains, in its insistent return, absolutely *true* to the event. (5)

23. From Celan's reply to a questionnaire from the Librairie Flinker in Paris (1958), the text concludes: "Hence never—forgive the truism, but poetry, like truth, goes all too often to the dogs—hence never what is double" (Celan, *Collected Prose*, 23).

24. This is the double etymology of *bleiben*: from the Indo-European root **leip-*, to remain fixed, adherent, and also from **leik-*, to remain as residue or a remnant. Thus, in German, the number eleven, *elf*, is the small one that remains after having counted from one to ten. *Leben* and *Leib* have the same origin.

25. *Stiften* means "to erect," "to found," "to give," but it seems to be related to *Stift*, a large peg, a sharp and pointed point, extreme (one will recall the etymology of *Ort* indicated by Heidegger); thus, the foundation of place would primordially consist in the erection of a building with posts.

26. In English, italics, and quotation marks in the original. The Spanish word I've been translating as "remnant" in anticipation of Celan's "Singable remnant [*Singbarer Rest*]" is *resto*, since this is also the word with which Oyarzun translates Celan's poem: "Resto cantable." The relation to the English "rest" is apparent.—Translator.

27. This is the second poem of the second part of *Breathturn* (*Atemwende*). See the brief commentary that Derrida dedicates to it in "Shibboleth" (37–38). How to render—I will not mention other difficulties—"entmündigte Lippe," which oscillates between the defenselessness of what has not yet reached maturity (*munt* is "defense" in old German), what lies under interdict and therefore requires guardianship, and a sort of mutilation of a lip without a mouth (*Mund*), of a literally unbridled lip? ["Unbridled" translates the Spanish *des-bocado*. *Desbocar* means "to run off" or "run wild," but in response to Celan's German formulation *entmündigte Lippe* Oyarzun activates a more literal meaning by hyphenating the word: *des-bocado*, "dis-mouthed."—Translator.]

Notes to Chapter 3

1. What does "today," *heute, das Heutige*, that word so accentuated in *The Meridian* mean? (Accentuated, indeed, because the word designates the time that, in contrast to the historical and the eternal, bears an "acute" accent [Celan, *Meridian*, 10b]). Is it the "today" when the speech was given before a specific audience and in the determined context not only of the German literary institution but also of that Germany that never completely dominates its past (*Vergangenheitsbewältigung* was the political, moral, and cultural slogan that designated the national task of facing the abyss of what happened and what was perpetrated), takes responsibility

for it and controls it, overcomes it while symptoms of the past's ominous latency present themselves again? With the feverish clarity of one who knows of his brittle individuality from the harassment and imminence of brute negation, Celan wanted to mark—with his "22 October 1960"—the complexity of a historical, political, and ethical present in which the poet had to make himself entirely responsible for his word and to make his word entirely interpellative. In his brilliant biography of Celan, John Felstiner recounts that

> some 314 pages of notes and drafts accumulated as he looked for words, turns of speech, metaphors, memories, precedents, and citations that might release the truth of poetic experience. "It was a dark summer," he wrote to a friend. "And the Büchner Prize was, up to the last minute, an ordeal, i.e., it was both temptation and affliction. [. . .]" Celan composed "The Meridian" in three days. Yet this nuanced, layered, elaborately qualified, covertly and overtly allusive speech has nothing hurried about it, forming with all its questioning Celan's authoritative statement on poetry. (Felstiner, *Paul Celan*, 163)

But, then, would the date that fixes a juncture end up bound in turn to the conflict of the meanings and interests in which that date consists? And would the today that it once named remain immured as one milestone among others in the history of that conflict? How could that milestone's force be communicated to another knot and juncture? How and where, if not in the hermeneutic *medium* of language (of language, that is to say, experienced hermeneutically), is a "historical dialogue" established that does justice to the difference in times? Insistent and reiterative, this is the problem of universality that already showed up with respect to Hans-Georg Gadamer's glosses. How does one today speak to another if not—necessarily—through mediation and only in the horizon of intelligibility, of commonality? Or does there exist, perhaps, a strict passage between singularity and singularity? And how to cross it? What is the *shibboleth* that opens the path? Whatever it might be, in this speech that speaks of dates obstinately, that places the date at the root of the poem, and that dates today's poem precisely by the necessity of commemorating dates, the speech itself also complies with this requirement. Marking its "today," it allows itself to be inscribed by a destiny, and it destines itself; "our" present, our "today" belongs to the destiny that continues to subscribe to that date. There is also, for us, a "22 October" that brings and continues to bring its imminence. In question, to be sure, is the enigma of dates. The enigma of dates if, that is, an "enigma" is that which constitutively exceeds all possibility of our knowledge while provoking it as an obsessive pressure, perhaps because one feels in the enigma, precisely, the principle and the prescription of knowledge's possibility. Dated is that concerning the destinal force of which one has an obscure knowledge. In what concerns *The Meridian*, this presentiment is called upon to direct the reading and its questions.

2. See Levinas, *Proper Names*, 41–42, and Oyarzun's commentary thereon in chapter 1 above.—Translator.

3. "*All art*, as the letting happen of the advent of the truth of beings [*des Seienden*], is, *in essence, poetry*" (Heidegger, *Off the Beaten Track*, 44). Such is the fundamental proposition with which Heidegger introduces the aforementioned thesis in the text. Later, I will have to return to the question of *truth*, which balances the relation of art and poetry.

4. Not only is it unclear what "the specific character" is for "modern art"; it is also unclear where art seeks it, as Heidegger says at the end of his *Spiegel* interview in 1966, and with this doubt it would be necessary to raise the even purer doubt of *whether* art seeks it at all (see "Only a God" 64). In what follows, it is essential to observe how these doubts or, rather, certain doubts related to these doubts are also present in Celan.

5. In addition to a dramaturg, Mercier (1740–1814) was an author of novels and *Du théâtre, ou nouvel essai sur l'art dramatique* (*On Theater, or a New Essay on the Dramatic Art*, published in 1773), which has been important in the history of literary conceptions. Opposing classicism, the essay contains the formulation of principles akin to those of the coming romanticism. The imperative mentioned by Celan can be considered the epitome of that discussion.

6. Celan, *Meridian*, 10a. *Ach, die Kunst!*, the counterpoint of Mercier's motto speaking from its own depth, would exclaim the awakening memory that art is the only dimension that, wittingly or not (above all not) and willingly or not, we have never abandoned; it is a perpetual awakening that bears diverse accents: actual, historical, eternal. Celan lends his ear not only to accents but also to tones. In Büchner, it is a question of the parody that ridicules art admirers who succumb to its power to astound, to its ostentatious thaumaturgy (one hears the disfigured echo of its enchantment: "ah" . . . "oh" . . .). But "oh" is also the lament for the wound that art inflicts upon the "real," the wound that art *is* in the "creaturely" (*Meridian*, 14c). And Celan does not believe in the curative, healing virtue of art.

7. Plato, as I already said, wanted to keep them apart; the infinite irony he employed in his attempt to do so adopted a history to which we still belong, with at least one foot planted on the nutrient soil; the contemporaneity that hurries us along began its spadework some time ago.

8. The whole magnitude of an excursus would be necessary to link the aforementioned to Heidegger's noteworthy analysis of the celebrated chorus of *Antigone* (verses 332–75) in the fourth chapter of *Introduction to Metaphysics*. Here, I will limit myself only to establishing a few features. As is well known, that analysis is one of the crucial sites in which Heidegger develops his concept of *Unheimlichkeit*. To translate the Greek *deinon* that Hölderlin had earlier rendered as *ungeheuer*, that is, "monstrous," "atrocious," "excessive" (Hölderlin, *Sämtliche Werke*, 2:331), Heidegger makes use of the term *das Unheimliche*: *pollà tà deinà koudèn anthrópou deinóteron pélei* (Sophocles, *Sophocles I*, 340); "Vielfältig das Unheimliche, nichts doch / über

den Menschen hinaus Unheimlicheres ragend sich regt" (Heidegger, *Einführung*, 155); "Manifold is the uncanny, yet nothing / uncannier than man bestirs itself, rising up beyond him" (Heidegger, *Introduction*, 163). The chorus relates the awe imposed by the consideration of the human essentially to the unfolding of *technē*, and Heidegger defines the latter, precisely, as one of the meanings of the double *deinon* in Sophocles's text: on the one hand, the surpassing power of *dikē* (*das Überwältigende*), that is, of the articulated and imperious unfolding of beings in their totality; on the other hand, the power of the human feat (*das Gewalt-tätige*, *technē*) that opens a path among beings (162–83). It is true that, in the outline on which this note serves as a commentary, I redouble the meaning of the *Unheimliche* somewhat abusively. Heidegger did not apply this term to the process of planetary desertification that modern technology carries out (the general effect of which is uprooting and statelessness, *Entwurzelung* and *Heimatslosigkeit*); rather, he reserved the term for that type of experience that offers testament to a knowledge of the excessive character of being itself, a knowledge that, moreover, has no theoretical or doctrinal range, a knowledge of which existence itself—in its irruption and finitude—provides proof. *Technē* would still belong to the circle of that experience, but precisely *technē* as it is "projected" in poetic diction, which after its fashion entails the seal of violence (*Gewalt*) with which the human measures itself against the immeasurable (which is immeasurable not because it is infinite but, rather, because it is measure itself). So, the duplication I inflict upon the concept is not entirely arbitrary. One must reckon with a certain ambiguity of *technē*, splintered between the *Unheimlichkeit* of its controlled impetus and the *Unheimlichkeit* of the experience of that impetus (poetically phrased), as well as with a certain ambiguity of poetry, which names the experience but needs the controlled impetus to deploy the force of nomination. Not far from here (but also not so absolutely close) lies the duality between the "fire from heaven" and the "clearity of the presentation" that Hölderlin explains to his friend Casimir Ulrich Böhlendorff in a famous letter from 4 December 1801 (Hölderlin, *Essays and Letters*, 149).

9. Bender had invited Celan to collaborate in the anthology *Mein Gedicht ist mein Messer* (My poem is my knife), which he was preparing at the time. Celan's delicately expressed refusal is one of the few occasions on which, with maximum economy, Celan formulates his understanding of the poem. Here, too, one finds that formulation celebrated by Levinas: "I cannot see any basic difference between a handshake and a poem" (Celan, *Collected Prose*, 26). For what concerns the fascination that I mentioned above, abundant in what has been said, it is worth considering that sequence of "making," "making it," and "machinations"; *Machenschaft* is the first name that Heidegger coins (in the latter half of the 1930s) to designate what he will later call *Gestell* (see Heidegger, *Contributions*, 85–129). And, of course, the theme of "hands," toward which language folds back upon itself to concentrate in the pure efficacy of the fatal (hands no longer thought in terms of making and productivity, no longer "poietic," that is, neither instrumental nor the beginning or

model of instrumentality), preserves an emphatic link to the authority of the hand (*Hand*) in Heidegger, from the allusive meanings that proliferate in the margins of *Vorhandenheit* and *Zuhandenheit* in *Being and Time* to the assertion that the hand has its own, irreducible, and never merely intraworldly peculiarity ("mit der Hand hat es seine eigene Bewandtnis") and the conception of thinking as "handiwork [*Handwerk*]." See Heidegger, *What Is Called Thinking?*, 16–17.

10. Previously, in a legendary tone, Heidegger says, "There was a time [*einstmals: in illo tempore*] when it was not technology alone that bore the name *technē*. Once that revealing that brings forth truth into the splendor of radiant appearing also was called *technē*. / Once there was a time when the bringing-forth of the true into the beautiful was called *technē*. And the *poiēsis* of the fine arts also was called *technē*" (Heidegger, *Question Concerning Technology*, 34). How to avoid evoking, with respect to these lines, what Celan says with so much emphasis and visible irritation in his letter to Bender? "Don't come with *poiein* and the like" (Celan, *Collected Prose*, 26).

11. That is to say, to the meaning of the offering (*Opfer*) that is, moreover, a principal trait of essential thinking.

12. I will address this in the next chapter.

13. ". . . what happened [*das, was geschah*]" is the extremely discrete formulation, almost a whisper, with which Celan refers to the Holocaust (*Collected Prose*, 34).

14. I have employed this turn almost stupidly. If I speak of art's "unique dimension" and unidimensionality, it is in order to underscore something that, to me, seems to belong to the structure of occidental art. For the mode in which it is experienced, the "real" entails the seal of the polydimensional: "real" is that which manifests or suggests the index of a severance [*excedencia*], of an external border with respect to the representable. In this same context, the marvel of art depends on something like a loss; the algorithm of art is, to use Duchamp's literally caustic formula, n-1 dimensions.

15. This *trans* is the oft-repeated *meta* that, always surprising, defines the double coordinate (vertical, horizontal) by virtue of which the possibility of thinking, imagining, representing a being and the totality of beings is established. *Meta*physics (in the vertical) and *meta*phor (in the horizontal) have the same root. Heidegger has insisted on this. But we will still have to concern ourselves more closely with the theme of metaphor and also, of course, with Heidegger's insistence. In the meantime, I note the following: if vertical metaphysics measures the distances between the sensible and the intelligible (and a metaphorical output will always be necessary to make it possible to understand this distance), the horizontal of metaphor measures that other distance between the living and the dead (and a metaphysical valence, by metaphorical extension, must be supposed in these concepts). The supreme power recognized in metaphor consists precisely in provoking in and with words, despite their petrified fixity or *mutatis mutandi* their facile evanescence, the feeling of an intensity of being of which we receive news only in the experience of that which

we call "life." This being the case, and abbreviating here several things that would have to be said with less haste, I think that it can be hypothetically suggested, supplementing what I have previously said, that prosopopoeia would be the fundamental figure of art: to attribute life to inanimate beings, to put words in the mouths of the dead. Prosopopoeia would secretly govern the power of metaphor in the determination of art with which Celan debates.

16. This revocation is already present in *Being and Time* through the distinction between the hermeneutical "as" (*Als*) that, originally rooted in Dasein's comprehending structure, therefore has a behavioral character and the apophatic "as" that characterizes the structure derived from the proposition and that has a representational character. While the first "as" remains linked to performative processes of understanding (as being-potential), constituting the structural principle for expressing what is understood, and is therefore nothing other than the explicitness of the projective articulation in which being-potential itself consists through its concern for a "totality of relevance [*Bewandtnisganzheit*]" (*Being and Time*, 84; see 138 ff. and 143 ff.), the apophatic "as" supposes a *leveling* of the "at-hand" set in that totality, which makes it present as merely given (*vorhanden*) such that it becomes inscribable in comparative relations (see 151 ff.). Whatever its degree of refinement, the analogical perspective thus implies a certain indifferentiation of beings, which buries the trait of the incomparable that the latter still tenuously highlights in Dasein's worldly drudgery. (In fact, what palpitates more gravely at the bottom of that equivalence between beings is the indifferentiation of beings and being.) If, from this perspective, one attends to the pertinent developments of Heidegger's conception, it could perhaps be said that poetry enjoys the power to make explicit that incomparable condition, that is to say, the singularity of manifestation (which is at the same time refuge) of the truth of being in beings. From here one could understand the fretwork of Heidegger's critique of metaphor in diverse moments of his work, not only because it pays tribute to the metaphysical difference between the sensible and the intelligible, but also because it bears within itself, even in its supreme and fulgurating force, the imprint of the leveling—of the forgetting—of the unrepeatable. I will have to return to this in the following chapter.

17. I want to recall here a brief text by Benjamin included in *Short Shadows*, which in turn belongs to the cycle of 1931–32 texts from his *Denkbilder*. Translating this title as "images of thought," with everything debatable and truly inadequate that results, at least helps suggest that species of dialectic divorce that takes place between image and thought in the text (a dialectic divorce: this is a knot). The text is as follows:

> *Too Close.* I dreamed I was on the Left Bank of the Seine, in front of Notre Dame. I stood there, but saw nothing that resembled Notre Dame. A brick building loomed, revealing the extremities of its massive shape, above a high wooden fence. But I *was* standing in front of Notre Dame, overwhelmed. And what overwhelmed me was yearn-

ing—yearning for the very same Paris in which I found myself in my dream. So what was the source of this yearning? And where did this utterly distorted, unrecognizable object come from?—It was like that because I had come too close to it in my dream. The unprecedented yearning that had overcome me at the heart of what I had longed for was not the yearning that flies to the image from afar. It was the blissful yearning that has already crossed the threshold of image and possession, and knows only the power of the name—the power from which the loved one lives, is transformed, ages, rejuvenates itself, and, imageless [*bildlos*], is the refuge of all images. (Benjamin, *Selected Writings*, 2:1 269)

In 1968, Celan declared: "At bottom my word formations are not inventions. They belong to language at its very oldest. My concern? To get free of words as mere designations. I'd like to hear again in words the *names* of things." (I take this citation from John Felstiner's *Paul Celan* [324n17]; Felstiner in turn refers to Clemens Podewils's article "Namen / Ein Vermächtnis Paul Celans" [69].) "To hear again in words the *names* of things": this does not suppose, despite appearances, the ambition of returning to linguistic archaism, to a supposedly "naturalness" of language's link to "things" irrevocably immured in their identity. What is "oldest" concerning language is the supreme effort to phrase what is *perceived*.

With respect to the question of the "Name," which oscillates so sensibly in these citations, I will attempt to offer a few signs in the last chapter.

18. This difference between Celan and Heidegger, which I describe very precariously here, is impoverished above all in the following way: it might suggest that a simple opposition is at stake, as if the relation between the two had an "either-or" structure. I do not say that the relation absolutely does not have this structure; I only want to suggest that one must heed the bar or the dividing line, the comma, as a limit in that structure.

19. ". . . death is a master from Germany [*der Tod ist ein Meister aus Deutschland*]" (Celan, *Poems*, 32–33). Repeated four times between the fourth and fifth stanzas of "Todesfuge," this—unhinging—articulation or hinge incites with the density of an *omen* the memory of that which is called "German art" and even "sacred German art" (Richard Wagner: his portentous sounds resonate deafly in the poem's *playback*, if I might put it thus), in its sublime musicality (Johann Sebastian Bach: *die Kunst der Fuge*) and sublime language (Johann Wolfgang von Goethe: allusion to the "golden hair Margarete" in *Faust* [lines 6, 14, 22, 32, 35]). Without ceasing to preserve the unmistakable echo, this musicality and language begin to clog here through the work of another "mastery." (By another "mastery" I mean that shouting mastery that commands "his Jews" [line 8] "more sweetly play death" [line 24] with their violins and commands they play—precisely—the "Tango of Death," which was a favorite piece in the Janowska concentration camp in Lviv, near Czernowitz, from which Celan borrowed the early title of his "fugue." On which, see Felstiner,

Paul Celan, 26–30.) But how is one to ensure that it is indeed an "other" mastery? How to keep the masteries apart? How to ensure that some secret communication does not exist between them? Pointing to the "radical calling-into-question," the Benjaminian memento—"There is no document of civilization which is not at the same time a document of barbarism" (Benjamin, *Illuminations*, 278)—does not lose its edge but, on the contrary, sharpens it.

Perhaps the most profound reticence before that secret and deaf communication dictates a poem like "Keine Sandkunst mehr" ("No sandart anymore"), in which the poet interpellates himself. The poem belongs to the second part of *Breathturn* (*Atemwende*), the title of which already announces the transformation of poetic speech, of the poetic *canto* in Celan's work. In its rigorous diction, it seals the end of a historical matrix of poetry in which the author sees his own production implicated. "Death Fugue" was at that time converted into an irreplaceable part of German poetry anthologies, as if a debt could thereby be paid off, as if recognition of and homage to Celan as a new "master" of German art could cover the flagrant wound with a scar. The poet refuses anthological proliferation of the famous "fugue" and withdraws from the lyricism of its moving musicality: his poetry becomes more fractured, more elliptical. The poem formulates—as a sentence, as a new contract with itself—the renunciation of art, of the book, of mastery ("No sandart anymore, no sandbook, no masters [*Keine Sandkunst mehr, kein Sandbuch, keine Meister*]"), the renunciation of the generous chance of the dice (one will think of Mallarmé) and winnings (*erwürfeln* can be read in this way) that fail due to the uneven cipher of the "mutes" (of the dead, of the broken mouths): "Nothing in the dice. How / many mutes? / Seventeen [*Nichts erwürfelt. Wieviel / Stumme? / Siebenzehn*]" (Celan, *Collected Later Poetry*, 24–25). If the poem is still a question, which would wish to hold itself up into the opening through the work of its sweetest rhythm, it is a question that sinks into itself. It is not a rhetorical question that already has its answer but rather—suspended through the caesura of the "dash of thought" or *Denkstrich* ("Your question—your answer [*Deine frage—deine Antwort*]"), which is the interval of respiration and pure expectation—a question that is fatally its own answer: knowledge, the only knowledge of the canto ("Your chant, what does it know [*Dein Gesang, was weiß er*]?"), namely, what remains buried "Deepinsnow [*Tiefimschnee*]" (Celan, *Collected Later Poetry*, 24–25). [The words "omen" and "playback" in this note are in English and italics in the original.—Translator.]

Notes to Chapter 4

1. In what immediately follows and with respect to the essential connivance of art and discourse, it is opportune to bear in mind the motif of enlargement (*Elargissez l'art !* once again) that predominates everywhere here: an enlargement

that is required by art for its entry onto and development in the scene, and an enlargement that is open, configured, and arranged by discourse.

Furthermore (and I hurry to note this, which I believe must be understood as a footnote to what I said in the previous chapter), this enlargement—this movement of enlarging—is the secret beginning of "history," which in the Büchnerian context to which Celan refers also, in complicity with discourse, forms a single system with "art." As one sees, Büchner presents Lucille—"blind to art" (*Meridian*, 6c)—as foreign to history (she does not follow the "thread" of the conversation about history, the historical account), and with her gesture, with her absurd exclamation, her freedom, and her *step*, she breaks the puppet's string, interrupts the rhetorical circle of history and art, its *theater*, and restitutes Camille to *his* death from the "theatrical" death that the latter enacts for himself and for the rest (see *Meridian*, 6).

2. Consequently, what I argue here is a continuation and—indispensable—complement to the indications essayed in the previous chapter concerning the consummation of art in the "discourse of art," the "death of art" as the condition for art to accede to its unconditionality. There, it was a question of showing the inevitable link between art and discourse; here, it is a question of the inverse.

3. On this point, I previously mentioned Emmanuel Levinas; I could add the name of Ernst Tugendhat. In any case, it is opportune to designate the general context of this issue insofar as the abovementioned "authority" should be referred more strictly to the recognition of language's "anteriority." One could say this recognition (which to a certain point was already prepared by Georg Wilhelm Friedrich Hegel, for whom language is the general space of mediation) is the common premise of all contemporary thought. The premise can be modulated in various ways. We *already* move in language; we always arrive late to it: we are late and evening creatures of the *Abend, abendländisch*, "occidental." (The Occident itself could perhaps be described in accordance with the protocol of this event: the sun of the word sets; we bathe in its tenuous light; this light is language.) But we *already* move in language not only for the structural reason that language finds itself preconstituted the instant we enter into it since, as a structure, it always precedes the empirical outputs of speech. No, more radical than Ferdinand de Saussure is Heidegger's absolute postulation of "anteriority": *die Sprache spricht*. *We are* on the basis of language; we are *through* it. Precisely *this sentence* lies in the gravitational center of my reflections here; its powerful force of attraction, it seems to me, should be emphasized if one seeks to discover the relation between Celan and Heidegger. *This sentence*, with all its implications and difficulties. Whether the vibrant metaphysics of Levinasian alterity or the strict affirmation of analytic sobriety—two modes of responsibility—this same sentence is energetically resisted on dissimilar fronts. (To say something about this responsibility: that forceful phrase scandalizes Tugendhat, who sees the epitome of philosophical obscurantism in it: "Heidegger's dictum that language thinks belongs to the darkest of what has ever been said in philosophy,

because it declares the bankruptcy of all philosophy and is the deepest expression of counter-enlightenment [*Gegenaufklärung*]" [Tugendhat, "Die Seinsfrage," 176].) But the phrase has been coined as the radicalized—and to that extent entirely consistent—form of the attempt to think the genesis of the categorial dimension in which what is most decisive in contemporary thought has been engaged. Moreover, established early in Heidegger's work (its very first inklings already appear in his two youthful theses; on this issue, I refer to my essay on "El problema del lenguaje en el temprano Heidegger"), this attempt belongs to the most originary determination of philosophy, on the basis of which Heidegger claims the right to be measured. If the "anteriority" of language is for contemporary thought effectively the kind of premise that I have said, it is important to calibrate in its specificity (which is here conceived in terms of extreme radicalization) the Heideggerian modulation as it is expressed in the sentence *die Sprache spricht*. The step that makes this sentence possible—the extreme from which it is coined—implies abandoning the question of the categorial because it is derivative. And precisely *that* step leads to poetry in Heidegger, to the understanding of the poetic essence of language.

4. I am referring to the "turning around," the *retournement* of which Lacoue-Labarthe speaks, which relates to the "categorial turning point" that divides beginning and end; "turning around" in a forced "self-forgetting," man (i.e., Oedipus) must "continue" obeying the law of caesura, which is to say, of infidelity that dialectically unites the memory of the Heavenly (*das Gedächtnis der Himmlischen*) and their omission. The *caesura* (to which I will later return) is the interruption of eloquence, of language. See Hölderlin, *Sophocles*, 67–68.

5. The *se* is *unheimlich*. In Spanish, it renders not only the "impersonality" of the German *man* ("one"), the neutral locality of which the artist conjures and convokes ("one wishes to does of course not mean here: *I* wish to" [*Meridian*, 16b]), but also that other sort of neutrality that belongs to the return, to the turn, that is to say, to the "self [*sí*]," to the "itself [*sí mismo*]" (*sich, sich selbst*). In Heidegger, certainly, not only *Man* is neutral; so is *Dasein* (Heidegger, *Metaphysical Foundations of Logic*, 136 ff.). The *se* (this therefore bivalent word of ours) folds over itself two "strangenesses": the tacit, imperceptible strangeness in which we find ourselves everyday, and the other strangeness, sharp when itself announced. The *se* is *unheimlich*; its law is *unheimlich*. And here, at the same time, the *Unheimlichkeit* of the law echoes.

6. The "enrichment" of which I spoke above, of course, alludes to what Celan says in his Bremen speech, and the adjective *angerreichert* ("enriched") that he employs there (Celan, *Collected Prose*, 34) resonates with the word *Reich* with an exact and terrifying irony, leading one to understand what the source of such a treasure was. The reader will bear in mind the grammar of *danken* (here "to thank," "to owe") with the play on which the same speech opens.

7. An essential lesson of "Stimmen," the poem already cited with which *Language Behind Bars* begins:

Stimmen, ins Grün
der Wasserfläche geritzt.
Wenn der Eisvogel taucht,
sirrt die Sekunde:
(*Language Behind Bars*, 2)

Voices, etched
into the green of the water's surface.
When the kingfisher dives,
The moment vibrates:
(*Language Behind Bars*, 3)

I refer to the remarkable analysis that Werner Hamacher offers in his essay "The Second of Inversion" (233 ff.).

8. One can put this another way, I think, which would establish—in a conditioned manner—that old idea of instrumentality the pertinence of which is not unrelated to its menacing truth. What I call the operation of *Rede* would be, in this other version, instrumentalization properly speaking: that character of *organon* attributed to language—which, as I just indicated, cannot be quickly dismissed—in any case would not consist in its availability for human intentions but, rather, in being the *medium* in which the human begins to recognize itself—and misrecognize itself—in its budding intentionality. Language, in the final analysis, can only be the *organon* of itself, and this relation—this "self-relation," if one can say so—defines the space (the "medium") of such a play of knowledge and ignorance by which the human is constituted as such.

9. In "Paul Celan: 'Tübingen, Jänner' " (180), Bernhard Böschenstein suggests that the young poet Christoph Theodor Schwab recorded this uncertain alternative in his diary (14 January 1841). See Fioretos, "Nothing," 317. In fact, Schwab made this observation in his *Hölderlins Leben*: "One of his favorite expressions was the word *pallaksch!* One could at times take it for Yes, at other times for No, but he usually didn't think anything when uttering it; rather, he used it when his patience or the rest of his intellectual capacity was exhausted, and he was not willing to take the trouble of pondering if Yes or Nor should be said" (quoted by Wiedemann in Celan, *Die Gedichte*, 681–82).

10. Naming would happen in the depths of language: Celan made this declaration in conversation with Dietlind Meinecke, according to the latter's *Wort und Name bei Paul Celan* (189; cited by Fioretos, "Nothing," 316, 338n41). Fioretos alludes to the etymological relation between *taufen* ("baptize") and *tauchen* ("submerge").

11. According to the nihilation of the origin in the Kabbalah, above all in the astounding formulation of Isaac Luria (1534–1572) and in contrast to the theory of emanation, the world is possible only through God's act of withdrawal,

contraction, or autolimitation—the *Tzimtzum*—such that creation is nothing but the trace (filler in an emptied container) of a divinity that has always been and always will be absent. Following this first moment is the *Shevirat HaKelim*, the breaking of vessels (*sephirot* inferior to the first three) by way of a "compulsion of light" that is at the same time writing and that to a degree governs the displacement of all world authorities, leading to a state of general exile. There must follow still a third moment, the *Tikun* or the restoration of vessels, which is the task of humanity. See Andrés Claro, *La Inquisición y la Cábala*, 291–95.

12. For instance, see Oyarzun, *Baudelaire*, 18 and 142. —Translator.

13. And will that question from *The Meridian* that, in a crucial passage of the "calling-into-question of art" (Celan, *Meridian*, 19), so essentially concerns Stéphane Mallarmé not have something to do with this? That one should (*sollen wir*) think Mallarmé first of all (*vor allem*) "through to the last consequences [*konsequent zu Ende denken*]" (19; translation modified) would follow not only from the fact that the unconditional presupposition of art is affirmed in Mallarmé but also from the mode in which this affirmation is solely possible for the author of *Un coup de dés*, that is, in the form of what could be called the nihilating poem or, to put it another way, that which Maurice Blanchot called "writing" with respect to Mallarmé and the impossibility of the Oeuvre (see Blanchot, "The Absence of the Book," in *Infinite Conversation*, 422–34).

14. Lend an ear to the original diction, with its strongly accentuated, almost enchanting rhythm: "Das einmal, das immer wieder einmal und nur jetzt und nur hier Wahrgenommene und Wahrzunehmende" (Celan, *Gesammelte Werke*, 3:199).

15. I say "coming without arrival" not to mark a fact or delay or defect of an incident. The coming of the other as other, the coming to the poem that "lets the most essential aspect of the other speak: its time" (*Meridian*, 36b), is only the coming and never the arrival because the poem itself, as a poem, does not obey any intentionality that could conjure up the arrival; rather, it only projects the space of such a coming: "the open, empty and free" (36c).

16. Incommensurability of the gift and the debt? I am still alluding to the Derridean theme of the "one time" so ingeniously articulated in "Shibboleth"; I am still alluding to my own lucubration on that theme and, therefore, to the question of the date. In a note ("Shibboleth," 194), Jacques Derrida refers to Jean Greisch's analysis in "Zeitgehöft et Anwesen (La dia-chronie du poème)" and, with respect to the date and the gift, to the references that Greisch makes to certain passages in Heidegger's work. The first, in Heidegger's *Hölderlin's Hymn "The Ister"*:

> Poetic time is also different in each case, in accordance with the essential nature of the poetry and of the poets. For all essential poetry also poetizes "anew" the essence of poetizing itself. This is true of Hölderlin's poetry in a special and singular sense. No calendrical date can be given for the "Now" of his poetry. Nor is any date needed here at all. For this

> "Now" that is called and is itself calling is, in a more originary sense, itself a date—that is to say, something given, a gift; namely, given via the calling of this vocation. (9)

The second, from the paragraph of *The Basic Problems of Phenomenology* on "The structural moments of expressed time: significance, datability, spannedness, publicness":

> By the term "datability" we denote this relational structure of the now as now-when, of the at-the-time as at-the-time-when, and of the then as then-when. Every now dates itself as "now, when such and such is occurring, happening, or in existence." [. . .] The date itself does not need to be calendrical in the narrower sense. The calendar date is only one particular mode of everyday dating. The indefiniteness of the date does not imply a shortcoming in datability as essential structure of the now, at-the-time, and then. These must belong to it in order for it to be able to be indefinite as a date. [. . .] The dating can be calendrically indeterminate but it is nevertheless determined by a particular historical happening or some other event. [. . .] The "now when," "at-the-time when," and "then when" are related essentially to an entity that gives a date to the datable. The time that is commonly conceived as a sequence of nows must be taken as this dating relation. This relation should not be overlooked and suppressed. (262–63)

To these indications, one would have to add a third, taken from Heidegger's *Contributions to Philosophy*: "*Solely what occurs once* [das Einmalige] *stands in the possibility of re-petition*" (45).

17. The relation of the image to perception contains at least two essential consequences: on the one hand, it cancels the mediating function of the image that predisposes what is punctual and particular in experience for its universal clarification, its reading in a conceptual key; on the other hand, it also cancels the image's aptitude for deception (as a fantastic or fictional product) by referring it to the testimonial truth of *Wahr-nehmung*.

18. Celan, by contrast, defends the irrevocable inalienability of experience, not as property or privacy, not for its exclusive and excluding reference to a particular subject, but rather precisely as an equally irrevocable moment of alterity: inalienable is not the enclosure in my I or its avatars but, rather, what opens me to the other.

19. In order to specify that contexture and what plays out in its crisis, it should be opportune to refer briefly to a brilliant essay by Werner Hamacher that, without ever touching the structure of metaphor directly, allows one to understand the principle of its articulation, at least for what concerns modern metaphor. This principle would be that of *inversion*, which Hamacher considers "the canonical shape of the lyric" (Hamacher, "Second of Inversion," 222) in modernity and at

the same time proposes as the key for understanding Celanian poetry, in which its crisis would occur in the form of a deobjectivating language that cannot yield anything other than "the articulation of the withdrawal of the world" (233). Organized around its semantic function, according to Hamacher, the entire occidental conception of language is caught in the aporia of suppressing language in search of the reality to which it refers on the one hand and, on the other, elevating language to a transcendental condition that makes possible and models all reality; the latter critical version is, in truth, an inversion of the naïve understanding of the world, and for it to win philosophical credit requires awaiting the culmination of absolute subjectivity with which, by way of Immanuel Kant and Hegel, "the metaphors of turning, of overturning and transforming, of perverting, reverting, and returning make their entrance . . . with unprecedented density" (220). One can argue that these metaphors are not simple "metaphors." I think it is tenable to hold that metaphor is the vehicle that permits one to traverse the entire orbit of what is, linking the most distant with the most distant; as in every voyage, the danger of perdition also lurks in this: an integrally metaphorized speech plunges the significant *vis* that metaphor favors and facilitates into the abyss; every metaphorical excursion, then, should have its return ensured. In the modern configuration of knowledge and discourse, moreover, this return—which must bring back what is treasured in the adventure as the capital of reality won even in the subject's extreme exposure—is accomplished only by virtue of inversion: the metaphor of inversion radicalizes the inveterate metaphorical principle and is indistinguishable from the concept of the operation and structure in which the return is consummated along with subjectivity as the essential pole to which language returns in the supreme achievement of its significative vocation. Upon reaching its speculative form, such a radicalization consumes the inversion as a recuperation of self *through loss* (*a priori* deciding the overcoming of this loss) and therefore in the experience of death as resistance to death (which is in turn absolute resistance to signification), which is only possible in said form insofar as it is possible to determine and configure death as nothing-of-something, thus incorporating it into subjectivity's semiotic process of autoconstitution and universalization. Hamacher characterizes this configuration as prosopopoeia. See Hamacher, "The Second of Inversion," 219 ff.

20. Thus declared Ingeborg Bachmann at the end of her second lecture at the University of Frankfurt in 1960, titled "Of Poetry," with respect to what was at the time Celan's latest publication, *Sprachgitter*:

> It walks across a new and still unfamiliar terrain. Metaphors have entirely disappeared; words have removed all clothing, all disguises; no word flies toward or intoxicates another any longer. After a painful turn, after an extremely hard examination of the relations between word and world, it comes to new definitions. [. . .] They [poems] are

uncomfortable, groping, reliable, so reliable in naming that it must be said: hereto and no further.

Suddenly, however, because of the severe restriction, it is once again possible to say something very directly and non-cryptically. It is possible for anyone speaking of him- or herself, wounded by reality and in search of it [*wirklichkeitswund und wirklichkeitsuchend*], to go toward language with their existence [*Dasein*]. (Bachmann, *Frankfurter Vorlesungen*, 40)

21. I say this to accentuate the Celanian diction of the word "perception": *Wahrnehmung*. In the inherited semantics of this concept, we find something double: taking for true or the truth (which, of course, can always be deceived), but also truly taking (which entails certainty). With sensible modulations, the double persists from Aristotle to René Descartes and beyond. The acceptation that the word has in Celan does not adhere to either member of this alternative. It points toward something more originary. Following the thread that links perception to the absurd, let me venture the following: *Wahr-nehmung* is not taking possession or assimilating (*Aufnahme*) something or someone in a predesigned, preknown, and (due to its congruency with a preestablished standard) as such true figure but, rather, the opening onto difference, onto radical alterity, that is to say, onto its exception (*Ausnahme*)—if "to perceive" is "to take," the latter requires above all exposure to the "outside" (*aus*). This opening in turn has the nature of waiting. The *Gegenwart* of the human (of the other) is not a being that can be observed or determined but, rather, the *Gegenwart* of a being that from itself (from its *gegen* as angle and direction) comes but comes without arriving. At stake is the waiting (*Warten*) of the encounter (*Begegnung*) that defines what we call "present." But this waiting is not strengthened by anticipation or with a self-certain hope. The hope that has always belonged to the poem, to speak "*on another's behalf*" (a speaking that is not prosopopoeia), is sustained here only by a "who knows" hanging weakly from a "perhaps" (*Meridian*, 31b–d). And *this* waiting therefore has the nature of an expectation in suspense (*verhoffen*), suspended and paused breath of the creature exposed to extreme danger's trance. Difficult not to evoke on this point the doctrine of historical truth that Walter Benjamin formulates in his so-called "Theses": "Articulating the past historically [. . .] means appropriating a memory as it flashes up in a moment of danger" (Benjamin, *Selected Writings*, 4:391).

22. "A roar [*Ein Dröhnen*]," included in *Breathturn*, says that "truth itself" has made its resounding appearance in the midst of mankind, "right into the / metaphor-flurry [*mitten ins / Metapherngestöber*]" (Celan, *Collected Later Poetry*, 86–89).

23. As anticipated a little vaguely in note 11 of the first chapter, this vigilant wait would determine what we call "present" *in its experience*.

24. What is forgotten when one forgets oneself? Perception, the absurd, the deafening is forgotten. But this same forgetting is not self-enclosure like the *cogito*;

rather, it ex-poses the self-forgotten to the perception of the other—the feminine other: Lucille.

25. What doubt remains that, in this appeal, Celan refers to that other essential inscription of "language" in *The Meridian* that is the *Mallarmean poem*? Not only, to be sure, each particular poem that Mallarmé wrote but also *the* poem as Mallarmé conceived, thought, and prescribed it. As is known, Mallarmé measures the distance between the particular poem and the absent totality to which it alludes: the *Work*, the *Book*, for the sake of which the world exists. The measure is *chance*. *Un coup de dés jamais n'abolira le hasard* speaks of the essential failure that determines every poem, but also of chance as the law of production of the poem itself. *Chance* is art as such (*hasard* = *art*) at the height of its enlargement, of cosmic scope, embracing all possible experience; it is the supreme act of possibility as the transcendental key of the Occident's poetic. In this act, language no longer measures the possible; it *is* the dimension of possibility and, therefore, also pure universality.

26. The note is dated 26 March 1969 (Celan, *Gesammelte Werke*, 3:181). ["Poetry no longer imposes itself; it exposes itself."—Translator]

Notes to Chapter 5

1. One is Walter Benjamin's well-known warning in that spellbinding essay "The Task of the Translator," which he wrote as an introduction to his German translation of Charles Baudelaire's *Tableaux parisiens* and which Paul de Man glosses in his "Conclusions" to *The Resistance to Theory*. (See Benjamin's "On Language as Such and on the Language of Man" in the first volume of *Selected Writings* and Elizabeth Collingwood-Selby's commentary in *La lengua del exilio*.) The other, older warning comes from Novalis: "The particular quality of language, the fact that it is concerned exclusively with itself, is known to no one" (Novalis, *Philosophical Writings*, 83). Heidegger cites this warning at the beginning of "The Way to Language" (*On the Way*, 111), originally the last text of *Unterwegs zur Sprache*. I will soon address what he says about the issue that I am now beginning to weave.

2. I cannot but invoke here that astonishment of which Friedrich Nietzsche speaks in the preface to *On the Genealogy of Morals* with respect to the paradox that "we knowers" are "unknown to ourselves": the astonishment that makes us miscount the "twelve reverberating strokes of our experience, of our life, of our being" (Nietzsche, *Genealogy*, 3) at the very moment (that is to say, every moment) they resound in full force.

3. I borrow the notion of "exscription" from Jean-Luc Nancy; although introduced by Nancy in relation to Georges Bataille's writing, I think it is very pertinent in a reading of Celan because, among other things on which I will have to pause later on, it elaborates in the most rigorous way the relation between writ-

ing and reading, in the knot of a crisis of sense, through a "reversal" of sense out of itself. At the beginning of his article, Nancy says: "This reversal of sense that *makes* sense, or this reversal of sense into the obscurity of its source of writing, I call *exscription* [*l'*excrit]" (Nancy, *Une pensée*, 55).

4. Dennis J. Schmidt formulates it thus:

> If the sounding voice is the achievement of language in the body, if this is the bearer of the poetic word and its idiom, then the countervalent idiom, the idiom in which the body robs language of voice—the "mouthfuls of silence"—is best spoken of in terms of the moment in which the body robs us of words, that is, in the moment at which pain interrupts language. [. . .] In pain, the ipseity of the body and the idiom of the silence meet. Ultimately, this contraction of the human space which happens in pain, the moment at which the body silences language, must be understood as a mime of death. (Schmidt, "Black Milk," 121–22)

5. I refer to the analysis that Ulrich Baer dedicates to the poem "All souls [*Allerseelen*]" in *Language Behind Bars*, especially its last stanza:

> Und einmal (wann? auch dies ist vergessen):
> den Widerhaken gefühlt,
> wo der Puls den Gegentakt wagte.
> (Celan, *Language Behind Bars*, 64)

> And once (when? this too is forgotten):
> the barbed hook, felt
> when the pulse dared its counter beat.
> (Celan, *Language Behind Bars*, 65)

Ulrich Baer says:

> When the pulse changes its rhythm, life itself is momentarily threatened. Between life and death, the interruption or reversal of the pulse is a living being's turning back to the past, and thus a momentary refusal to go on with life. But this change of direction may not qualify as an experience at all. Rather, when the pulse changes its "rhythm" and sinks its "hooks" into life, the possibility of "crossing through" life in an "ex*peri*ence" is momentarily suspended. The poem takes leave of musicality when it forsakes rhyme for an emphasis on *Gegentakt*. Harmony is left behind, physicality reigns. (Baer, *Remnants of Song*, 291)

6. Throughout this chapter, Oyarzun comments upon and weaves between two texts originally published together as the first two essays of *Unterwegs zur Sprache*: "Language [*Die Sprache*]" and "Language in the Poem [*Die Sprache im Gedicht*]." "Language" has been included in *Poetry, Language, Thought*, while "Language in the Poem" is included as the last essay in *On the Way to Language*.—Translator.

7. This is the etymological meaning of the adjective *einsam*, which contains the idea of unity (*ein*) and the theme of gathering or uniting (*sam*).

8. Of course, I do not pause on the grounds for this exegesis, which relate to the Heideggerian theory of the "fourfold," the moments of which were registered in parentheses.

9. *This* actuality gives the tone and above all the *tempo* of that present; I say the *tempo* because the present of art that unfolds in a long duration or perhaps in eternity—of which we have a hint in the happy but transitory calm of contemplation—is probably nothing but the effect of a peculiar "speed" (Celan, *Meridian*, 31f) that compresses times and distances and differences into the polished surface of the spectacle.

10. It would also be necessary to take into account what Heidegger says in this other essay by following the thread of an exegesis of what Trakl's poetry calls "spirit" (*Geist*), that is, the "flame that inflames, startles, horrifies, and shatters us," the flame that chases the soul off to a peregrination of the world, throwing it "into strangeness [*in der Fremde*]" (*On the Way*, 179–80). "An essence in itself opposition [*gegenwendiges*]," Heidegger affirms, "is proper to pain" (180; translation modified). In accordance with the same motif of "rift," interpreted in a stanza of "Thunderstorm" ("O pain, thou flaming vision / Of the great soul!"), this internal opposition is explicated, on the one hand, as the violent uprooting that launches the soul to storm the heavens and, on the other, as the rifting that by virtue of the "vision" sweeps back to pain and its intimate mildness (see *On the Way*, 180–81).

11. One could also pause here to inquire into what this has to do with, I will not yet say "lived experience [*vivencia*]," but rather the *experience* [experiencia] of pain to which, in one way or another, the Heideggerian notion must remain faithful.

12. And there is a secret community between *logos* and *algos*, between word and pain.

13. Heidegger is commenting upon the final stanza of the third part of "Bright Spring" (second version): "So painful good, so truthful is what lives, / And softly touches you an ancient stone: / Truly! I shall forever be with you. / O mouth! that trembles through the silvery willow" (cited in Heidegger, *On the Way*, 183). Here, in the distance, one perceives the echo of that other talking "stone" that—hospitable and loquacious, ambivalent in its mortuary task—figures in Celan's "Engführung":

Ja.
Orkane, Par-
tikelgestöber, es blieb
Zeit, blieb,

es beim Stein zu versuchen—er
war gastlich, er
fiel nicht ins Wort. Wie
gut wir es hatten:

Körnig,
körnig und faserig. Stengelig,
dicht;
traubig und strahlig; nierig,
plattig und
klumpig; locker, ver-
ästelt —: er, es
fiel nicht ins Wort, es
sprach,
sprach gerne zu trockenen Augen, eh es sie schloß.

Sprach, sprach.
War, war.
(Celan, *Language Behind Bars*, 96)

Yes.
Hurricanes, part-
icle storms, there was
time, still,
to try it out with the stone—it was
hospitable, it
didn't interrupt. How
good we had it:

Grainy,
grainy and stringy. Stalked,
thick;
clustered and radiant; kidney-shaped,
level and
bumpy; loose, branch-
ing—: it
did not interrupt, it
spoke,
spoke gladly to dry eyes, before it shut them.

Spoke, spoke.
Was, was.
(Celan, *Language Behind Bars*, 97)

14. As an *innuendo*, I hold: reverberation of the traditional, metaphysical, and theological concept of pain, the *crux* of theodicy—to justify pain, to make sense of pain; the intolerable for thinking in that tradition is the idea of a senseless pain.

15. I think the translation of *Stille* into Spanish as *queda*, postverbal of *quedar*, is opportune: *quedo*, from *quietus*, since long ago in Spanish means "quiet, immobile, calm," as well as "silent." As one knows, the noun *queda* designates that vespertine or nocturnal time during which, in states of emergency, the free movement of citizens is prohibited. It is also the name given to the bell that announces this time. [Oyarzun silently alludes here to the curfew (*toque de queda*) implemented after the 1973 coup d'état in Chile and at times of massive unrest in the dictatorship that followed.—Translator.]

16. David Young has omitted Celan's emphasis on "E s s e i" in the German transcription of his bilingual edition. Since Oyarzun insists upon this spatial form of emphasizing in German, I have also exchanged expanded spacing for italics in the English "Let there be."—Translator.

17. "Celan's poetry comes into being as the pain of language itself: a syntactically wounded stutter breaking down language into its smallest elements: *Buch-staben*" (Fioretos, "Nothing," 331).

Notes to Chapter 6

1. Let us repeat: "close together, and in one and the same direction." In the original: *dicht beieinander*. It is a matter of discerning one strangeness from another, even if they are close together, precisely because they are so and insofar as they are so. That discernment is the task of poetry—of *Dichtung*—not as a function of densification, not as a mission for synthesis, but rather as knowledge of closeness or narrowness. But uncertain knowledge, of course, which knows of such narrowness insofar as it relates to strangeness or projects it for itself.

2. Published posthumously, as is known, Celan's *Zeitgehöft* contains in three folios (the first of which bears the aforementioned title) and in chronological order poems written between 25 February 1969 and 13 April 1970, with the exception of "Almonding you [*Mandelnde*]," which is dated 2 September 1968 and opens the second folio. Celan prepared neither the collection nor its pieces for publication.

3. This is the fourteenth poem from the second folio.

4. The allusion is to the translation of Pindar's *Olympian Odes* and *Pythian Odes* that Hölderlin carried out at the beginning of the century; there is no agreement over their date, and conjectures oscillate between 1800 and 1803. Aris Fioretos conjectures that Celan's poem could refer to Pindar's fifth fragment (Fioretos, "Introduction," 18–19), which Hölderlin translates and upon which he comments:

> Das Gesez,
> Von allen der König, Sterblichen und
> Unsterblichen; das führt eben
> Darum gewaltig
> Das gerechteste Recht mit allerhöchster Hand.
>
> The law,
> King of all, mortals and
> Immortals; just for this reason it wields
> Powerfully
> The most rightful law with the very highest hand.
> (quoted in Fioretos, "Introduction," 18–19; see Hölderlin, *Sämtliche Werke*, 2:381)

Hölderlin's commentary stipulates that "the immediate, taken strictly, is impossible for mortals, as well as for immortals" (2:381), because both must distinguish diverse worlds: the former in favor of the sacred purity of their goodness; the latter since "knowledge [*Erkentniß*] is only possible through opposition [*Entgegensezung*]" (2:381). By contrast, "the law is . . . strict mediation" (2:381). Celan's verbal neologism *zackern*, translated in the poem as "harrows," contains a reference to *Zacke* ("point," "tooth," "prong").

    5. One will recall the following passage, which concludes the draft of the first stanza of "In Lovely Blueness . . . ," a composition from after 1806:

> But the Heavenly, who are always good, all things at once, like the rich, have these, virtue and pleasure. This men may imitate. May, when life is all hardship, may a man look up and say: I too would like to resemble these? Yes. As long as kindliness, which is pure, remains in his heart not unhappily a man may compare himself with the divinity [*misset nicht unglüklich der Mensch sich mit der Gottheit*]. Is God unknown? Is He manifest as the sky? This rather I believe. It is the measure of man [*Des Menschen Maaß ist's*]. Full of acquirements, but poetically, man dwells on this earth. But the darkness of night with all the stars is not purer, if I could put it like that, than man, who is called the image of God. (Hölderlin, *Poems and Fragments*, 601)

In the beginning of the sketch for the second stanza, Hölderlin continues: "Is there a measure on earth? There is none [*Giebt es auf Erden ein Maaß? Es giebt keines*]" (Hölderlin, *Poems and Fragments*, 601). All too famous is Heidegger's discussion of the theme of measure in ". . . Poetically Man Dwells . . ." (Heidegger, *Poetry*, 216 ff.), in which he constructs upon this disputed text his thesis concerning poetry as "measure-taking" (*Maßnahme*) and concerning poetizing as "measuring" (*messen*). I cannot address here the complications of this reading (its validation of the fragment as a product from Hölderlin's hand, its preference for the version in verse reconstructed by Norbert von Hellingrath, the elisions and forcings); characteristic of Heidegger's powerful, hermeneutical *will*, they leave too many doubts concerning the fidelity to the Hölderlinian radical experience of a lack of measure, of the *non datum* of measure as the essential determination of the modern world, a lack stretched between the "Yet each of us has his measure [*Nur hat ein jeder sein Maas*]" in the grand poem "The Rhine" (Hölderlin, *Poems and Fragments*, 421), the question concerning the dation of measure and its negative on earth, and the affirmation of the patency of God qua patency of heavens as the measure of man. On this, I refer to the critique that Peter Fenves proposes in his essay "Measure for Measure." But I do not believe it inadmissible to think that Celan's *Deut* is an acute way of prolonging the question of the *non datum* of measure in modernity as an epoch of the caesura.

6. Here, I limit myself to venturing one possible link to—an echo of (to use Hölderlin's own word)—this poem in Celan's "I drink wine." In recent decades (following Arne Melberg's "Turns and Echoes"), scholars of Hölderlin's hymnic poetry have managed to reconstitute a single poem of four stanzas with the title "The Nymph Mnemosyne" on the basis of the three versions recorded in the Stuttgart edition ("The Nymph," "Mnemosyne" [draft], and "Mnemosyne"). The verses in question would belong at the beginning of the second stanza (at least in the order that Melberg prefers), which would be organized around a turn the pivot of which would be, in the stanza's exact middle, the mention of the "One," "He," an "other" that is—with respect to mortals—"God" (Melberg, "Turns and Echoes," 349–50). "God" also occupies the center of Celan's poem. Yet, if in Hölderlin the movement governed by the turn leads from the passivity of "a state of inhuman alienation" to the activity of memory, history, and mourning (350), in Celan we find—perhaps according to the law of the echo—the inversion of this movement.

7. Joel Golb argues that a contradiction afflicts Szondi's commentary: the claim that reading the poem rests upon itself, upon its formal and thematic universe, is validated only with recourse to the poem's "outside," that is to say, the historical world (Golb, "Reading Celan," 193). And Fioretos thinks that Szondi's remarkable analysis does not take into account the complexity he thinks observable insofar as the text can even be read only by disobeying the imperative that the poem itself announces at the beginning—"Read no more"—and thus by opposing violence to it (Fioretos, "Nothing," 323). Both objections, which of course begin by recognizing the vigor and depth of Szondi's commentary, agree in resisting the central theoretical idea that the poem—but also poetry as such—is not the mimesis or representation of a reality, whatever the latter might be, but rather reality for itself: text. It must also be said that, albeit in different ways, the question of allegory occupies a fundamental place in both of these discussions. I will return to this.

8. I have restored the capitals to the first word in the English translation, along with the initial asterisk.—Translator.

9. To this extent, there does not seem to me to be an exclusive opposition here—like the one Fioretos supposes—between "read" and "walk" or, therefore, a violence that must be exercised against the command to read or to continue reading; rather, as I just suggested, there seems to be the *demand* for a different type of poetic reading capable of maintaining itself on the border between "poem" ("language") and "reality." But this reading can be nothing other than *a reading of the trace* (or of the *remainder*), as the unequivocal trace of violence and loss. (The verb *verbringen* also means "to lose," "to squander," "to waste.")

10. It is perhaps legitimate to say that this empty infinitude marks the difference between Hölderlin's idealism and that of his fellow students Friedrich Wilhelm Joseph Schelling and Georg Wilhelm Friedrich Hegel. The fragment "The Fatherland in Decline" makes such "emptiness" intelligible as the plexus of possibilities in the trance of the end of one world and the beginning of another.

11. Commenting upon this passage, José Manuel Cuesta Abad (*La palabra tardía*, 82–83) rightly refers to the notion of the "expressionless [*das Ausdruckslose*]," which Walter Benjamin formulates in his essay on "Goethe's Elective Affinities" (*Selected Writings*, 1:340). In fact, Benjamin himself affirms that there is no other place in which to find a stricter definition of the inexpressive, as "a category of language and art and not of the work or of the genres" (1:340), than this very passage from Hölderlin's "Notes." He signals that in the caesura,

> along with harmony, every expression simultaneously comes to a standstill, in order to give free reign to an expressionless power inside all artistic media. Such power has rarely become clearer than in Greek tragedy, on the one hand, and in Hölderlin's hymnic poetry, on the other. Perceptible in tragedy as the falling silent of the hero, and in the rhythm of the hymn as objection. Indeed, one could not characterize this rhythm any more aptly than by asserting that something beyond the poet interrupts the language of the poetry. (1:341)

12. In English and italics in the original.—Translator.

13. The grammatical form of this passage is similar to the one we find in the last stanza of "Ashglory," which has its center in the preposition *für*. Already in the second chapter, I referred to the attention Derrida pays to this word and to the undecidable play of meanings that it foments.

14. "One can also *fall* upward [*in die Höhe*], as well as down [*in die Tiefe*] (Hölderlin, *Sämtliche Werke*, 2:58). Without mentioning Hölderlin and having cited Johann Georg Hamann and his meditation on the identity of reason and language as an abyss, Heidegger alludes to this reflection to suggest what is at stake in his *dictum* "language speaks": "If we let ourselves fall into the abyss denoted by this

sentence, we do not go tumbling into emptiness. We fall upward, to a height [*Wir fallen in die Höhe*]. Its loftiness opens up a depth. The two span a realm in which we would like to become at home, so as to find a residence, a dwelling place for the life of man" (Heidegger, *Poetry*, 189–90).

15. In chapter 5 above, I had occasion to cite the poem "To stand [*Stehen*]" from *Breathturn*. I am inclined to think that the "für dich" from line 5, a modulation of the "for-no-one-and-nothing" in line 3, also obeys the intricate regime of the "für" in "Ashglory," (un)determined by the "trivium" crossroads with Oedipal resonances. This "to stand" (but we already know: in the abyss) has testimonial fiber (it is "to be there," *da stehen, da sein*); "nothing" and "no one" comes to confirm it, and "all that has room in it" (line 7) is assigned by the justness of narrowness.

16. One will recall the passage from "Stretto" that alludes to the atomic theory of ancient materialism (Democritus, Epicurus, Lucretius) that, with its description of the primordial whirlwind of particles, excludes "the other" as "opinion" (mere *doxa*):

Orkane.
Orkane, von je,
Partikelgestöber, das andre,
du
weißts ja, wir
lasens im Buche, war
Meinung.
(Celan, *Language Behind Bars*, 94)

Hurricanes.
Hurricanes, from the past,
particle storm, the other,
you
know it, we
read in the book, it was
opinion.
(Celan, *Language Behind Bars*, 95)

17. Let us recall again what was implied in the final declaration of the "Speech at Bremen": as a wound and at the same time as that which is to be sought, reality is never, for the poet, that which is merely evident [*consta*].

18. In the German column of the bilingual edition of *Language Behind Bars*, "Stern" is transcribed with a lowercase. I have restored the capital here.—Translator.

19. Baer (*Remnants of Song*, 188–89) refers to Celan's brief essay on Osip Mandelstam in which he defines the essence of poetry with the expression *zeitoffen*, which no doubt—and this is how Baer himself takes it—can be and demands to be understood according to diverse readings. It seems to me, in any case, that one

would have to take into account a double opening: the opening of the poem to time and the opening of time itself; this double opening could be considered the very structure of the date.

20. "Huhediblu" speaks this "when" (*Wann*) of madness (*Wahn*):

Wann,
wann blühen, wann,
wann blühen die, hühendiblüh,
huhediblu, ja sie, die September-
rosen?

Hüh—on tue . . . Ja wann?

Wann, wannwann,
Wahnwann, ja Wahn,—
Bruder
Geblendet, Bruder
Erloschen, du liest,
du liest und du,
dies hier, dies:
Dis-
parates –: Wann
blüht es, das Wann,
das Woher, das Wohin und was
und wer
sich aus- und an- und dahin- und zu sich lebt, den
(Celan, *No One's Rose*, 130)

When,
when do they bloom, when,
when-bloom-they, whodotheybloom,
hoodootheyblue, yes, them, those September-
roses?

Whoooo—there's killing going on . . . Yah, when?

When, whenwhen,
wodewhen, yes, wode,—
brother
blinded, brother
extinguished, you read,
you read and you,

> this here, this:
> dis-
> parity —: When
> does it bloom, the When,
> the Wherefrom, Whereto, and what
> and who
> lives out of, and on to, and out to, and to oneself lives, the
> (Celan, *No One's Rose*, 131)

Derrida comments upon the madness of this "When," which makes the poem delirious in the question concerning its unassignable punctuality, as the madness of the date, which the final verse of the stanza preceding those I have cited here calls "this date, the Nevermansday [*Nimmermenschtags*] of September" (Celan, *No One's Rose*, 130–31; see Derrida, "Shibboleth," 38 ff.). On 15 September 1935, the Nürnberg Racial Laws were enacted by the German Nazi regime, depriving Jews of all civil rights. How to think of the abyssal "when" of the September roses, which evoke the final line of Paul Verlaine's sonnet "L'espoir luit comme un brin de paille dans l'étable [Hope gleams like a strand of straw in the stable]": "Ah, quand refleuriront les roses de septembre [Oh, when the September roses will bloom again]!" (Verlaine, *Sagesse*, 82)? The final line of "Huhediblu" recalls the line with a telling modification: "Oh quand refleuriront, oh roses, vos septembres [Oh when, oh roses, will your Septembers bloom again]?" As always in Celan, one *Unheimlichkeit* needs to be separated from the other. There are, perhaps, two madnesses here, along with the crevice of time in between. Scratching on the wall of the *Nimmer* and *Immer* is perhaps the madness of poetry itself, *zeitoffen*, which *The Meridian* formulates as "this infinity-speaking [*Unendlichsprechung*] full of mortality and to no purpose!" (Celan, *Meridian*, 44).

Notes to Chapter 7

1. *Partners* in English and italics in the original.—Translator.
2. See Allemann, "Paul Celan."
3. Heidegger, "Hölderlin and the Essence of Poetry," in *Elucidations*, 51–66. The examination of this third "guideword" takes place on pages 56–58. Its location in the middle of the five guidewords scanning Heidegger's reflection, demanded by the argument, is in no way innocuous: it defines the center that animates the poem from "*the poet's poet*" (Heidegger, *Elucidations*, 52). The draft corresponds to the second versified project of "Celebration of Peace [*Friedensfeier*]," which dates from between 1801 and 1802. Hölderlin conceived the canto shortly after the announcement of the peace treaty between Austria and France in Lunéville on 9 February 1801. The four verses reproduced here—which are in fact three: the first two occupy the same

line—lie at the end of the draft and are followed by a final verse that reads: "For behold, it is the evening of time [*Denn siehe es ist der Abend der Zeit*]" (*Sämtliche Werke*, 2:361). In its definitive version, the poem contains another version of the passage that interests Heidegger but which he does not consider:

> Viel hat von Morgen an,
> Seit ein Gespräch wir sind und hören voneinander,
> Erfahren der Mensch; bald sind wir aber Gesang.
> (Hölderlin, *Poems and Fragments*, 438)

> Much, from the morning onwards,
> Since we have been a dialogue and have heard from one another
> Has human kind learnt; but soon we shall be song.
> (Hölderlin, *Poems and Fragments*, 439; translation modified)

The exclusion of the latter variant implies a voluntary double omission in Heidegger's citation, which neglects to mention the cycle of morning and evening and the promise or enthusiastic annunciation. For a painstaking analysis of "Fiedensfeier," see Szondi's "Er selbst, der Fürst des Fests."

4. This poem is a response to the beginning of the second stanza of Brecht's "To Those Born Later [*An die Nachgeborenen*]": "What times are these, in which / A conversation about trees is almost a crime / Because it implies silence about so many horrors!" (Brecht, *Poetry and Prose*, 70–71; translation modified). In both poems, the word for "conversation" is *Gespräch*, the properly German word for "dialogue." It sounds here like a distant and destitute reverberation of Hölderlin's above-quoted verses and their noble expectation ("but soon we shall be song").

5. This is the infinite project of "Romantic poetry," which Philippe Lacoue-Labarthe and Jean-Luc Nancy famously term "*theory itself as literature* or, in other words, literature producing itself as it produces its own theory" (Lacoue-Labarthe and Nancy, *Literary Absolute*, 12).

6. One would have to invoke here the first paragraph of "Notes to *Oedipus*," which contain the notes of obfuscating light that Hölderlin appends to his version of Sophocles's *Oedipus Rex*. This beginning—the first paragraph—suffices to indicate the historically decisive knowledge that Hölderlin possessed concerning the destinal link between poetry and politics: "It will be a good thing, giving poets even in our country a secure social existence [*eine bürgerliche Existenz*], if poetry, even in our country and notwithstanding the differences of the times and of the political systems, is raised to the *mechane* of the Ancients" (Hölderlin, *Sophocles*, 63).

7. Hölderlin, *Poems and Fragments*, 439. The first draft of the poem, in prose, begins with the sentence: "A chorus are we now [*Ein Chor nun sind wir*]" (Hölderlin, *Sämtliche Werke*, 1:355).

8. Literally, Joyce's joke in *Ulysses* reads, "Jewgreek is greekjew. Extremes meet" (504). I would be tempted to add yet another modification to the modification: "Extremes hardly meet, even with themselves." [Oyarzun's citation of Joyce and his two modifications of it are in English in the original.—Translator.]

9. In question, in truth, is a modulation: Celan's declaration repeats the poetic hope, the fundamental poetic desire, the expectation of *pure* language [*lengua*], refracted multifariously in those fragmentary shards of tongues [*idiomas*] scattered to all latitudes. Yet, in the terms in which they are apprehended here, the modulation is *extreme*: for it supposes that *one* of those tongues retains the original stele of that absolute language. Because of what I perceive as an extreme modulation, with respect to what Felstiner says, I speak—in a voluntary paradox—of the *thesis* of the Name: the Name, thus with a capital letter, is that which can be neither posited nor imposed in any way; if there is such a thing, in the absolutely unique way of its being there, the Name would be that which becomes insofar as it comes in a movement of pure and unapproachable imminence. And therefore Hebrew, in its spoken facticity, would not simply be the place of that coming; rather, it would harbor receptivity for this imminence exemplarily.

10. I will not say that Jean Bollack conceives it in exactly these terms, but his brilliant essay "Le mont de la mort," which centers on the visit that the poet paid the philosopher in his Black Forest refuge and, of course, on the poem "Todtnauberg," takes a turn and sees in Celan's visit the execution of a plan; it attributes a sort of irresistible power to Celan by virtue of which he can extort the reticent answer from Heidegger, the "monstrous word" (Bollack, "Le mont de la mort," 170). Bollack imagines this aside the moment when Celan leans over to take a sip from the fountain placed before the cabin:

> "What you see me do has its own meaning; perhaps it escapes you, and yet what I have just asked, by accepting to drink from this water— your water—is clear. The expected answer will no doubt be refused to me. One might fear this. But one must not be mistaken: I will have already obtained it over the course of this visit. I will have rerouted the refusal to my advantage." Interpreters have been mistaken or have not wanted to read it, refusing to make the visit something so mortuary, the response to a denial of murder. (162)

The "something so mortuary," let us point out in the meantime, is ominously inscribed in the very name of the cabin's location, which Celan transfers to the poem's title: "*Todt*nauberg" homophonically contains "tot" (dead) and "Tod" (death) and, prolonged by the "n," sounds like "Toten" (the dead). Together with the latter reading (the dead—meadow [*Au*]—mountain [*Berg*]), Bollack follows Israel Chalfen's biography of the young Celan and recalls that the Third Reich had a "Todt Organization," so-called because of its founder, Fritz Todt, who was Minister of

Armaments. Pierre Joris also plays with the name in his article "Celan / Heidegger: Translation at the Mountain of Death."

11. Unless one were also, vaguely, to hear the echo of "wound," and in any case one loses the strength of the German *w*, a sign of the wound made by biting one's lip. And certainly the guttural "g" of "gain" does not manage this, not to mention that the alliteration is prolonged and consummated in *Welt*.

12. Excluding the issue that I am interested in accentuating, I cannot resist hearing in this piece the distorted echo of the poem by Stefan George that Heidegger examines (*On the Way*, 140); it begins precisely with the word *Wunder* ("Wonder or dream from distant land") and its penultimate distich concludes with the word *gewann* ("The treasure never graced my land . . ."). Adding "of both the single name" that is the "sore gain / of a world," Celan's verse "not a word, not a thing" seems to epitomize the unblemished "Where word breaks off no thing may be [*Kein ding sei wo das wort gebricht*]" with which George's poem concludes. See above, 72 ff.

13. See what I have said about the wound above.

14. Derrida's emphasis in italics: the origin becomes the absolutely unappropriatable.

15. Felstiner calls attention to the precise wording of Celan's citation: in the original, reproduced in the epigraph in Russian Cyrillic, one reads, "All poets are Yids [*Vse poety* zhidy]" (Felstiner, *Paul Celan*, 197), "Yids," "Jews" not in the sense of an established and originary identity, as it has been frequently understood, but rather as a problematic identity, oppressed with grave derogatory undertones. "Zhid," as Felstiner points, is "a popular Czarist epithet . . . used ironically by Tsvetaeva" (197).

16. In "Conversation in the Mountains," "Jew Klein," and "Jew Gross"—respectively, as is known, Celan and Theodor W. Adorno ("his cousin, a quarter of a Jew's life older" [Celan, *Collected Prose*, 18])—are the names of the two who meet and chat desolately in the fiction of the failed appointment in the Upper Engadin. The whole text invites us to read it as Celan's reflection on "being Jewish" ("Jewish being").

17. "Greek" and "Jew" are in English and italics in the original.—Translator.

18. Celan's poem is found in his *Collected Later Poetry* (322–23). Szondi's essay bears the title "Eden" and has been published in *Celan Studies* (83–92).

19. Gadamer's commentary, initially published in its first version in 1972, was republished in *Wer bin Ich und wer bist Du* and also, with the title "Was muß der Leser wissen?," in the volume *Gedicht und Gespräch*. I have consulted the German text in volume 9 of Gadamer's *Gesammelte Werke* (443–47). [In what follows, I cite the English translation included in *Gadamer on Celan*.—Translator.]

20. In the *Times Literary Supplement*, Enzensberger had said: "*In fact, we are not confronting communism, but revolution. The political system of the German Federal Republic is irreparable. We can either accept it or replace it with a new system. Tertium non dabitur*" (quoted in Celan, *Collected Prose*, 27). *Der Spiegel* asked various intellectuals and artists to react to this dilemma.

21. On some of the poem's allusions and in particular the allusion that, as in so many other poems by Celan, encrypts the name of Osip Mandelstam, whom Celan admired, cf. Felstiner, *Paul Celan*, 188.

Bibliography

Adorno, Theodor W. *Negative Dialectics*. Translated by E. B. Ashton. New York: Continuum, 2007.
———. *Prisms*. Translated by Samuel and Shierry Weber. Cambridge, MA: MIT Press, 1983.
Allemann, Beda. "Paul Celan." In *Deutsche Dichter der Gegenwart: Ihr Leben und Werk*, edited by Benno von Wiese, 436–51. Berlin: Erich Schmidt, 1973.
Bachmann, Ingeborg. *Frankfurter Vorlesungen: Probleme zeitgenössischer Dichtung*. Munich/Zurich: R. Piper, 1982.
Badiou, Alain. *Manifesto for Philosophy*. Edited and translated by Norman Madarasz. Albany: State University of New York Press, 1999.
Baer, Ulrich. *Remnants of Song: Trauma and the Experience of Modernity in Charles Baudelaire and Paul Celan*. Stanford, CA: Stanford University Press, 2000.
Baumann, Gerhard. *Erinnerung an Paul Celan*. Frankfurt am Main: Suhrkamp, 1986.
Benjamin, Walter. *Illuminations: Essays and Reflections*. Translated by Harry Zohn. Edited by Hannah Arendt. Boston: Mariner, 2019.
———. *Selected Writings*. Vol. 1, *1913–1926*. Edited by Marcus Bullock and Michael W. Jennings. Cambridge, MA: Harvard University Press, 1999.
———. *Selected Writings*. Vol. 2, part 1, *1927–1930*. Edited by Michael W. Jennings, Howard Eiland, and Gary Smith. Translated by Rodney Livingstone and others. Cambridge, MA: Harvard University Press, 1999.
———. *Selected Writings*. Vol. 4, *1938–1940*. Edited by Michael W. Jennings and Howard Eiland. Translated by Rodney Livingstone and others. Cambridge, MA: Harvard University Press, 2006.
Blanchot, Maurice. *Infinite Conversation*. Translated by Susan Hanson. Minneapolis: University of Minnesota Press, 1992.
Bollack, Jean. "Le mont de la mort: Le sens d'une rencontre entre Celan et Heidegger." *Lignes* 3, no. 29 (1996): 157–88.
Böschenstein, Bernhard. "Paul Celan: 'Tübingen, Jänner.'" In *Studien zur Dichtung des Absoluten*, 177–80. Zurich: Atlantis, 1968.

Brecht, Bertolt. *Poetry and Prose*. Edited by Reinhold Grimm and Caroline Molina y Vedia. New York: Continuum, 2003.
Brockhaus Conversations-Lexikon. Amsterdam: Im Kunst- und Industrie-Comptoir, 1809.
Brockhaus Enzyklopädie in Zwanzig Bänden. 17th ed. Wiesbaden, Germany: F. A. Brockhaus, 1966.
Büchner, Georg. *The Complete Collected Works*. Edited and translated by Henry J. Schmidt. New York: Avon, 1977.
Caruth, Cathy. "Trauma and Experience: Introduction." In *Trauma: Explorations in Memory*, edited by Cathy Caruth, 3–12. Baltimore, MD: The John Hopkins University Press, 1995.
Celan, Paul. *Breathturn into Timestead: The Collected Later Poetry*. Translated by Pierre Joris. New York: Farrar, Straus and Giroux, 2003.
———. *Collected Prose*. Translated by Rosemarie Waldrop. Manchester, UK: Carcanet Press, 2003.
———. *From Threshold to Threshold*. Translated by David Young. Grosse Pointe Farms, MI: Marick Press, 2010.
———. *Die Gedichte: Kommentierte Gesamtausgabe*. Edited by Barbara Wiedemann. Frankfurt am Main: Suhrkamp, 2003.
———. *Gesammelte Werke*. Vol. 1. Edited by Beda Allemann and Stefan Reichert. Frankfurt am Main: Suhrkamp, 1983.
———. *Gesammelte Werke*. Vol. 3. Edited by Beda Allemann and Stefan Reichert. Frankfurt am Main: Suhrkamp, 1983.
———. *Language Behind Bars*. Translated by David Young. Grosse Pointe Farms, MI: Marick Press, 2012.
———. *Lichtzwang: Vorstufen Textgenese Endfassung*. Tübinger version. Frankfurt am Main: Suhrkamp, 2001.
———. *Le Méridien*. Translated by André Bouchet. Paris: Fata Morgana, 1995.
———. *The Meridian: Final Version—Drafts—Materials*. Edited by Bernhard Böschenstein and Heino Schmull. Translated by Pierre Joris. Stanford, CA: Stanford University Press, 2011.
———. "The Meridian." Translated by Jerry Glenn. In *Sovereignties in Question: The Poetics of Paul Celan*, edited by Thomas Dutoit and Outi Pasanen, 173–85. New York: Fordham University Press, 2005.
———. *No One's Rose*. Translated by David Young. Grosse Pointe Farms, MI: Marick Press, 2014.
———. *Poems of Paul Celan*. Translated by Michael Hamburger. New York: Persea, 2002.
Chalfen, Israel. *Paul Celan: Eine Biographie seiner Jugend*. Frankfurt am Main: Suhrkamp, 1983.
Claro, Andrés. *La Inquisición y la Cábala: Un Capítulo de la diferencia entre metafísica y exilio*. Vol. 2, *Ontología y Escritura*. Santiago: Arcis/Lom, 1996.

Collingwood-Selby, Elizabeth. *La lengua del exilio*. Santiago: Arcis/Lom, 1997.
Cuesta Abad, José Manuel. *La palabra tardía: Hacia Paul Celan*. Madrid: Trotta, 2001.
Derrida, Jacques. "Shibboleth." In *Sovereignties in Question: The Poetics of Paul Celan*, edited by Thomas Dutoit and Outi Pasanen, translated by Joshua Wilner, revised by Thomas Dutoit, 1–64. New York: Fordham University Press, 2005.
———. "'A Self-Unsealing Poetic Text': Poetics and Politics of Witnessing." Translated by Rachel Bowlby. In *Revenge of the Aesthetic: The Place of Literature in Theory Today*, edited by Michael P. Clark, 180–207. Berkeley: University of California Press, 2000.
Dostoevsky, Fyodor. *A Writer's Diary*. Edited by Gary Saul Morson. Evanston, IL: Northwestern University Press, 2009.
Emery, H. G., and K. G. Brewster, eds. *The New Century Dictionary of the English Language*. New York: D. Appleton-Century, 1946.
Felman, Shoshana. "Education and Crisis." In *Trauma: Explorations in Memory*, ed. Cathy Caruth, 13–60. Baltimore, MD: The John Hopkins University Press, 1995.
Felstiner, John. "Goodbye Silence: Paul Celan's Conversation in the Mountains." *Stanford Humanities Review* 1, no. 1 (1989): 33–43.
———. *Paul Celan: Poet, Survivor, Jew*. New Haven, CT: Yale University Press, 1995.
Fenves, Peter. "Measure for Measure." In *The Solid Setter. Readings of Friedrich Hölderlin*, edited by Aris Fioretos, 25–43. Stanford, CA: Stanford University Press, 1999.
Fioretos, Aris. Introduction to *The Solid Letter: Readings of Friedrich Hölderlin*, edited by Aris Fioretos, 1–21. Stanford, CA: Stanford University Press, 1999.
———. "Nothing: History and Materiality in Celan." In *Word Traces: Readings of Paul Celan*, edited by Aris Fioretos, 295–341. Baltimore, MD: Johns Hopkins University Press, 1994.
Friedrich, Hugo. *Die Struktur der modernen Lyrik von der Mitte des neunzehnten bis zur Mitte des zwanzigsten Jahrhunderts*. Hamburg: Rowohlt, 1979.
Fynsk, Christopher. *Language and Relation: . . . That There Is Language*. Stanford, CA: Stanford University Press, 1996.
Gadamer, Hans-Georg. *Gadamer on Celan: "Who Am I and Who Are You?" and Other Essays*. Translated and edited by Richard Heinemann and Bruce Krajewski. Albany: State University of New York Press, 1997.
———. *Gedicht und Gespräch: Essays*. Frankfurt am Main: Insel, 1990.
———. *Gesammelte Werke*. Vol. 9. *Ästhetik und Poetik*. Tübingen, Germany: J. C. B. Mohr (Paul Siebeck), 1993.
———. "Under the Shadow of Nihilism." In *Hans-Georg Gadamer on Education, Poetry, and History: Applied Hermeneutics*, translated by Lawrence Schmidt and Monica Reuss, 111–24. Albany: State University of New York Press, 1992.

Golb, Joel. "Reading Celan: The Allegory of 'Hohles Lebensgehöft' and 'Engführung.'" In *Word Traces: Readings of Paul Celan*, edited by Aris Fioretos, 185–218. Baltimore, MD: Johns Hopkins University Press, 1994.

Hamacher, Werner. "The Second of Inversion: Movements of a Figure through Celan's Poetry." In *Word Traces: Readings of Paul Celan*, edited by Aris Fioretos, 219–63. Baltimore, MD: Johns Hopkins University Press, 1994.

———. "Wasen: Um Celans Todtnauberg." In *Das Robert Altmann Projekt*, edited by Norbert Haas et al, 35–83. Notebook 3, *Paul Celan in Vaduz*. Schaan, Liechtenstein: Edition Eupalinos, 2012.

Hannover-Drück, Elisabeth, and Heinrich Hannover. *Der Mord an Rosa Luxemburg und Karl Liebknecht: Dokumentation eines politischen Verbrechens*. Frankfurt am Main: Suhrkamp, 1967.

Heidegger, Martin. *The Basic Problems of Phenomenology*. Rev. ed. Translated by Albert Hofstadter. Bloomington: University of Indiana Press, 1982.

———. *Contributions to Philosophy (of the Event)*. Translated by Richard Rojcewicz and Daniela Vallega-Neu. Bloomington: Indiana University Press, 2012.

———. *Einführung in die Metaphysik*. Gesamtausgabe 40. Frankfurt: Vittorio Klostermann, 1983.

———. *Elucidations of Hölderlin's Poetry*. Translated by Keith Hoeller. Amherst, NY: Humanity, 2000.

———. *Erläuterungen zu Hölderlins Dichtung*. Gesamtausgabe Edited by Friedrich-Wilhelm von Herrmann. Frankfurt am Main: Vittorio Klostermann, 1981.

———. *Four Seminars*. Translated by Andrew Mitchell and François Raffoul. Bloomington: Indiana University Press, 2003.

———. *Hölderlin's Hymn "The Ister."* Translated by William McNeill and Julia Davis. Bloomington: Indiana University Press, 1996.

———. *Introduction to Metaphysics*. 2nd ed. Translated by Gregory Fried and Richard Polt. New Haven: Yale University Press, 2014.

———. *Metaphysical Foundations of Logic*. Translated by Michael Heim. Bloomington: Indiana University Press, 1984.

———. *Off the Beaten Track*. Translated and edited by Julian Young and Kenneth Haynes. Cambridge: Cambridge University Press, 2002.

———. *On the Way to Language*. Translated by Peter D. Hertz. New York: HarperCollins, 1982.

———. "Only a God Can Save Us." Translated by William J. Richardson, S. J. In *Heidegger: The Man and the Thinker*, edited by Thomas Sheehan, 45–67. New York: Routledge, 1981.

———. *Poetry, Language, Thought*. Translated by Albert Hofstadter. New York: Harper & Row, 1971.

———. *The Question Concerning Technology and Other Essays*. Translated by William Lovitt. New York: Garland, 1977.

———. *Unterwegs zur Sprache*. Gesamtausgabe 12. Edited by Friedrich-Wilhelm von Herrmann. Frankfurt am Main: Vittorio Klostermann, 1985.

———. *What Is Called Thinking?*. Translated by Fred D. Wieck and J. Glenn Gray. New York: Harper & Row, 1968.

Hoefler, Walter. "Todtnauberg: Un poema intraducible." *El Espíritu del Valle* 4/5 (1998): 39–43.

Hölderlin. *Essays and Letters on Theory*. Translated and edited by Thomas Pfau. Albany: State University of New York Press, 1988.

———. "The Fatherland in Decline." In *The Death of Empedocles: A Mourning-Play*, translated by David Farrell Krell, 153–58. Albany: State University of New York Press, 2008.

———. *Hölderlin's Sophocles*. Translated by David Constantine. Northumberland, UK: Bloodaxe, 2001.

———. *Hymns and Fragments*. Translated by Richard Sieburth. Princeton, NJ: Princeton University Press, 1984.

———. *Poems and Fragments*. Translated by Michael Hamburger. Ann Arbor: University of Michigan Press, 1967.

———. *Sämtliche Werke und Briefe*. 3 vols. Edited by Michael Knaupp. Munich: Carl Hanser, 1992.

Joris, Pierre. "Celan/Heidegger: Translation at the Mountain of Death." UPenn Writing. Last accessed September 8, 2021. http://writing.upenn.edu/epc/authors/joris/todtnauberg.html.

Joyce, James. *Ulysses*. New York: Random House, 1992.

Lacoue-Labarthe, Philippe. *Heidegger and the Politics of Poetry*. Translated by Jeff Fort. Chicago: University of Illinois Press, 2007.

———. *Poetry as Experience*. Translated by Andrea Tarnoowski. Stanford, CA: Stanford University Press, 1999.

Lacoue-Labarthe, Philippe, and Jean-Luc Nancy. *The Literary Absolute: The Theory of Literature in German Romanticism*. Translated by Philip Barnard and Cheryl Lester. Albany: State University of New York Press, 1988.

Levinas, Emmanuel. *Proper Names*. Translated by Michael B. Smith. Stanford, CA: Stanford University Press, 1996.

Lewis, Charlton T., and Charles Short. *A Latin Dictionary*. Oxford: Clarendon Press, 1975.

Meinecke, Dietlind. *Wort und Name bei Paul Celan: Zur Widerruflichkeit des Gedichts*. Bad Homburg, Germany: Gehlen, 1970.

Melberg, Arne. "Turns and Echoes." In *The Solid Letter: Readings of Friedrich Hölderlin*, edited by Aris Fioretos, 340–55. Stanford, CA: Stanford University Press, 1999.

Mendicino, Kristina. "An Other Rhetoric: Paul Celan's *Meridian*." *MLN* 126 no. 3 (2011): 630–50.

Nancy, Jean-Luc. *Une pensée finie*. Paris: Galilée, 1991.

Nietzsche, Friedrich. *On the Genealogy of Morals*. Edited by Keith Ansell-Pearson. Translated by Carol Diethe. Cambridge: Cambridge University Press, 1997.

Novalis. *Philosophical Writings*. Translated by and edited by Margaret Mahony Stoljar. Albany: State University of New York Press, 1997.

Oyarzun, Pablo. "Ah, el arte." In *La filosofía como pasión: Homenaje a Jorge Eduardo Rivera Cruchaga en su 75 cumpleaños*, edited by Juan Pablo Brickle, 275–90. Madrid: Trotta, 2003.

———. *Baudelaire: La modernidad y el destino del poema*. Santiago: Metales Pesados, 2014.

———. "Diálogo." *Extremoccidente* 3 (2003): 73–75.

———. "Entre Celan y Heidegger." *Seminarios de Filosofía* 9 (1996): 193–212.

———. "Lugar." *El espíritu del valle* 4/5 (1998): 22–27.

———. "El problema del lenguaje en el temprano Heidegger." *Seminarios de Filosofía* 8 (1996): 161–97.

Petzet, Heinrich Wiegand. *Auf einen Stern zugehen: Begegnungen und Gespräche mit Martin Heidegger, 1929–1976*. Frankfurt am Main: Societäts-Verlag, 1983.

Pfeifer, Wolfgang, ed. *Etymologisches Wörterbuch des Deutschen*. 2nd ed. Berlin: Akademie-Verlag, 1993.

Plato. *Republic*. 2 vols. Loeb Classics Library. Translated by Paul Shorey. Cambridge, MA: Harvard University Press, 1937/1942.

Podewils, Clemens. "Namen: Ein Vermächtnis Paul Celans." *Ensemble* 2 (1971): 67–70.

Pöggeler, Otto. " '—Ach, die Kunst!' Die Frage nach dem Ot der Dichtung." In *Über Paul Celan*, edited by Dietlind Meinecke, 77–94. Frankfurt: Suhrkamp, 1970.

———. "Spur des Wortes: Zur Lyrik Paul Celans." In *Zu Dir hin: Über mystische Lebenserfahrung von Meister Eckhart bis Paul Celan*, edited by Woflgang Böhme, 270–304. Frankfurt am Main: Insel, 1987.

Random House Webster's Unabridged Dictionary. 2nd ed. New York: Random House, 1998.

Safranski, Rüdiger. *Martin Heidegger: Between Good and Evil*. Translated by Ewald Osers. Cambridge, MA: Harvard University Press, 1998.

Schmidt, Dennis J. "Black Milk and Blue: Celan and Heidegger on Pain and Language." In *Word Traces: Readings of Paul Celan*, edited by Aris Fioretos, 110–29. Baltimore, MD: Johns Hopkins University Press, 1994.

Sophocles. *Sophocles I*. Loeb Classics Library. Translated by F. Storr. New York: MacMillan, 1912.

Steiner, George. *Martin Heidegger*. Chicago, IL: University of Chicago Press, 1987.

Szondi, Peter. *Celan Studies*. Translated by Susan Bernofsky, with Harvey Mendelsohn. Stanford, CA: Stanford University Press, 2003.

———. "Durch die Enge geführt: Versuch über die Verständlichkeit des modernen Gedichts." In *Schriften II*, 345–89. Frankfurt/Main: Suhrkamp, 1978.

---. "Er selbst, der Fürst des Fests: Die Hymn *Friedensfeier*." In *Hölderlin-Studien: Mit einem Traktat über philologische Erkenntnis,* 62–94. Frankfurt am Main: Suhrkamp, 2015.
Tugendhat, Ernst. "Die Seinsfrage und ihre sprachliche Grundlage." *Philosophische Rundschau* 26, no. 3 (1977): 161–76.
Verlaine, Paul. *Sagesse*. Paris: Société Générale de Librairie Catholique, 1881.
Walde, Christian, et al. "Obscuritas." In *Historisches Wörterbuch der Rhetorik*, vol. 6, edited by Gert Ueding, 358–83. Tübingen, Germany: Max Niemeyer, 2003.
Waldrop, Rosemarie. Introduction to *Collected Prose*, vii–x. Translated by Rosemarie Waldrop. Manchester: Carcanet Press, 2003.

Index

"A leaf [*Ein Blatt*]," 95
"A roar [*Ein Dröhnen*]," 135n22
absurd, xii–xiii, xvi, xxvii–xxxii, 23–24, 55–56, 59, 63, 77, 86, 91, 106, 117n9, 129n1, 135n21, 135n24
Adorno, Theodor W., 110n11, 119n17, 149n16
"All souls [*Allerseelen*]," 137n5
allegory, 91, 142n7
Allemann, Beda, 94, 96–98, 146n2
"Almonding you [*Mandelnde*]," 140n2
alterity, 28, 72, 129n3, 133n18, 135n21; *see also* other
"And with the book from Tarussa [*Und mit dem Buch aus Tarussa*]," 101
Aristotle, 55, 135n21
art, xi–xiv, xviii, xxi, xxv–xxvi, xxviii, xxxvii, 18, 27, 33–44, 45–48, 50, 65, 77, 86, 123n3, 123n4, 123n6, 125n10, 125n14, 126n15, 127n19, 128n19, 128–29n1, 129n2, 132n13, 136n25, 138n9, 143n11; artist, artistic, xiii, 27, 33, 37, 40–42, 46, 48, 65, 130n5, 143n11, 149n20
Artaud, Antonin, 87
articulation, 31, 36, 43–44, 46, 67, 70–71, 83, 85, 89, 94, 124n8, 126n16, 127n19, 132n16, 133–34n19, 135n21; inarticulate, 62; disarticulation, xxiv–xxv
artifice, xiii, 33–34, 46, 82
"Ashglory [*Aschenglorie*]," 25, 70–71, 85–86, 117n10, 143n13, 144n15

Bach, Johann Sebastian, 127
Bachmann, Ingeborg, 134–35n20
Badiou, Alain, xxxvii, 111n2
Baer, Ulrich, 87, 137n5, 144n19
Bataille, Georges, 136n3
Baudelaire, Charles, 38, 87, 136n1
Baumann, Gerhart, 111n1
Bender, Hans, 12, 39, 115n18, 124n9, 125n10
Benjamin, Walter, xxiv, 44, 57, 87, 91, 98, 126–27n17, 128n19, 135n21, 136n1, 143n11
Benn, Gottfried, xi, xiii, 112n2
Blanchot, Maurice, 132n13
body, xxxviii, 3, 29, 32, 46, 61–63, 69, 88, 103, 107, 115n22, 119n18, 137n4
Böhlendorff, Casimir Ulrich, 124n8
Bollack, Jean, 148n10
Böschenstein, Bernhard, 131n9
Bouchet, André du, 47
Breathturn (*Atemwende*), xx, 59, 70, 103, 121n27, 128n19, 135n22, 144n15
Brecht, Bertolt, 95–96, 147n4

Brentano, Clemens, 107
Brickle, Juan Pablo, 111n3
Büchner, Georg, xi–xiii, xvi, 15, 17, 26–27, 33, 35, 37, 45–46, 65, 114n13, 115n22, 122n1, 123n6, 129n1

caesura, xix, 51–52, 63, 78, 84–86, 88, 100, 104, 128n19, 130n4, 142n5, 143n11
Caruth, Cathy, 120n22
"Cello-entry [*Cello-Einsatz*]," 12, 70–71
Chalfen, Israel, 148n10
chiasmus, 88–89
Claro, Andrés, 132n11
Collingwood-Selby, Elizabeth, 136n1
community, xvii, xxxi, 26, 29–31, 95–96, 99, 101, 138n12
"Conversation in the Mountains [*Gespräch im Gebirg*]," 118–19n17, 149n16
creature, 24, 33, 57, 61, 91, 123n6, 129n3, 135n21
Cuesta Abad, José Luis, 143n11

date, x–xi, xiii–xiv, xxiii, xxvi, xxix, xxxii, 19, 24–32, 43, 45, 50, 52, 62, 100–1, 104, 106, 118n12, 118n15, 118n16, 119n18, 122n1, 132–33n16, 136n26, 145n19, 146n20, 146n3; dation, 142n5
de Man, Paul, 136n1
death, 8, 27, 42, 44, 46, 57, 63, 72, 82, 84–85, 106, 117n9, 127–28n19, 129n1, 134n19, 137n4, 137n5, 148–49n10; of art, 36–38, 129n2
"Death Fugue [*Todesfuge*]," 44, 55, 82, 119n18, 120n21, 127–28n19
Democritus, Democritean, 71, 144n16
Derrida, Jacques, xxi, xxix, 25–26, 30, 80, 99–102, 105, 114n10, 117n10, 118n16, 119n18, 121n27, 132n16, 143n13, 146n20, 149n14
destination, destiny: x, xiii, xxvii, 10–11, 21, 23, 27–29, 31, 34, 38–39, 42, 44, 45, 62, 79, 81, 85, 105, 118n15, 122n1, 147n6
dialogue, x, xiv, xviii, xx–xxii, xxvi–xxviii, xxx–xxxi, 1–15, 21, 23, 37–38, 44, 93–107, 115n21, 116n7, 122n1, 147n3, 147n4
difference, xvii, xix, xxx, 12, 15, 19, 26–27, 29, 34, 36–37, 47, 51–52, 54, 64–66, 68, 84, 87, 96, 100, 104–6, 110n13, 113n6, 119n19, 122n1, 124n9, 126n16, 127n18, 135n21, 138n9, 143n10, 147n6
discourse: xi–xiii, xvi, xviii–xix, xxv–xxvi, 8, 11–13, 18, 28, 34, 36, 38, 43, 45–6, 48–51, 56, 62, 69, 86, 96, 116n2, 128–29n1, 129n2, 134n19
doit, xvii, xxvii, 77–92, 101
Dostoevsky, Fyodor, x
dream, 30, 120n21, 126–27n17, 149n12
Duchamp, Marcel, 125n14

ego, 28; *see also* I; self
Eichmann, Adolf, 27
ellipsis, 83, 88
encounter, x, xii, xvii, xx, xxii–xxiv, xxviii–xxx, 6, 9, 28, 30–31, 52, 56, 62, 70, 77, 86, 102, 112n5, 114n10, 116n3, 118–19n17, 120n19, 135n21
Enzensberger, Hans Magnus, 105, 149n20
Epicurus, 144n16
estrangement, 23, 37–38, 48, 50, 86
event, xvii, xx, xxiii, xxv, xxvi, xxviii, 2, 6–7, 23, 25–27, 30–31, 34, 59,

71–72, 82–83, 114n10, 118n12, 118n16, 120–21n22, 129n3, 133n16
existence, xxvi, xxxii, 7, 19, 23–26, 28–31, 33–36, 39, 41, 48, 60, 61–62, 78–79, 81–82, 86, 91, 100–1, 104–5, 109n7, 110n13, 113n10, 124n8, 133n16, 135n20, 147n6
experience, ix, xxi, xxv, xxvi, xxviii–xxxiv, 1, 5, 7, 10–11, 17–18, 20, 27, 38, 40–41, 43–44, 50–51, 55, 58, 66, 70, 74–75, 77, 79, 81–82, 86–87, 94, 96, 103–4, 106, 114n11, 120n22, 122n1, 124n8, 125n14, 125n15, 133n17, 133n18, 134n19, 136n23, 136n25, 137n2, 137n5, 138n11, 142n5
experiment, 39, 55, 100

Felman, Shoshana, 120n21
Felstiner, John, 97–99, 107, 119n17, 122n1, 127n17, 128n19, 148n9, 149n15, 150n21
Fenves, Peter, 142n5
Fioretos, Aris, 88–90, 131n9, 131n10, 140n17, 140–41n4, 142n7, 143n9
foreign, foreignness, xv, xxii, 13, 34, 46, 81, 129n1; *see also* strangeness; *Unheimlich*
forget, forgetting, 7, 35, 46–50, 87, 103, 118n12, 126n16, 130n4, 135n24; *see also* memory
Franzos, Karl Emil, xvi, 15
From Threshold to Threshold (*Vom Schwelle zu Schwelle*), 117n9
Fynsk, Christopher, 116n3

Gadamer, Hans-Georg, xviii–xix, 3–7, 102–3, 109n7, 112n2, 113n6, 113n9, 114n13, 119n18, 122n1, 149n19

gathering, xvii, xxvii–xxviii, 20–21, 23, 31, 56, 64, 66–68, 70–72, 74–75, 116n7, 119n18, 138n7
George, Stefan, x, 72, 149n12
Geviert, das, xvi, 111n1
gift, 13–14, 22–23, 26–27, 30, 35, 39, 41, 43–44, 49, 56, 58, 68, 85, 101, 117n9, 121n25, 126n16, 132n16, 133–34n16
Goethe, Johann Wolfgang, ix, 127, 143n11
Golb, Joel, 142n7
Greisch, Jean, 132n16

Hamacher, Werner, xxi, xxiii, 110n8, 110n13, 131n7, 133–34n19
Hauptmann, Gerhart, 35
Hebrew, 97–100, 148n9
Hegel, G. W. F., xix, 36, 118n12, 129n3, 134n10, 143n10
Hellingrath, Norbert, 142n5
hermeneutics, xviii–xix, xxi–xxiii, 3–5, 7, 17, 102–4, 113n6, 113n8, 119n18, 122n1, 126n16, 142n5
hermeticism, ix, xviii, 2–3, 109n1, 112n2
Heydrich, Reinhard, 27
Hoefler, Walter, 111n1
Hölderlin, Friedrich, xxviii, xxxi, 13, 31, 38, 48, 50–51, 78–79, 81, 84–86, 88, 94–97, 99, 106–7, 111n1, 118n13, 123–24n8, 130n4, 131n9, 132n16, 140–41n4, 141–42n5, 142n6, 143n10, 143n11, 143n14, 146–47n3, 147n4, 147n6, 147n7
"Hoodootheyblue [*Huhediblu*]," 145–46n20
Huchel, Peter, 103

I, xii–xiii, 19, 27–28, 30–31, 46–49, 60; *see also* ego; self

"I drink wine [*Ich trink Wein*]," 78–80, 142n6
"In one [*In eins*]," 99, 105
indifference, 6, 27, 29, 36, 47, 87, 99, 100, 104, 126
inscription, xxii, 1, 7, 9, 15, 18, 26–28, 30–32, 36, 42, 50, 62, 71–72, 77–79, 82, 84, 90, 94, 101, 104, 118n13, 122n1, 126n16, 136n25, 148n10
insignificance, 80–82, 101; *see also* doit
inversion, xii, xix, 88–89, 117n9, 133–34n19, 142n6

Joris, Pierre, 149n10
Joyce, James, 97, 148n8
Judaism, xxix, xxxi, 8, 26–27, 97–99, 101–2, 106, 119, 127n19, 146n20, 148n8, 149n15, 149n16, 149n17

Kafka, Franz, 38, 118n11
Kant, Immanuel, 18, 134n19
Kasack, Hermann, 116n1
Kaschnitz, Marie Luise, 116n1
"Knock [*Klopf*]," 58–59

Lacoue-Labarthe, Philippe, xviii, xxi, xxiv, xxvi, 3–4, 10–11, 36–37, 47, 110n8, 111n2, 113–14n10, 115n20, 130n4, 147n5
Language Behind Bars (*Sprachgitter*), 82, 112n5, 130–31n7, 134–35n20, 137n5, 144n18
Lenz, Reinhold, xii, xvi, 24, 26–28, 35, 37, 46, 65, 86
"Letter to Hans Bender [*Brief an Hans Bender*]," 12, 39, 115n18, 124–25n9, 125n10
Levinas, Emmanuel, xvii–xviii, xxi–xxii, 11–15, 33, 115n20, 123n2, 124n9, 129n3
Lewis, Charlton T., xv

Liebknecht, Karl, 103–4
light, xxx–xxxii, 2–3, 17, 24, 43–44, 57–60, 74, 90, 116n7, 129n3, 132n11, 147n6
Lightduress (*Lichtzwang*), xxxi, 1, 17, 57–58, 98, 107, 110n14, 110–11n1
Lucretius, 144n16
Luria, Isaac, 131n11
Luther, Martin, 98
Luxemburg, Rosa, 103–4
lyric, lyricism, xiii, xxiii, 31, 82, 98, 128n19, 135n19

Malebranche, Nicolas, xxiv
Mallarmé, Stéphane, ix, 7, 35–36, 95, 114n13, 128n19, 132n13, 136n25
Mandelstam, Osip, 144n19, 150n21
map, 18–19, 116n4
meaningfulness, 7–8; significance, 101, 133n16
Mendicino, Kristina, xi
Meinecke, Dietlind, 131n10
Melberg, Arne, 142n6
memory, 18, 25–29, 31, 40, 43, 45, 49, 87, 96, 106, 114n12, 118n16, 119n18, 122n1, 123n6, 127n19, 130n4, 135n21, 142n6; immemorial, 61; *see also* forgetting
Mercier, Louis Sébastien, 34–38, 42, 123n5, 123n6
The Meridian (*Der Meridian*), ix–xxiv, xxvi, xxviii–xxx, xxxii, 11, 13, 15, 17–19, 24–29, 31, 33–35, 38–39, 41–43, 45–47, 49, 52, 54–55, 57, 61, 65, 77, 79, 83, 86, 96, 100–1, 105, 106, 109n3, 109n4, 109n7, 114n13, 115n19, 115n20, 115n21, 116n5, 118n15, 120–21n19, 121–23n1, 123n6, 129n1, 130n5, 132n13, 132n15, 135n21, 136n25, 138n9, 146n20

metaphor, xii, xx, xxix–xxx, 7, 43–44, 54–56, 66, 77, 84, 115n16, 122n1, 125–26n15, 126n16, 133–34n19, 134n20, 135n21
metaphysics, 7, 20–22, 44, 66, 68, 123n8, 125n15, 126n16, 129n3, 130n5, 140n14
Michel, Wilhelm, 107
mimesis, xix, xxiii–xxx, 37, 42, 48, 53–54, 87, 142n7
Mistral, Gabriela, 62

name, xiv, 9, 19, 21–22, 24, 26, 42, 44, 57, 59–60, 64–65, 71, 83, 87–89, 94–95, 97–100, 103–4, 127n17, 148n9, 149n12; see also pronoun
Nancy, Jean-Luc, 136–37n3, 147n5
narrowness, 10, 19, 22, 29, 35, 41, 62–63, 78, 82, 92, 96, 133n16, 140n1, 144n15
nature, x–xiii, xxiv, xxx–xxxi, 3, 10, 13, 23, 33–37, 42–44, 48, 50, 61, 65–66, 73–74, 85, 97, 99, 116n7, 119n18, 120n22, 127n17, 132n16, 135n21; naturalism, 35–36
Neumann, Gerhard, xx
Nietzsche, Friedrich, 38, 136n2
no one, 25, 47, 70, 86, 91, 136n1, 144n15
No One's Rose (*Die Niemandsrose*), 50, 71, 91, 99
"No sandart anymore [*Keine Sandkunst mehr*]," 128n19
nothing, xvii, 4, 7, 12, 14, 24, 63, 67, 70, 78, 81–82, 89–92, 101, 103, 114n14, 115n16, 119n18, 128n19, 134n19, 138n9, 144n15; see also existence
Novalis, 95, 136n1

obscuritas, xxix, xxiv, 110n10

"Once [*Einmal*]," 54
other, x, xi–xiv, xxi–xxv, xxviii–xxxii, 10, 13–14, 18–19, 29–31, 38, 49–50, 52, 54–55, 57–58, 62, 77–79, 84, 86–87, 91–92, 96–98, 101–2, 105–6, 113n6, 113n10, 120n19, 128n19, 132n15, 133n18, 135n21, 136n24, 142n6, 144n16

pain, 61–75, 81, 83, 106, 113n10, 115n16, 118n10, 135n20, 137n4, 138n10, 138n11, 138n12, 138n13, 140n14, 140n17
"Pain, the syllable [*Die Silbe Schmerz*]," 60, 71–72, 104
perception, xii, xviii, xxii, xxx, xxxii, 3, 11, 14, 27, 54–55, 61, 80–82, 90, 104, 118n15, 119n19, 127n17, 133n17, 135n21, 135–36n24, 138n13, 148n9
Petzet, Heinrich Wiegand, xx
Pfeifer, Wolfgang, 80
Pindar, 78–79, 140n4
place, xii–xiii, xv–xvii, xxi, xxviii–xxxii, 8, 10, 13, 17–32, 34–35, 39, 41, 43–44, 49, 52–53, 55–57, 59, 63–64, 77, 83–84, 86, 96, 98, 100, 104, 106, 109n5, 116n6, 116n7, 117n9, 117n10, 120n19, 121n25, 144n14, 148n9
Plato, 37, 42, 123n7
Podewils, Clemens, 97, 127n17
Poe, Edgar Allan, 38
Pöggeler, Otto, 109n6, 111n1
political, xxxi, 26, 95–96, 99, 105–6, 111n2, 118n10, 121–22n1, 147n6, 149n20
presence, xiii–xiv, xvii, 24, 28, 40, 43, 52, 55, 61, 64–65, 69, 73–74, 86, 101
present, xxiii, 4, 28, 52, 55–56, 65, 72–73, 77, 82–83, 91, 112n5,

present *(continued)*
  114n11, 119n19, 122n1, 135n21, 135n23, 138n9
pronoun, 30, 71–72, 78
prosopopoeia, 126n15, 134n19, 135n21
"Psalm [*Psalm*]," 91

raw, xxi, xxiii, xxviii, 4–9, 11, 24, 30, 36, 70, 115n15, 115n16, 120n21
Regime of Terror, xiii
remainder, 39–40, 86, 88, 91, 143n9
repetition, xi, xxx, xxxii, 10, 23–26, 29–30, 50, 87, 118n12, 119n18, 120n22, 127n19, 148n9
"Reply to a Questionnaire from the Flinker Bookstore [*Antwort auf einer Rundfrage der Librarie Flinker*]," 31, 49, 121n23
revenge, 98
Rilke, Rainer Maria, x, 13
Rivera, Jorge Eduardo, 111n3
Rosenberg, Alfred, xxxvii

Safranski, Rüdiger, 111n4
Schelling, Friedrich Wilhelm Joseph, 143n10
Schlegel, Friedrich, 95
Schmidt, Dennis J., 137n4
Scholem, Gershom, 53
Schwab, Christoph Theodor, 131n9
self, xii, xxii, 47–49, 73–74, 114n10, 130n5, 131n8, 134n19; *see also* I; ego
shadow, 24, 69–70, 83, 95, 117n9, 117n10
shibboleth, 80, 99–101, 105, 122n1
Short, Charles, xv
silence, 9, 21, 24, 32, 50, 52, 62–63, 67–68, 79, 82, 93, 110n13, 112n5, 114n10, 119n17, 137n4, 140n15, 143n11, 147n4

"Singable remnant [*Singbarer Rest*]," xxxv, 32, 121n26
Snowpart (*Schneepart*), 95, 102
"So many constellations [*Soviel Gestirne*]," 92
Sophocles, 123–24n8, 147n6
speech, ix, xi, xviii, xxi, xxiii–xxiv, xxvi–xxviii, xxx, 5, 7–9, 11, 13, 15, 17–18, 20, 22–23, 37, 48, 45–58, 60, 61–64, 67–68, 71, 75, 77, 79, 82, 86–87, 96, 112n5, 113n10, 114n10, 115n16, 116n2, 117n9, 122n1, 128n19, 129n3, 132n15, 134n19, 135n21, 143n14, 146n20
speech act, xxvii
"Speech on the Occasion of Receiving the Literature Prize of the Free Hanseatic City of Bremen [*Ansprache anläßlich der Entgegennahme des Literaturpreises der Freien Hansestadt Bremen*]," ix–x, xxv, xxvii, 9–10, 19, 30, 43, 83, 96, 113n10, 114n12, 125n13, 130n6, 144n17
Steiner, George, 111n1
strangeness, 13–14, 19, 23–25, 33–34, 37–38, 44, 47–48, 50, 52, 65, 77, 86, 119n17, 130n5, 138n10, 140n1; *see also* foreignness; *Unheimlichkeit*
"Stretto [*Engführung*]," xix, 71, 82–84, 88–91, 110n12, 112n5, 138–39n13, 144n16
Szondi, Peter, xviii–xix, xxiv–xxv, 82–84, 88–89, 102–4, 110n12, 119n18, 142n7, 147n3, 149n18

technē, technology, xi–xiii, xxiii, 33, 38–41, 82, 124n8, 125n10; *see also* art
testimony, x, xiii, xx, xxv, 8, 25, 33, 56, 81–82, 85–86, 88, 101, 112n5, 113n6, 117n10, 133n17, 144n15
"The left-to-me [*Die mir hinterlassne*]," 110–11n1

thinking, x, xiv, xxiv, xx–xxi, xxvi–
xxxii, xxxvii, 1, 3, 5, 10–11, 14,
17, 20–23, 26, 33, 38–40, 44,
60, 66–68, 70, 75, 93–94, 106,
110n13, 113n9, 116n7, 118n12,
125n9, 125n11, 125n15, 126n17,
128n19, 129–30n3, 140n14
time (one time, at the same time),
xxvi, xxix, xxxii, 27–31, 54–55, 59,
79, 84, 119n18, 132–33n16
Timestead (*Zeitgehöft*), 79, 140n2
"To one who stood at the door
[*Einem, der vor der Tür stand*]," 91
"To stand [*Stehen*]," 69–70, 86,
144n15
Todt, Fritz, 148n10
"Todtnauberg [*Todtnauberg*]," xx,
xxxvii, 1–2, 9–10, 81, 93, 106,
110n8, 110n13, 111n1, 112n2,
112n3, 113n10, 115n21, 148n10
Trakl, Georg, x, xxvii, 13, 20–21, 38,
63–67, 116n6, 138n10
trauma, 29–30, 120–21n22
Tsvetaeva, Marina, 101, 149n15
"Tübingen, January [*Tübingen,
Jänner*]," 50–51, 79–81, 131n9
Tugendhat, Ernst, 129–30n3

Unheimlichkeit, xii, xxxiv–xxxv, 18, 30,
34, 37–38, 40–44, 47–48, 50, 77,
116n4, 123–24n8, 130n5, 146n20;
see also foreignness; strangeness
unrepeatability, 10, 23, 26–27, 30, 39,
54–55, 86, 118n12, 126n16; *see also*
repetition
utopia, xxxii, 15, 19, 24, 56–57, 59,
105–6, 117n9

Vallejo, César, 62
"Voice [*Stimmen*]," 18–19, 130–31n7

Wagner, Richard, 127n19
Walde, Christian, xxiv, 110n10
"Wan-voiced [*Fahlstimmig*]," 98
we, us, 7, 9, 29, 47, 57, 77–78, 90,
116n7, 120n21, 129n3
"We already lie [*Wir lagen*]," 58
"Webbing [*Schwimmhäute*]," 59
"Whichever stone you pick up
[*Welchen der Steine du hebst*]," 49
witness, xi, xx, xxxviii, 3–5, 24–25,
39–40, 43, 55, 81, 85, 103, 107,
117–18n10, 119n18
word, xiii–xiv, xvi, xix–xx, xxviii, 8–10,
15, 17, 22–24, 30, 39, 43–47,
49–50, 52, 56, 58–59, 67, 71–75,
77–83, 85, 89, 97–101, 106,
117n9, 125–26n15, 127n17, 129n3,
134n20, 138n12, 148n10, 149n12;
coming word, xxxvii–xxxviii,
4–6, 106, 112n5, 113–14n10;
counterword, xiii–xiv, xvi–xvii, 34,
50, 55, 86, 101; poetic word, 13,
137n4
wound, xxi, 8, 19, 29–31, 62–63,
69–70, 72, 82, 98–99, 113n10,
115n15, 120n21, 123n6, 128n19,
135n20, 140n17, 144n17, 149n11,
149n13

"You lie [*Du liegst*]," 102–3, 119n18,
149n18
"You too speak [*Sprich auch du*]," 58,
117n9
"Your dream [*Dein vom Wachen*]," 30